Contents

List of Figures and Tables

The Interplay Between Gender, Markets and the State in Sweden, Germany and the United States

LILJA MÓSESDÓTTIR

ASHGATE

Published by
Ashgate Publishing Limited
Gower House
Croft Road
Aldershot
Hants GU11 3HR
England

Ashgate Publishing Company
Suite 420
101 Cherry Street
Burlington, VT 05401-4405
USA

Ashgate website: http://www.ashgate.com

British Library Cataloguing in Publication Data
Mósesdóttir, Lilja
   The interplay between gender, markets and the state in
   Sweden, Germany and the United States
   1. Sex differences 2. Sex role - Sweden 3. Sex role - Germany
   4. Sex role - United States 5. Sexual division of labor -
   Sweden 6. Sexual division of labor - Germany 7. Sexual
   division of labor - United States
   I. Title
   305.3'0943

Library of Congress Control Number: 2001088802

ISBN 0 7546 1745 9

Reprinted 2004

Printed in Great Britain by
Antony Rowe Ltd, Chippenham, Wiltshire

Acknowledgements

This work could not have been completed without the encouragement and assistance of many people and it is a great pleasure to have now the opportunity to thank them.

I would like to start by thanking Ivar Jonsson for our constructive discussions about my work. I am also in debt to Professor Jill Rubery, for encouraging me to break out of disciplinary cleavages and for her valuable collaboration throughout the writing of this book. Moreover, I would like to thank Professor Rosemary Crompton and Jordan Goodman for constructive comments on this work.

During the couse of writing this book, I have benefited from comments on earlier drafts made by anonymous readers at the British Journal of Sociology and Acta Sociologica as well as by Collete Fagan, Damian Grimshaw, Susanne Schunter-Kleemann, Jordan Goodman, Guðný B. Eydal, Tómas Bjarnason, Mary Daly, Birte Siim, Jackie O'Reilly and Dominique Anox. I would also like to mention people who have been very helpful at different stages of this work. Among these are Ian Gough, Ann S. Orloff, Traute Meyer, Bengt Furåker, Ruth Emerik, Diana Perrons, Anne Kovalainen, Pertti Koistinen, Ilona Ostner, Katarina Katz and Donald Storrie. I would also like to thank Elísabet Andrésdóttir for her valuable assistance with formatting the final manuscript.

As this book is about three countries and has been written in four countries, I have had to rely on the generosity of many institutions. I would especially like to mention Reykjavík University, University of Manchester Institute of Science and Technology (UMIST), the University of Greenland, the Centre for European Labour Market Studies, University of Gothenburg, Sweden, Wissenschaftszentrum Berlin (WZB), Germany, the Institute of Social Policy at the Georg-August-University, Germany, FREIA Feminist Research Centre in Aalborg, Denmark, Harvard University, Boston, the United States and Institute for Women's Policy Research, Washington, the United States. Finally, I would like to acknowledge that my past experiences as an economist for the Icelandic Federation of Labour, ASÍ, and as a political activist within and outside the Women's List (Kvennalistinn) in Iceland have been a valuable source of ideas throughout the writing of this work.

Introduction

The development of gender relations during the post-war period in Sweden, Germany and the United States forms the core of this work. Gender relations refer to the hierarchical relations between men and women in which women are subordinated to men. The hierarchical relations are based on economic, political, social and biological differentiation between men and women. We compare forms/patterns of gender relations across the three countries and their development through time. Our analytical focus is primarily on how actors, cultural norms and institutional arrangements interrelate and affect the relative position of men and women creating certain patterns/forms of gender relations that vary across countries and change through time. Hence, we are not concerned with explaining the origin of women's subordination but the particular form it takes across space and time. Comparing patterns of gender relations across countries with different histories of social relations and institutional settings reveals the importance of social structures (actors and institutions) in shaping common trends in the industrialised societies. An integration of women into paid work and politics has, for example, occurred in Sweden, Germany and the United States. However, the speed at which this common trend has taken place and its implications in terms of pay and segregation differs across the three countries. Sweden was, for example, among the first to establish the dual breadwinner model while Germany is only slowly moving away from the male breadwinner model. The United States is positioned between the other two countries.

Our main assertion as concerns the development of gender relations in Sweden, Germany and the United States during the post-war period is that incremental changes have accumulated into a shift from one form/pattern of gender relations to another or from the male breadwinner model to the dual breadwinner model. However, the shift has involved overlapping developments with dual, breadwinner and one-headed models existing at the same time and multi-linear development across countries. Hence, different models or patterns of gender relations exist in each country but it is possible to identify one dominant model by examining how gender relations are regulated through norms and institutional

1

arrangements. These norms and institutional settings constitute a mode of regulation that is influenced by political struggles and compromises. A mode of regulation adjusts the behaviour of men and women to certain pattern of gender relation. Moreover, each country adopts its one variant of the male breadwinner and/or the dual breadwinner models. We term the Swedish variant of the dual breadwinner model as the egalitarian regime of gender relations and the modified male breadwinner model in Germany is captured by the ecclesiastical regime of gender relations. The liberal regime of gender relations in the United States is positioned between the other two regimes with male and dual breadwinner models coexisting, although the latter is becoming more dominant than the former.

Our study of the development of gender relations is comparative and historical, i.e. the same issues are examined in more than one country and the historical development of these issues is also explored. One of the main advantages of a comparative study is that it highlights the differences and the similarities of the countries being compared. Sweden, Germany and the United States are comparable as they are highly industrialised and have similar structures of representative democracy. These countries differ, however, with respect to the patterns of gender relations (the dependent variable). In this book, we argue that social blocks (independent variable) involving a stable system of relations that have challenged and become embedded into institutional arrangements are the main force creating differences in the patterns of gender relations across the three countries. Our choice of Sweden, Germany and the United States is based on the belief that differences are more revealing about the forces shaping the patterns/forms of gender relations than similarities. Our historical approach rests on the assumption that actors can only change social structures through existing relations and institutional arrangements. Hence, present social structures can only be understood in view of past struggles and institutional compromises. A historical approach in comparative studies is essential as variation across space is the outcome of previous similarities and dissimilarities underlying the variation (see øyen 1992; Kalberg 1994).

Our study is inter-disciplinary as well as being comparative and historical. In order to explain variations across the three countries, we find it necessary to break out of the sharp division of work between economics, sociology and political science. These disciplines were not developed to explain cross-country differences in the development of gender relations. Rokkan (1978 quoted in øyen 1992) claims that it is difficult to conduct

2

acceptable comparisons between countries without bringing in broader ranges of variables than those of only one discipline. Hence, this study has required knowledge and methodological skills in sociology and political science with which the author was not previously familiar. Finally, our study of the development of gender relations during the post-war period is to a large extent limited to the aggregated level or structures involving institutional structures and collective actors at the national level. A more disaggregated analysis of the role individuals have played in shaping gender relations as well as of regional and local variations in the patterns of gender relations would enrich our study of the development of gender relations in the three countries but is beyond the scope of this work.

In chapter 1, different approaches and in particular recent feminist approaches to the nature of the state are discussed. The aim is to explore how women as a social force both influence, and are constrained by the state. Thereafter, we develop a new 'feminist-relational' approach to the study of the state as gendered social relations or a site of gender strategies and a regulator of gender relations as well as a product of past gender struggles. The role of the welfare state in the labour market and social reproduction has expanded at the same time as women have intensified their participation in paid work. Hence, the importance of the state in regulating gender relations has increased which has contributed to the formation of a certain pattern/form of gender relations. In order to capture the patterns/forms gender relations take in Sweden, Germany and the United States, three typologies are developed on the basis of three variations in the mode of regulation, i.e. norms, institutional arrangements and the political relations underlying the regimes. The mode of regulation reveals what is the most dominant pattern/form of gender relations. These typologies are: the egalitarian regime of gender relations, the ecclesiastical regime of gender relations and the liberal regime of gender relations. The names refer to the most significant societal principles shaping gender relations. The chapter concludes with some thoughts about the processes of change affecting the regimes of gender relations but regimes are under constant pressure to change and/or adjust.

We developed our 'feminist-relational' approach further in chapter 2 by studying women's struggles in relation to other social and political relations. Work within the Regulation school that focuses on the interrelationship between social blocks and the women's movement is discussed in order to enhance our understanding of how social movements have challenged and become embedded in the development of political and social institutions. The theoretical insights given by the Regulation school are then used to study women's political struggles in relation to the main social blocks prevailing since the early part of this century in Sweden, Germany and the United States. As political actors, women have fought for recognition by the prevailing social blocks and for a place in the forming of social blocks but political and social actors will after a period of struggles form alliances and agreements as well as institutional compromises around a certain mode of regulation. Our main argument is that the particular form of integration or exclusion from political influences will determine to what extent women are able to influence/challenge norms about their role in society that have become embedded in institutional settings across time and space. The success of women's struggle is affected by the institutional arrangements of the state that include the form of the state, policy formation and policy implementation. Moreover, the institutional arrangements of the state influence how homogenous the conditions of women are within the national borders.

In chapter 3, we expand our 'feminist-relational' approach by examining the role of the state in regulating employment changes in the labour market that have affected gender relations or the patterns/forms of gender relations. Our focus is on how demand for labour in the production sphere has given rise to supply responses on the one hand and on the role of the state in mediating between demand pressures and supply response on the other hand. Our main assertion is that the interrelationship between the household, the labour market and the state is relatively autonomous, such that there is no direct causal relationship between the nature of the welfare state and employment structures. Moreover, the interrelationship has been shaped by actors involved in power struggles which in turn have contributed to divergent labour market patterns across space. In the empirical part, we start by studying demand pressures or the development of the aggregated demand since the 1960s. We apply shift-share analysis to reveal how much of the changes in female and male employment is accounted for by structural developments and how much is the result of employers' labour use strategies. Although the focus of our analysis is on the demand side, we recognise that it has become difficult to isolate demand and supply pressures as the latter has increasingly come to condition the former. In the second part of the empirical analysis, we analyse how the state has affected the responses of the supply by altering

4

the volume of the labour supply through immigration and by creating incentives/disincentives to participate in paid work.

Gender segregation is studied in chapter 4 as it reveals how the division of work between men and women has been altered by the integration of women into paid work. Secondly, gender segregation is an important source of pay inequalities between men and women. We start our analysis by discussing explanations given by neo-classical and segmentation theories of the processes underlying gender segregation. We claim that gender segregation is the outcome of a dynamic interaction between individual tastes and country-specific social structures. Moreover, the size of the labour force will influence how much power employers have over the segmentation processes. Immigration also affects the composition of the labour force and thereby the scope for segregation. When the working population consists of more than one race, differences between men and women become infused with race. In our empirical investigation, we measure changes in gender segregation over time with the Index of Dissimilarity and the Index of Segregation in order to evaluate whether the three countries are converging around a more desegregated labour market. After discussing the forces behind changes in the level of gender segregation in the three countries, more disaggregated national data is then studied to obtain some insights into men's and women's concentration in certain occupations and the extent to which labour market segmentation is based on social norms about men's and women's perceived abilities. As we are interested in uncovering the role of the labour unions and the state in the segmentation processes, we relate differences in gender segregation across the three countries to variations in the vocational training systems and to the different nature of service sector employment. The chapter concludes with a discussion of how the relationship between gender segregation and the gender pay gap in the three countries has been shaped by the national system of pay determination as well as by the national vocational training system.

In chapter 5, we analyse how changes in the production sphere during the post-war period have contributed to a shift from the male breadwinner model towards the dual breadwinner model. In the theoretical part, we discuss approaches used to explain changes over time but very few analyses have been undertaken to explain changes in gender relations across time and space. We claim that changes in gender relations arise from the dynamic interaction of country-specific social, political and economic institutions and actors (social structures) creating both designed and unintended processes that are evolutionary. The outcomes of these evolutionary processes involve overlapping developments with male and dual breadwinner models coexisting at the same time. Moreover, the development is multi-linear across space as the speed at which countries adopt variants of, for example, the dual breadwinner model differs. In our empirical analysis, we study how the interaction of the industrial system and industrial relations system has shaped the feminisation of the labour force and the conditions under which men and women are employed. The feminisation of the labour force has generated a move from the male breadwinner household model towards the dual household model. In recent years, decentralisation and international regionalisation has occurred in the three countries. These developments have further strengthened the dual breadwinner model in Sweden and the move towards the dual breadwinner model in the United States and Germany. International regionalism has also exacerbated differences between the United States on the one hand and Sweden and Germany on the other hand.

In the concluding chapter, we integrate the theoretical and empirical arguments developed in chapters 2 to 5 into our regimes of gender relations (chapter 1). The aim is to introduce time into our analysis of regimes of gender relations that were developed to highlight the forms/patterns of gender relations prevailing during the early 1990s in Sweden, Germany and the United States. Central to our analytical framework of the regimes of gender relations is the mode of regulation which is a concept applied within the regulation theories. As the concept of mode of regulation has not been developed to analyse how a particular form of hierarchical relationships between men and women are established and reproduced, further theoretical work is needed on the concept of the state as gendered social relations on the one hand and on the processes of change which result in new patterns of gender relations on the other hand. We therefore start by introducing the concept of the state as gendered social relations and processes of change into the framework of regimes of gender relations. Moreover, we conclude with remarks about the difficulties involved in classifying countries according to modes of regulation involving norms, institutional arrangements and political relations underlying the mode. We then summarise the results of our empirical analysis within two periods. The first period involves mounting tension over the male breadwinner model in the three countries. The second period is characterised by compromises or by the establishment of the dual breadwinner model in Sweden, modifications to the male breadwinner in Germany and a move towards the dual breadwinner model in the United States. The chapter concludes with a discussion of the new contradictions and tensions created by these country-specific compromises.

1 A Theoretical Framework for the Study of the State and Gender Relations

Even though the state is recognised to be an important regulator of gender relations, it has been largely ignored as social relations in economic and feminist research. The implications of the state's activities and policies are the main concerns of economic and feminist writings. Very limited attention has been paid to social forces such as the women's movement and their influences on policy outcomes as well as their resistance to the state's activities and policies. Women have primarily been treated as objects with very limited control over their lives. However, women have been and are active in influencing and contributing to the development of the state from outside and inside. By examining how women's interests are articulated into the state's activities and policies, a better understanding will be attained of the nature of the state as a regulator of gender relations. Women's interests and strategy towards the state may vary from one country to another due to different functioning and structure of the cultural, economic, political and social system. The regulation of women's lives depends on linkages and interactions between societal (economic, political and social) forces and the state. At the same time as women have increased their participation in paid work, the role of the welfare state in the labour market and social reproduction has expanded. Hence, the importance of the state in regulating gender relations has increased and its nature has also changed through time as welfare states are not constants. In recent years, economic, social and political changes have affected the development of the welfare state and its role in shaping gender relations. These changes and women's greater involvement in paid work has and will continue to fragment women's interest towards the state such that different groups of women may increasingly adopt different strategies. Divisions among women as an interest group will weaken their influence on and resistance to the state. Moreover, the state may use these divisions to implement policies and legislation contrary to the interest of most women.

In this chapter, we attempt to construct a comparative analytical framework for the study of the state as gendered social relations. In the first part, the aim is to explain how women as a social force both influence, and are constrained by the state. Different approaches and in particular recent feminist approaches to the nature of the state are discussed in order to develop a new 'feminist-relational' approach to the study of the state. In the second part, the state is analysed as a regulator of gender relations. State regulation has become the main source of divergences in forms/patterns of gender relations across space. Typologies will be developed in order to capture the form gender relations take in Sweden, Germany and the United States. These typologies are; the egalitarian regime of gender relations, the ecclesiastical regime of gender relations and the liberal regime of gender relations. As regimes are under constant pressure to change and/or adjust the transformation of regimes and transition to new regimes will also be analysed.

The State as Gendered Social Relations

The analyses of the role of the state in modern capitalist societies are dominated by four fundamentally different approaches. These approaches are; Keynesian and neo-classical approaches, Marxist approaches, state-centred approaches, and strategic-relational approaches. However, feminist approaches to the state have emerged in recent years as a product of the expansion of feminist studies in social science. The state as an institution is a neglected field of study in economics both in theories that presume an active role for the state as well as in those which presuppose a more restricted role. In neo-classical economics, the state is a factor which structures and limits the applications of economic principles and in Keynesian economics the state is a set of neutral policy instruments applicable to various economic goals (Jessop 1990). On the other hand, Marxist approaches to the capitalist state analyse the nature of the state in terms of long term accumulation strategies and hegemonic projects on the one side and in terms of class struggle on the other side.

Within the tradition of radical and political economy, particularly neo-Marxist approaches to the state have developed in recent decades.

9

These approaches can be divided into three groups, i.e. instrumentalist approaches, structuralist approaches and form-determination approaches. In the instrumental approaches, the state is employed by capital to pursue its interests at the expense of other classes or societal forces, be it individual capitalist, particular firms, certain fractions or sectors of capital, or the capitalist class as a whole. The structuralist approaches are mainly concerned with the different functions the state has to perform to ensure reproduction of the capitalist mode of production. The form-determination of state policies refers to the structure of the capitalist state itself that ensures that the interests of capital are realised in policy making and policy implementation (Jessop 1990:145-194). The state-centred approaches, on the other hand, conceive the state as an institutional reality and as such able to act independently of accumulation requirements and class domination. The state is hence considered to be autonomous and in some cases 'potentially' or relatively autonomous from structural factors and class domination. Even though the state-centred approaches have anti-Marxist assumptions, many of their concerns can also be found within the Marxist tradition. Most Marxist approaches allow, for example, for some degree of state autonomy. The strategic-relational approach is a Marxist approach to the capitalist state that attempts to take the role of political and social agents into account, as well as the importance of the institutional features connecting state, economy and society. In this approach, the state is a social relation and relatively autonomous from structural features and class domination. The main attributes of the instrumental approaches, structural approaches, form-determination approaches and state-centred approaches are incorporated into the strategic-relational approach. We will therefore leave out a further discussion of these approaches (see Mósesdóttir 1994 for more detailed discussion).

Besides these different approaches to the state, feminist approaches emphasise the role of the state as an instrument of patriarchal control and/or capitalism. These recent feminist approaches are to some extent based on the above mentioned approaches. As our comparative analytical frame-work for the study of the state as gendered social relations is a synthesis of the strategic-relational approach and feminist approaches to the state, we will start our analysis by discussing these approaches in more details.

In his strategic-relational approach, Jessop argues that the state is the site of social relations, i.e. the site of strategies, a producer of strategies, and a product of strategies. First, the state system is the site of strategy whose structure and operations are more open to some types of political strategy than others. A given type of state (for example feudal or capitalist), state form (for example liberal or corporatist) and form of regime (for example liberal Fordism or corporatist Fordism), will be more accessible to some forces than others depending on the strategies they adopt to gain state power. Moreover, the particular type of state will be more appropriate for certain types of economic or political strategy than others due to the modes of intervention and resources that characterise the system, i.e. the state is a system of *strategic selectivity*. The success of political forces influencing the state is determined by the degree of class mobilisation and the strategies they adopt. A successful strategy is the one to which the state form is vulnerable. Secondly, the state is the site where strategies are produced. Whereas the state is the site of class struggles as well as the site of struggles among its different departments, state managers may try to develop different strategies and tactics to impose a measure of coherence on its internal and external activities. Third, the state is a product of strategies such that the structure and the operation of the state system can be understood in view of their production in and through past political strategies and struggles (Jessop 1990:260-261). The strategic-relational approach uses the concept of strategy as involving a reciprocal relation between institutional, or structural features and political agents. Thus, strategies affect both structures and forces and in turn structures influence strategies and forces (Bertramsen 1991:109).

Jessop's theory is 'capital-centred' as he deduces the interrelationship between state, economy and society from capital interests in the form of accumulation strategies. Hence, the interrelationship between state and civil society is not adequately accounted for. It is not apparent how social movements, for example the women's movement, shape, and are shaped by the state apparatus and policies. To analyse the state in terms of different societal interests, a theory of the politics of interest mediation in capitalist society is needed (Jonsson 1989:228-31; 1993:68-73). Moreover, Bonefeld criticises Jessop for equating 'class struggle with capital strategies such that the Marxian notion of contradictory constitution of a social relation is destroyed' (1993:26). Bonefeld argues that the strategic-relational theory can not capture essential historical developments or contingencies in labour-capital relations as the theory separates social relations into different regions with distinct internal logic in which labour plays no role. Historical developments are lost within the strategic-relational theory as it fragments social relations and then searches for interconnections. Finally, Jessop's analysis is gender blind as he ignores the fact that resources are not equally as available to women and men. Although men and women use the same strategies, the state may be more vulnerable to men's efforts as they have greater access to resources.

The interrelationship between the state and the family/household or social reproduction is missing in the strategic-relational approach. Humphries and Rubery (1984) identify two methodologies in economic analysis concerning the interrelationship between social reproduction and production. First, there is *absolute autonomy* implying that social reproduction is independent of the system of production. The second methodology is *reductionist/functionalist* in which social reproduction is either entirely structured by the capitalist system (reductionist) or dependent on that system but plays nevertheless a significant part in its operation and reproduction. Finally, Humphries and Rubery develop the *relative autonomy* approach that entails that social reproduction is an integral part of the economy but relatively independent of the sphere of production. The relationship between social reproduction and production is historically determined and non-functional.

We can apply these approaches to the interrelationship between social reproduction and the state. In instrumentalist, structuralist and form-determination approaches, social reproduction is either entirely structured by the capitalist system, such that the state shapes social reproduction in accordance to the needs of capital (reductionist) or dependent on the capitalist system but influences its operation and reproduction such that the state meets the needs of the social reproduction as long as they are in line with the accumulation requirements of capital (functional). In the state-centred approach, on the other hand, social reproduction is independent of the system of production and of the state, such that gender relations are, for example, only governed by patriarchal or men's power. Finally, in the strategy-

12

theoretical approach, social reproduction is more open to some of the state's activities and policies than others and the openness may vary from time to time as each sphere needs time to adapt to the other (relative autonomy). Hence, the interrelationship between the state and the family/household can be described as relative autonomy.

The State in Feminist Approaches

The main feminist approaches to the analysis of gender and the states are Liberal feminism, Marxist feminism, Radical feminism and Dual-systems theory. Liberal feminists see the state as a biased arbiter. The structural conditions shaping the nature of the state are at the centre of Marxist feminism. Radical feminists see the state as pursuing the interest of patriarchy. Finally, the Dual system theorists, on the other hand, argue that the state is governed by structural conditions and patriarchy.

Liberal feminists regard the state as a biased arbiter between conflicting interests as men are overrepresented in the state structure. Thus, the policies of the state would be more favourable for women if there were more women in decision making posts (see Connell 1990:512-513; Walby 1990:153). It is, however, not evident that numerical majority will translate into advantageous policies for all groups of women. Women who are, for example, disadvantaged in the labour market due to their lack of training and education will not benefit from a policy promoting equality between individuals (Franzway et al. 1989). The feminist liberal theory of the state ignores also power relations between men and women, structural conditions, and the influences of gendered social forces in its analysis of the state.

McIntosh (1978) provides a Marxist analysis of women's oppression by the state. The state is capitalist as it intervenes both in the family, and in the capitalist workplace and labour market to secure social conditions that allow capitalist production to continue. By supporting certain forms of household in which women provide unpaid domestic services for a male, the state maintains the oppression of women. A particular form of household that ensures the cheap reproduction of labour and the availability of women as a reserve army is beneficial to capitalism. The oppression of women by the state is indirect as it is based on the maintenance of a particular household (Walby 1990:154-155). McIntosh's theory is mainly concerned with capitalist relations and it reflects the contradictory pressures and demands under which the state acts and are reflected in ambivalent policies (Franzway et al. 1989:22). However, McIntosh disregards men's benefits from women's oppression in particular within the household. Moreover, the state as a relatively autonomous institution and the influences of gendered social forces are not considered.

A crucial theme of Radical feminism is that the *personal is political.* By extending the analysis to include the personal as political, they have broadened the definition of politics to include sexual harassment, domestic violence, pornography, etc. Men's domination of women, i.e. patriarchal domination is rooted in the biological differences of the sexes and does not derive from any other system of social inequality (see, for example Firestone 1970). Radical feminists regard the state as an instrument of patriarchal domination, especially when it adopts policies of non-intervention. Men use the state to control women's bodies through, for example fertility controls like abortion. The state reinforces patriarchal control by failing to intervene in men's violence against women (Hanmer and Saunders 1984). Radical feminists' account of the state is confined to the personal implications of the state's policies for women and it does not take into account structural conditions, the relative autonomy of the state and of social forces from male domination.

Instead of focusing on either capitalism or patriarchy, Dual system theory claims that both systems influence and structure gender relations (Tong 1989:175). There are two approaches within the Dual systems theory; one that sees patriarchy and capitalism as fused into one system of capitalist patriarchy (for example Eisenstein 1981) and another that sees patriarchy and capitalism as analytically distinct but empirically interacting systems (Hartmann 1979). Hartmann defines patriarchy as a set of social relations between men which have a material base. Although hierarchical, the social relations establish or create interdependence and solidarity among men that enable them to dominate women (1981:14). According to Eisenstein (1984), patriarchy contributes to order and control, while capitalism provides the economic system driven by the pursuit of profit. Moreover, patriarchy and capitalism fuse at the state level where patriarchal interests are represented by capitalists and the form of the state, especially its separation from the family, is regarded as patriarchal. Walby (1990) supports Eisenstein's theory of a fusion of capitalism and patriarchy at the state level but claims that political struggle has a degree of autonomy from the material base of patriarchy and of capitalism. Hence, women's political struggle is able to affect the state's activities.

In Scandinavian feminist theory of the state, it is claimed that women have moved from private to public dependence (see Hernes 1987a; Borchorst and Siim 1987). This transition has not changed women's subordination in any fundamental way but rather strengthened it in, for example new areas such as paid employment. However, women are not subject to the same dependency across different countries. In countries like Sweden and Denmark, women rely on the state as public workers and as consumers of social services. Women in Britain and the United States, on the other hand, rely on the state as clients (Borchorst and Siim 1987:143-146).

Our comparative analytical framework synthesises Jessop's strategic-relational approach and feminist approaches. Jessop's approach incorporates the main contributions of Marxist approaches and state-centred approaches to the state. However, Jessop's strategic relational approach needs to be expanded to include social movements and contradictions in social relations. Whereas Jessop only considers the influences of economic determinants and struggle among classes and state bureaucrats on the state, we also need to incorporate gender relations into our analysis of the state. We will draw on the work of McIntosh (1978), Radical feminists, the Dual System theory as well as the Public Dependency theories (Hernes 1987a and 1987b; Borchorst and Siim 1987 and Dahlerup 1987) to integrate gender into our analysis of the state as gendered social relations. The analytical focus will be on the women's movements and their encounter with state rather than on the patriarchal nature of the state. In the first part, the focus will be on how the women's movements have sought to influence the state and how the state has shaped women's movement. Hence, the emphasis will be on the state as a site of strategies. The analysis will involve women's interests, mobilisation, strategies from outside and inside the state and contradictions in the activities and policies of the state.

Gendered Interests, Mobilisation and Strategies towards the State

The specific interests of women arise from their biological sex, their socialisation as women, their relations with men and their position within the capital-labour relations. Women's different biological conditions and socialisation from that of men will induce women to place greater emphasis on provision of certain services such as fertility control and maternity leaves. Moreover, women may demand better working conditions including training in technical skills in order to fight gender segregation based on technological competence. These specific gender interests will be met by employers if they contribute to social control and to the overall accumulation strategy. The extent to which the state meets these interests of women depends on how it mediates between different needs of various societal forces. Feminists have described gender relations as patriarchal relations involving hierarchical relations in which men dominate women. Men may maintain their superior position by restricting women's access to resources and by restraining women's control of their sexuality especially their reproductive capacities. Moreover, a highly gender segregated labour market reproduces hierarchical relations between men and women in the area of paid work. The undervaluation of women's work may force women into marriage and to adhere to gender division of labour. Employers will benefit from highly gender segregated labour market if they are able to use the division to differentiate between workers in terms of jobs and rewards. Unions may also enforce hierarchical relations between men and women by agreeing to lower wages, lower benefits and fewer advancement opportunities for 'female' jobs. However, structural conditions as well as the interests of employers, the state and men may be conflicting, leading to contradictory pressures and demands on women, especially in the area of paid and unpaid work.

Women's interests are historically determined and they will vary from one country/region to another and from one class, race and ethnic group of women to another. The interests being pursued depend on the groups of women mobilising that may vary from time to time. How aware women are of these 'common' interests will differ accordingly. Structural changes and/or hierarchical relations between men and women in which women are subordinated to men may give rise to women's mobilisation but the degree to which they mobilise is determined by their access to resources. As pointed out by Hernes (1987a), public policies may give women access to resources that will mobilise them to push for their interests in the development of the welfare state. The international flow of feminist ideas may also be a mobilising force. The interests that the women's movement chooses to promote are also influenced by what strategies are most likely to be successful as the state is 'strategic selective'. The form of representation shapes how the interests of women are articulated and can privilege some strategies over others. The influence of the women's movement and women in general on the state depends on their role in the overall mode of interest intermediation. If the women's movement plays a marginal role, it may easily be ignored by the state when it mediates between different political parties and/or interest groups. Moreover, women's influence may be further marginalised by their absence from the decision making bodies of powerful interest groups, for example the trade unions and employers' associations affecting directly and indirectly state's activities and policies. However, women's interests may be incorporated into the male dominated mode of interest intermediation as general interests. The need to mobilise on the basis of gendered interests is impaired, when women's interests become general interests.

The strategies women have used to pursue their interests vary from one country to another. A strategy adopted by the women's movement in one country may prove to be unsuccessful in another country. In general, the women's movement has chosen separatism from political parties as its basic strategy in order to establish common consciousness, a common identity and autonomy as a group (see, for example Hernes 1987a:47). This strategy of separatism has gone furthest in Iceland where a women's party was established in 1982 in order to articulate more effectively women's interests in local government and then in parliament. In the United States, the women's movement has made coalitions with the party or organisations and/or agents most likely to pursue their particular interests that may differ from time to time. Hence, the women's movement has made coalitions with the Democratic party, the unions, the bureaucracies and a range of other agents. In Western Europe, the women's movement has been more cautious in its coalition building and has been more inclined to appeal to the left. Socialist and Communist parties in Western Europe have also been more supportive of women's concerns than (Christian Democratic) Centre or the Right (Katzenstein 1987:6). The co-operation of many feminist groups with the Green Party in Germany during the 1980s forced the other parliamentary parties into competition for women's support (Lane 1993). Political coalitions have been more difficult to form in Britain than in the United States and

Sweden due to the relative weakness of Liberal and Right-wing feminists at the same time as Radical and Socialist feminists have been strong (Lovenduski and Randall 1993:362). In Sweden, the majority of women have supported the Social Democratic Party that is closely connected with the trade unions. Hence, equality strategy in Sweden has been implemented through the system of organised interests in which women are treated as a group of workers (see Lewis and Åström 1992). In other countries like the United States, equality strategy has mainly been implemented through the legal system where women are treated as individuals.

In order to understand women's interaction with the state, we need to distinguish between different levels of government. In most countries, more women participate in governing bodies at the regional and municipality level than at the level of the national government (see Munoz and Carey 1997). The women's movement has in some cases chosen to work at the municipality level as it is more open to women's interests than other levels of government and more in line with their grass-roots ideology. This strategy has been unsuccessful in Britain where federal structures do not exist (Franzway et al. 1989:44). During the early 1990s, the highest female political representation in Sweden was at the regional level while it was at the European level (the European Parliament) in Germany. Moreover, female political representation in the member-countries of the European Union (EU) is consistently higher at the European level than at the national, regional and local levels (Munoz and Carey 1997). Women's success at the European level may explain why the European Union (EU) has become a major force in the development of equal opportunities. The EU has, for example, made attempts to regulate part-time work such that part-time workers receive the same rights and benefits as full-time workers (see Walby 1997). Moreover, the EU has increasingly pushed through rights enabling men and women to reconcile work and family life (cf. the Directive on Parental leave). Moreover, women have had an easier access to and greater influence on governmental departments dealing with social affairs that are at lower levels in the state hierarchy than governmental departments dealing with financial affairs. The relative dominance of some departments over others has shaped the women's movement. Its strategy has been to pursue interests that are more in the social realm than in the financial realm as the state is vulnerable to such a strategy.

Women's increased representation at the municipality level and increased influence on the social realm does not appear to place a threat to men's power at the state level as the municipalities and social departments are under the control of the federal state and financial departments in which men are in control.

Many women or femocrats have tried as individuals to work for reforms within the state structure. Femocrats are those women who seek to promote women's interests within the state. More femocrats working within the state apparatus has contributed to the increased bureaucratisation of women's interests and in some cases the women's movement. The extent to which femocrats have been able to pursue women's interests within the state has depended on gaining senior positions within the highly gendered bureaucracy. It is doubtful, however, whether enough women occupy enough senior positions to affect policy outcomes. Even if femocrats gain access to senior positions, they are confronted with various tasks, conflicting demands of different societal forces, certain bureaucratic rules, and the need for coherence that will restrain them from promoting women's interests within the state. Equal opportunity programme are probably the most visible product of the interaction of the women's movement and femocrats with the state (Franzway et al. 1989: chapter 7). A greater involvement of feminists with the state apparatus has in some cases had negative consequences for the women's movement or led to its deradicalisation and even decline (see Lovenduski and Randall 1993).

The women's movement has not only sought to influence state policies and activities, but has also fought for changes in the institutional structure of the state. In some countries (the United States), a central agency such as the Equal Opportunity Commission has been established to monitor the status of women. The Equal Opportunity Commission has in many cases been an important force pressing for increased political participation of women and policy developments favourable to women. However, the existence of the Equal Opportunity Commission within the state apparatus does not necessarily mean that the state's bureaucrats are striving for equality between men and women as well as among women. It may as well seek to institutionalise gender conflicts and create difference between women (for example unskilled and professional women). The pressures from the women's movement will contribute to contradictions in the activities and policies of the state as it is also impregnated by other forces such as capital-labour relations and economic development. Hence, welfare programmes benefiting women may be cut due to structural conditions while equality policies are promoted as a result of mounting pressure from the women's movement (see Dahlerup 1987:118).

The state supports a certain form of gender relations by resisting or limiting women's demands, and by adhering to 'objectivity' in its activities and policies. 'Objectivity' may involve male norms and as such reinforces women's subordination. Equal opportunity policy based on merits only means equal opportunity among men and not between men and women. Women do not have the same access to resources as men such that equal treatment of unequal persons works in favour of men. Objectivity is widely used in legal procedures of the state and in its bureaucracy (Franzway 1989:29-31). The distinction between public sphere and private sphere is gendered as women tend to do most of the domestic work. Moreover, by making a clear distinction between a public sphere and a private sphere, the state cannot interfere with all aspects of domestic life such as domestic violence. The separation between public and private spheres has, therefore, served to marginalise and even obscure women's needs (Stivers 1993). However, the state does not only reproduce gender relations but also creates opportunities for women through, for example its employment creation and social services. The state's policies and activities have in many instances endowed women with resources essential for their mobilisation.

The activities and policies of the state may be inconsistent from one time to another and from one department to another. Moreover, the development of the welfare state may be contradictory as the state acts from time to time in the interest of different societal forces that have incompatible interests (Gough 1979). The department's response to societal changes and new demands will depend on managers' perception of the changes and on the functional flexibility of the department. Hence, some departments may adjust to a situation where the majority of women participate in paid work while others pursue policies assuming one breadwinner. Contradictions in the state's policies and activities demonstrate that the interrelationship between the state and the spheres of production and of social reproduction is relatively autonomous. Gender relations will also affect the state's policies and activities. Even when the state adapts to demands made by the women's movement, it cannot escape paradoxes as changes in one area may obscure women's needs in another. Moreover, policy areas in which there are no policies must be considered as it is as much a policy to deny needs as it is to meet them (Gordon, 1990:11).

During the 1980s, policies pursued by the state in the United Kingdom and the United States had contradictory implications. Women have on the one hand been forced to take on more caring work due to cut backs in social welfare. Both labour market and social policy have, on the other hand, encouraged the demand and the supply of low paid female labour. These apparently contradictory policies have led to greater utilisation of female labour in and out of the labour market. The lack of identified gender implications of different policies may be a reason for the contradictions (Rubery 1988c:135-139). In Germany where sexual division of work has been more distinct than in the United Kingdom and the United States, policies of the state have also been inconsistent. At the same time as the state has paid qualified and unqualified women working in the social service sector high enough wages to lead an independent family/household, limited public employment creation, absence of a continuous school day, and taxation policies have facilitated the economic dependence of women on a male breadwinner household (see Meyer 1994; Pfau-Effinger 1994).

Regimes of Gender Relations

The focus of our analysis has so far primarily been on how the women's movement has sought to influence the way in which the state regulates gender relations. We now proceed with our analysis and examine how the state regulates gender relations in the spheres of production and social reproduction across different countries. Hence, the analysis will move from the state as a site of strategies to the state as a producer of strategies. The state has become the most important regulator of gender relations and the main source of divergencies in the forms/patterns of gender relations across space. The main reason for the growing importance of the state as a regulator of gender relations is women's integration into paid work. However, the interrelationship between the state, the economy and the household is relatively autonomous. In order to capture the essential features or forms of gender relations in Sweden,

21

Germany and the United States, we will now develop the concept of regimes of gender relations.

The Egalitarian, Ecclesiastical and Liberal Regimes of Gender Relations

The concept of regimes of gender relations rests on the general principle of work organised along gender lines in the sphere of social reproduction and sphere of production. As the gendered work organisation is under constant threat of change, there exists a need for regulatory mechanisms or a mode of regulation. Gendered organisation of work involves hierarchical relationship between men and women in which women are subordinated to men. The concept of mode of regulation refers to explicit and implicit norms of institutions, of compensatory mechanisms and of information systems that constantly adjust the expectations and behaviour of individuals to the general logic of regimes of gender relations or to a certain pattern of gender relations. The general logic of regimes involves differentiation between men and women that legitimises the superior position of men. The consolidation of a mode of regulation will depend on political and social struggles, agreements and institutional compromises. Social forces will not devote themselves to endless struggle but build a stable system of relations of domination, of alliances and of concessions among different social forces, i.e. they will build social blocks that become hegemonic when this system of domination, alliances and concessions conform to the interests of the majority in the regime (see Leborgne and Lipietz 1991:28).

Three variations in the mode of regulation will be identified in order to establish what kinds of gender relations are promoted by the state in the spheres of production and social reproduction. The dimensions of variations include: the consolidation of the mode of regulation or the political relations underlying the modes of regulation as well as norms and institutional arrangement concerning paid and unpaid work. The more women and women's interests are involved in the consolidation of mode of regulation, the more 'women-friendly' the regime of gender relations. Norms about women as either wives or mothers and/or workers determine the basic assumptions behind activities and policies of the state, capital, organised labour and other social forces. These norms are engraved into the organisation of production and social reproduction as well as into state's activities and policies producing certain types of gender relations. The dimensions of variations in the mode of regulation can be used to constitute three distinct types of regimes of gender relations.

We propose three types of regimes of gender relations based on conditions prevailing during the early 1990s in Sweden, Germany and the United States; the *egalitarian regime of gender relations*, the *ecclesiastical regime of gender relations* and the *liberal regime of gender relations*. The names refer to the most significant societal principles shaping gender relations. A regime of gender relations is liberal when market ideology is the main force shaping gender relations[1]. In this regime, the state is more inclined to pursue the needs of capital than of other social forces. When, on the other hand, egalitarian principles structure gender relations, a regime of gender relations is egalitarian[2]. In this case, the state mediates between the needs of labour and to less extent capital. Finally, when the ideologies and the values of the religion/church affect how gender relations develop, a regime of gender relations is ecclesiastical[3]. These ideologies and values are mediated at the political level. The regimes are historically contingent. Our analysis of variations in the mode of regulation is based on Sweden, Germany (West) and the United States. Bailey (1994) calls this classification procedure the operational or indicator level that involves a combination of the conceptual and empirical levels. Although, the three types are applied to Western 'Christian' societies in the discussion below, the underlying dimensions of variations may also be used to analyse regimes of gender relations in societies characterised by different religions and organisations of the market and the state.

In the Swedish *egalitarian regime of gender relations*, the norms governing the activities and policies of the state are that women are working mothers who need certain social provisions to be able to combine paid and unpaid work and men are dual breadwinners. The organisation of production is based on generating full employment that requires the state to play an active role in employment creation whether in the private or public sector. The state is driven by egalitarian principles generated by the corporatist mode of interest intermediation such that everyone has a right to socially acceptable income. In order to integrate women into the economy as workers, the state has taken over many of the services involved in social reproduction. However, the state has guaranteed women access to the labour market without destroying the hierarchical relations between men and women. The state has allowed men to keep their privileges in the labour market and at home by not attacking gendered division of work in the household and gender segregation in the labour market. Women are still much more likely to do most of the unpaid work and paid work is organised along gender lines with women in welfare services and men in the private industrial sector. However, gender wage differentials are relatively low as wages have been negotiated centrally. Finally, the consolidation of the mode of regulation involves integrating women into the political and state system such that women's interests become part of the general interests. Women's co-operation with men has come under strain as a result of persistent and even growing gender differences. However, greater wage differentials and cost pressure at the level of the firm may reduce gender segregation in the labour market. Moreover, divisions among women in the private and public sectors are growing due to increasing wage differentials.

The underlying assumptions shaping the state's strategies in the German *ecclesiastical regime of gender relations* are that women are wives and to lesser extent mothers who should be enabled by indirect support to carry out their domestic responsibilities. Men, on the other hand, are assumed to be the main breadwinners. The organisation of production is based on generating employment that pays high enough wages to allow a male breadwinner to support a wife. This requires the state to pursue active industrial, education and vocational policies. Traditional gender divisions of work advocated by the Catholic Church are promoted by the state such that women with children are only enabled to work part-time (nurseries and schools are not continuous). Moreover, the family and/or voluntary organisations are responsible for social reproduction and the state provides 'last resort' services. Gender relations have remained largely unchanged as men have been able to hold full-time paid jobs and free themselves from domestic work. The organisation of work is gendered as most women entering the labour market during periods of lighter domestic responsibilities at the same time as men are in most cases full-time workers in the labour market. As concerns the consolidation of the mode of regulation, women have slowly started their integration into the political system. However, relatively few women have been able to enter into the state system and work there as femocrats. The general consensus among women on the one hand and men and women on the other hand regarding the traditional gendered division of work may come under threat as more women enter the labour market.

In the American *liberal regime of gender relations*, the norms shaping the activities and policies of the state are that men and women are presumed to be workers able to support themselves as long as they are not single parents. The organisation of production is based on generating enough employment in the private sector for those able to work. In order to ensure abundant employment opportunities, the state has enabled firms to create low pay jobs resulting in a wide disparity in wages. Moreover, individuals and the private sector are responsible for social reproduction. Driven by the needs of capital accumulation, the state has integrated women, especially less educated women, into the labour market as a cheap and flexible labour force by minimising welfare support and employment rights. The enforcement of non-discrimination laws has enabled educated women to compete with men for good paying jobs. As many unskilled women are low paid in precarious work that lack among other things employment security, hierarchical relations between men and women have not been destroyed. Less educated women are still forced to perform domestic work at home while educated women are able to buy the services of other women. Men and women work relatively long hours but inequalities exist concerning wage differentials. As concerns the consolidation of the mode of regulation, women are not an established part of the political system due to their fragmented interests arising from class and racial differences. However, women have entered the state system and pursued their interests as femocrats. Intensified divisions among the minority of highly qualified women and the majority of less qualified women will further fragment women's interests towards the state in the future. However, growing inequalities may induce men and women to collaborate even further to push for changes.

Our analysis of regimes of gender relations is related to the typologies constructed by Esping-Andersen (1990), Lewis (1992) and Schmid (1991 and 1992). Esping-Andersen examines variations in three concepts, i.e. decommodification, stratification and state-market relations to establish different types of welfare states. Lewis, on the other hand, looks at variations in the idea of the male-breadwinner family model and identifies the consequences for the relationship between paid work, unpaid work and welfare. Finally, Schmid study's variations in the wage formation and employment in order to locate what effects these dimensions of variations have on the 'sexual' division of work. In the following, we will discuss the typologies developed by Esping-Andersen, Lewis and Schmid and compare them with our regimes of gender relations.

The Political Regimes

Esping-Andersen's (1990) study of *liberal, social democratic and corporatist* welfare state regimes is useful for comparative research as it does not search for tendencies towards a universal model. Moreover, the analysis adds to our understanding of the state and gender relations since it does not only focus on social rights and state's expenditures but attempts to establish how different parts of society are systematically connected. However, feminist scholars and other welfare scholars have criticised various aspects of Esping-Andersen's typologies for economic reductionism. The main criticism is; the narrow policy scope, the gender blindness of the main analytical concepts used to classify welfare states, the applicability of the regimes to the labour market position of women and the clustering of welfare states. As concerns the policy scope, Esping-Andersen only compares employment related policy areas in which class alliances or coalitions may have the greatest influence. Policy areas such as reproductive rights and child care provisions, in which women's groups may have greater influence, are not considered (Cochrane and Clarke 1993:10).

The concepts of decommodification, stratification and state-market relations used by Esping-Andersen to classify welfare states have been criticised on various grounds. According to O'Connor, decommodification does not take into account that men and women are not equally commodified which may be a source of inequality. Women may have limited access to the labour market due to their caring responsibilities (1993a:513). Moreover, unpaid services provided by women decommodify male labour and must therefore be included in the analytical framework of decommodification (Orloff 1993:322). The process of decommodification is not only gendered, it may also vary between countries. Borchorst claims that women have, for example, been decommodified in the corporatist regime and commodified in the social democratic regime (1994:3). The concept of decommodification may also be problematic as an analytical concept since some activities and policies of the welfare state such as unemployment measures both commodify (active) and decommodify (passive) labour (see Furåker et al. 1990). Finally, it is not clear whether public employment involves decommodification or commodification.

Esping-Andersen has been criticised for ignoring how the welfare state as a system of stratification differentiates between men and women. According to Orloff, men's claims are in most welfare states based on paid work while women's claims are based on their familial or marital status. Claims based on motherhood or marriage have more restricted eligibility requirements and are associated with lower benefit levels than claims based on work (1993:314-315). The family as a provider of welfare is missing in Esping-Andersen's analysis as state-market relations are only considered (see Borchorst 1994:2). Moreover, very limited attention is paid to the sexual division of work within the states, markets, and families. Even though the effect of the state's services on women's ability to enter the labour market is considered, differences between countries in the provision of care are neglected (Orloff 1993:312-313). Orloff (1993) suggests two new dimensions to the analysis of welfare states in order to capture the effects of state social policies on gender relations. These are access to work or the right to be commodified and the capacity to form and maintain an autonomous household.

It has been pointed out that the three welfare state regimes are inadequate as they do not predict accurately the employment pattern, gender segregation, and full-time/part-time work of women. The social democratic regimes encourage labour market participation such that women's participation rates are high. In contrast, liberal regimes as, for example the United States and Canada do very little to facilitate labour market participation, but women's participation rates are still high. Moreover, in spite of progressive labour market policies of the Swedish welfare state, the labour market is very gender segregated, with high level of part-time work among women who do the bulk of unpaid work (O'Connor 1993a:507; Orloff 1993:313). Finally, the classification of the social democratic welfare state has been criticised by Leira (1993) as it does not hold when arrangements between mothers, fathers, state and the market are examined. The social democratic welfare states in the Scandinavian countries have, for example adopted relatively different approaches to working mothers with children. The Norwegian state treats women primarily as wives and mothers meanwhile the Swedish state treats women primarily as workers.

The Patriarchal Models

By including an analysis of the relationship between unpaid work and welfare, Lewis' models describe women's position in the sphere of production and social production better than Esping-Andersen's regimes. Even though Lewis claims that the male breadwinner family model has cut across established typologies of welfare regimes, it is not clear from her analysis whether the concept of male-breadwinner family model classifies countries differently than the concepts used by Esping-Andersen. The countries, Britain, Sweden and France, selected by Lewis as paradigms have also been identified by Esping-Andersen as belonging to three different welfare state regimes. Moreover, a classification that only allows for *strong, modified* and *weak* male-breadwinner models makes it difficult to classify countries like the United States where a weak male-breadwinner model (less educated women) and a dual breadwinner model (educated women) coexists. It is also doubtful that a country as Finland where the dual-breadwinner model prevails fits into classification based on strong, modified and weak male-breadwinner models (see Koistinen and Ostner 1994). Lewis' paradox that women have more options in countries such as Sweden and France where women's own demands have not played a significant role in determining their treatment are an incorrect interpretation of women's involvement in the consolidation of mode of regulation in these countries. Women's mobilisation is not a prerequisite for the realisation of women's demands. The demands or interests of women may be incorporated into the male dominated mode of interest intermediation as general interests reducing the need for women to mobilise on the basis of gender interests. Such incorporation is more likely to take place in countries where the activities and policies of the state are based on egalitarian values. Finally, the scope of Lewis' analysis is too narrow as it only considers policy outcomes and neglects how the male-breadwinner family model is engraved into the organisation of production.

Schmid's paradigms or the *integrated free market* model, the *integrated welfare state* model and the *disintegrated social market* model are an important augmentation to Esping-Andersen's and Lewis' typologies as they involve a detailed analysis of economic forces influencing the operation and structure of the state and of the labour market as well as the implications of these institutional arrangements for women's labour market participation in Sweden, the Federal Republic of Germany and the United States. Moreover, Schmid's analysis considers internal contradictions and tensions that may affect 'sexual' division of work. In Schmid's analysis, the state is an instrument used to achieve certain economic goals set by either the free market, the solidaristic wage policy or centrally co-ordinated agreement. By regarding the state as an instrument, contradictions in the state's activities and policies arising from the struggle of competing forces outside and inside the state are lost. Finally, the 'sexual' division of work is only explained by economic factors and the importance of social forces as, for example the religion/church, in shaping gender relations is ignored.

In the analysis of our regimes of gender relations, we use Esping-Andersen's ideal countries, i.e. Sweden, Germany and the United States, Lewis' concept of classification and Schmid's discussion of institutional arrangements. As pointed out by feminists scholars, gender is of limited concern in Esping-Andersen's analysis of different welfare state regimes. We therefore propose different concepts to classify countries according to variations in gender relations. However, we apply our concepts to the countries Esping-Andersen claims to be his ideal types in order to use his discussion of the welfare states in these countries. Moreover, we borrow Lewis' concept of the male-breadwinner to identify norms governing gender relations. However, Lewis' analysis is inadequate as the role of the organisation of production and the state as a social relation is not considered. Finally, our analyses of institutional arrangements concerning the organisation of production and work in the three countries are related to Schmid's paradigms. Schmid's analysis is, however, incomplete as it only involves economic dimensions of variations and treats the state as an instrument.

Our typologies are not based on a comparative statistical analysis. However, the underlying concepts, i.e. norms, institutional arrangements and consolidation of regimes or the political relations underlying the modes of regulation may be used to classify other countries. As the state must mediate between different needs of the economy and the interests of various social forces, the underlying concepts of classification may reveal contradictions as concerns regulation of gender relations. In Norway, for example, the religion/church has been a more significant force influencing the activities and the policies of the state than in Sweden. Instead of being interventionist in the sphere of social reproduction as in the case of the Swedish welfare state, the Norwegian welfare state has been non-interventionist. It has supported the traditional family ideology advocated by the Christian Democratic Party and treated women primarily as wives and mothers (see Leira 1993). The Christian Democratic Party in Norway had on average 11 per cent of the seats in parliament during the period 1973-1991. Even though Christian Democrats in Sweden have participated in parliamentary elections since 1964, it was not until 1991 that it entered the parliament as an independent party occupying 8 per cent of the total parliamentary seats (Lindblad et al. 1984; Nordic Council of Ministers). In 1994, the Christian Democrats received just over 4 per cent of the votes.

Institutional arrangements in Norway and Sweden concerning the sphere of production are, however, similar. Hence, a country can at a particular time in history resemble one type of a regime or it can be a hybrid of different types of regimes. By recognising that the underlying concepts of classification may reveal contradictions, I am able to identify and explain variations in norms and institutional arrangements concerning working mothers with children in countries that Esping-Andersen's concepts classify into one cluster or as social democratic welfare state regimes.

Transition/Transformation of Regimes

Regimes are not constants as the societal environment undergoes frequent changes that give rise to new demands by social forces. These new changes and demands put a pressure on the state to adjust or even change its activities and policies concerning the sphere of production and sphere of social reproduction. Conflicts and growing tensions may induce transition or transformation of the regime. In the case of regime transition the mode of regulation will change. Transition may either entail a change leading to the creation of a new regime of gender relations or a move from one existing regime to another. Institutional and policy changes/adjustment will not necessarily resolve tensions as they may generate conflicting social forces and different societal situations. Hence, regimes are under constant pressure to change and/or adjust its norms and institutional arrangements. The British regime of gender relations is an example of a regime undergoing a transition further away from an *egalitarian regime* closer to a *liberal regime*. This transition involves a greater support for the market by deregulating the private sector and by privatising state enterprises and welfare services (see Jessop 1991:96). Other regimes may only undergo transformation that involves adjustments within certain mode of regulation to societal changes and new demands by social forces. Such adjustments do not change the underlying principles of the particular regime. In the Swedish regime of gender relations transformation has taken place in recent years involving a weakening of the assumptions concerning women as working mothers in need of public assistance, welfare state cut backs and a decentralisation of the welfare state as well as greater scope for pay flexibility in the labour market. The transformation of the German regime of gender relations involves a weakening of the assumption of women as wives as more women participate in paid employment as well as further delegation of social affairs (for example, child care) to different intermediary organisations and greater employment flexibility.

After the Second World War, an *egalitarian regime of gender relations* was established in Sweden that involved a shift from personal (husband) to structural (state) dependency (see Hernes 1987a; Borchorst and Siim 1987). Change in the accumulation needs of capital and the growing strengths of organised working class generated the societal forces behind this transition (Lash and Urry 1987). In Sweden, women were drawn into the labour market on a large scale due to the expansion of the welfare state that entailed new employment opportunities and provisions of social services. This development made women dependent on the state as citizens, clients and employees of the state. As citizens and employees, women acquired less political power and working status than men. Moreover, women's client status was more fragmented than men's and more women than men became clients of the state (Hernes 1987a:37). Hence, the shift from private to public dependency did not change women's subordination in any fundamental way but rather strengthened it in new areas such as paid employment.

The transformation of the Swedish regime in recent years has also had important implications for gender relations. The decentralisation process has involved a shift from centrally negotiated collective wage agreements to sectoral wage negotiations and more individualised pay setting. Local trade union representatives and management are now responsible for wage negotiations and setting bonuses. The public sector has used individualised pay and performance pay as instruments to achieve more pay flexibility and more accountability and efficiency in government organisations. The implementation of individualised pay has since 1985 reversed the success of Swedish women in closing the gender wage gap and gender wage differentials have widened (Wise 1993; Delsen and Van Veen 1992). Higher wages in the private sector may, however, induce some women to move out of the public sector into different jobs offering higher wages, resulting in less occupational segregation and offsetting some of the the widening in the gender wage gap. In addition, Swedish women have been increasing their working hours during the 1980s that may indicate a move towards a less segregated labour market (see Jonung and Persson 1993:266). The move of some women out of the public sector will create divisions among the majority of women working in the public sector and women working in the private sector.

Britain is an example of a country in transition. The transition has involved various measures affecting gender relations. First, deregulation of employment rights has created greater dualism between core workers in permanent employment and peripheral workers in atypical employment. Deregulation of employment rights has increased gender differences in the labour market as women constitute the majority of part-time workers. Secondly, general erosion of individual rights has reduced legal distinctions between permanent and atypical work causing the status of all workers to shift down which reduces the tendency towards dualism (see Rubery 1989). This measure has led to a further deterioration in women's position in the labour market but may have left gender relations unchanged as all workers have seen their individual rights eroded. Finally, the vast majority of part-time jobs have been taken up by women married to employed men but not by unemployed persons or dependent on the unemployed (Deakin and Wilkinson 1991/2). However, it does not appear that women are being substituted for men. The expansion in part-time work has been in 'women's' jobs in the service sector leading to greater sharing of female jobs and a reduction in hours worked (Humphries and Rubery 1988). Hence, it seems that women's employment opportunities have been greater than those of men. However, women's increased partici-pation in the labour market has not been equally as beneficial to all women. Less qualified women have been integrated into the labour market at a low wage level making them economically dependent. More qualified women have, on the other hand, gained access to better paying jobs en-abling them to become economically independent on a partner (see Meyer 1994:18). The transition of the British welfare state seems to lead to a growing division between the increasingly proletarianized majority of women workers and an increasingly established minority of highly educated women with distinct different economic interests. A similar develop-ment appears to have taken place in the United States (see Power 1988; Boje 1993).

Conclusion

In this chapter, a comparative analytical framework for the study of the state as gendered social relations was developed in order to examine how women's interests are articulated into the state's activities and policies. In the first part, the focus was on how women have sought to influence the state and how the state has affected women's struggles and strategies. This contrasts with other economic and feminist approaches that are mainly concerned with how capitalists, capitalist development, state-managers and patriarchs mould the policies and activities of the state. Our approach to the state is 'feminist-relational' as it sees the state as gendered social relations or affected by and active in shaping women' struggles, i.e. as a site of gender strategies. At the centre of our approach is the interrelationship between women's strategies and the state. Strategies involve certain interests and form of mobilisation which are affected by the group of women mobilising and by the 'sensitivity' of the state to certain strategies. As the state is a product of country-specific political and social struggles, a strategy adopted in one country may not be successful in another country. The state influences gender relations through its policies and activities which may be inconsistent as the state has to mediate between different interests and institutional arrangements as well as state bureaucrats. Moreover, the institutional structures of the state many not be equally as adaptive to changes.

The state was analysed as a producer of strategies in the second part of this chapter. As a regulator of gender relations, the state has been the

33

main source of divergence in the forms/patterns of gender relations. The state adjusts the behaviour of men and women to certain patterns/forms of gender relations by creating/reproducing norms about men's and women's roles which are then supported by certain institutional arrangements in the area of production and reproduction. These norms and institutional settings constitute a mode of regulation that is influenced by political struggles and compromises or what has been termed as the consolidation. In order to establish what kinds of gender relations are promoted by the state in the spheres of production and social reproduction, three variations in the mode of regulation, i.e. norms, institutional arrangements and consolidation of regimes or the political relations underlying the modes of regulation were identified. On the basis of these variations in Sweden, Germany and the United States, three types of regimes were proposed; the egalitarian, ecclesiastical and the liberal regimes. Finally, regimes are under constant pressure to change as a result of the dynamic interactions between actors and structures. Growing conflicts and tensions may induce transition or a move from one regime to another on the one hand or a transformation or adjustment in the mode of regulation on the other hand.

Our comparative analytical framework of the state as gendered social relations included the state as a site of gender strategies and a regulator of gender relations. In the following chapter, our analysis of the state as a site of gender strategies will be expanded to include women's struggles in relation to other social political relations. Moreover, the interrelationship between social and political relations and the institutional arrangements of the state level will studied. The emphasis will be on the state as a product of past struggles and strategies in order to gain understanding of the functioning and structure of the state (cf. Jessop 1990).

Notes

[1] Following the tradition of Polanyi's (1944), I claim that market forces do not exist in their pure form. The economy is always 'embedded' in an institutional and historical context. This refers to contemporary capitalist economies as well as traditional economies (see Braudel 1979 and Holton 1993).
[2] Equality should not be confused with emancipation. Gender equality can involve integrating women into society constructed according to and defined by male standards.
[3] Even though the ethical message in Christianity and Islam is equality of all human begins, sexual hierarchy has been emphasised and institutionalised by the establishments of these religions.

2 Women's Encounter with the State during the Post-War Period

It appeared from the discussion in chapter one that Swedish women have been more successful than, for example, German and American women in closing the gender gap in political representation and labour market participation. American women, on the contrary, seem to have been the least successful in gaining political representation and social provisions enabling them to combine the roles of worker and mother. In Germany, the picture is more puzzling with a group of women advocating greater recognition of their unpaid work and another group struggling to enter the 'male-privileged' labour market. In order to explain why women's success in closing the gender gap has varied across the three countries, an inter-disciplinary and historical approach must be adopted that breaks the sharp division of work between economics, sociology and political science. Moreover, the state needs to be studied as gendered social relations or as a site of gender struggles, a regulator of gender relations and a product of previous history of struggles (see chapter 1).

Jessop's strategic-relational theory of the state forms the basis of our comparative analytical framework of the state. Bonefeld (1993) has criticised Jessop for destroying the notion of a contradictory constitution of social relations by focusing on the conceptualisation of the structural framework of struggle and not on the conceptualisation of class struggle. In order to overcome this deficiency in the strategic-relation theory of the state, women's struggles since the turn of this century will be analysed in relation to other social relations. The focus will be on political and social struggles in Sweden, Germany and the United States. Thereafter, the interrelationship between the institutional arrangements of the state and women's strategies towards the state will be studied. The institutional arrangements of the state, which are the outcome of previous history of social and political struggles, have affected the strategies adopted by the women's movements. As political actors, women have been involved in the consolidation of a certain mode of regulation. Consolidation refers to political and social struggles, agreements and institutional compromises around a certain mode of regulation. The particular form of integration or exclusion from political influences explain, for example, why certain norms have become embedded in institutional settings across time and space.

In the first part of the chapter, work within the Regulation school that attempts to supersede disciplinary cleavages and focuses on the interrelationship between social blocks and the women's movement will be discussed in order to enhance our understanding of how social movements have challenged and become embedded in the development of political and social institutions. The interrelationship between the women's movement and social blocks at the political level will give some explanations of why certain norms concerning the role of men and women have become more dominant than others across time and space. The theoretical insights given by the Regulation school will be used in the second part of the chapter to study actual conditions prevailing in Sweden, Germany and the United States during most of this century. The empirical analysis will start with an examination of women's political struggles in relation to the main social blocks prevailing during early part of this century. Thereafter, women's renewed political moblisation will be studied in light of the disintegration of the dominant social blocks. The chapter will conclude with a discussion of how the institutional settings of the state have affected women's position and political struggle.

Regulation of Social Relations

Regulationist theories give a framework for examining the shifting relationship between systems of production, reproduction and social blocks on the one hand and their regulation on the other hand. The Regulation school has developed as a reaction to the omission within Marxism and the Neo-classical school of the role of other mechanism than the value form and prices in ensuring a relative stabilisation of capitalism and market economies (Jessop 1995:316). Regulation refers to various modes by which activities within an economy and inter-actor relations are co-ordinated. During the 1980s, many Regulation theorists shifted their analytical focus from the regulation mechanism to new developments in the system of production and employment. This shift in focus by the Regulation school has been criticised for economic and technological determinism. For example, Tickell and Peck point out that the Regulationists' analyses of flexible production, flexible labour systems, and new industrial spaces have been very silent about the political and social institutions needed to maintain this economic development (1995:365). Regini (1995) has reacted to this deficiency by linking together changes in the organisation of production and work and changes in forms of regulation at the macro level that occurred in Europe during the 1980s[1].

According to Regini, the various modes or forms of regulation are the state, market, 'communitarian' regulation (family, subcultures and social movements) and 'associational' regulation. How these forms combine varies between countries and changes overtime. Changes are often only marginal, leading to small continuous adjustments (1995:5). However, a new form of regulation or the 'micro-social' regulation occurred during the 1980s in most of the European economies, replacing to a certain extent the 'macro-political' regulation. The boundaries between the two forms of regulation are not yet certain. At the 'macro-political' level of regulation, the state and large interest organisations engage in allocation of resources in order to counteract the socially undesirable outcomes of the market mechanism (1995:viii). At the 'micro-social' level of regulation, the site moves from that of the state to the level of the firm (in most cases) and initiatives are predominately taken by social actors such as associations, trade unions and firms as compared with political actors (1995:128).

Regini's analysis is reductionist as it focuses mainly on the changes in the regulation of capital-labour relations at the level of the state and the firm. More attention needs to be given to the regulation of other social relations such as gender relations at the level of, for example, social movements who have become more important during the 1970s and 1980s in order to understand the nature of the changes taking place within political and social institutions such as the welfare state as well as in organisation of work in the sphere of production and reproduction. Moreover, the fragmentation of various political alliances and the shift in the balance of power do not necessarily mean that initiatives are no longer made by the political actors, as it is not yet clear what this development will lead to. Although many have criticised Regulationists for not giving enough attention to the regulation of other social relations than that of capital-labour, very few have attempted to expand the Regulationist theories to include, for example, gender relations and social movements. The few exceptions include Jenson (1990) and Williams (1994) who have used the Regulationist framework to study how social movements have challenged and become embedded in the development of political and social institutions of the state.

In her analysis, Jenson (1990) attributes the failure of first-wave feminists' struggle or the suffragette movement in Canada to the timing of women's entry into the electoral institutions. At the time of women's entry, the political system was no longer open to the recognition of new actors and interests as it was a time of consolidation of the already firmly established institutions. Hence, Jenson claims that at certain moments the political discourse is in turmoil creating space for alternatives and at other moments '...the systems of social relations crystallise, stalling contradictions at least for a time' (1990:19). Williams (1994) on the other hand criticises the Regulationists for studying new challenges such as social movements only in terms of changes in class relations involving agency without power. Hence, Williams maintains that Regulationists' analyses of the welfare state are inadequate as social relations in this area are not only of class but of gender and race. According to Williams, analyses of social movements should be sensitive to their histories and consider the social relations from which they emerged and which they seek to challenge (1994:66-67). In our study of the women's movement, we have analysed how the women's movement has sought to influence the way the state regulates gender relations on the one hand and how the state has regulated gender relations in the spheres of production and social reproduction across different countries (see Mósesdóttir 1995). While Jenson only concentrates on the struggle of the Canadian first-wave feminists during the consolidation period, our focus was restricted to the second-wave feminist struggle. Williams' discussion also centres on more recent developments as it is confined to the role of social movements within welfare at the time of restructuring. Moreover, struggles and co-operation within and between social movements are missing in Williams' analyses.

Studies of social movements have led to important improvements in the theoretical framework of the Regulation school. However, more theoretical and empirical analyses are needed of the complex forms of collective identity, action, alliances, compromises and patterns of domination among social groups and of their historical development. Such analysis will enhance our understanding of the nature of the changes which have taken place within political and social institutions as well as in organisation of work in the sphere of production and reproduction. Moreover, greater attention should be given to individuals in relation to social movements and social blocks. Folbre (1994) has developed valuable insights into social relations in her approach to the study of collective identities, interests and action. According to Folbre, identities and interests that specify the context of individual choice are defined by assets, rules, norms and preferences. The mechanisms of group identity and interest shape and are shaped by social institutions which on the other side systematically strengthen certain groups and weaken others (1994:48). However, the interrelationship between various groups or agencies involving both co-operation and conflict as well as alliances and domination needs more elaboration in Folbre's discussion. The analysis in this paper uses insights from analysis of social movements by the Regulation school as well as from empirical studies of the historical development of social blocks in Sweden, Germany and the United States. Before proceeding to the conditions in the selected countries, we will discuss the historical development of social blocks in more analytical terms.

Our theoretical discussion will be multi-level, starting at the level of the individual and then moving to collective action and ending with structures. Individuals have a variety of interests or perceive themselves as belonging to a variety of groups organised around, for example, class, religion and race that may represent conflicting interests. Those individuals in similar situation may even designate themselves as belonging to different groups. The choice of group(s) will be influenced by how the individual perceives his/her position and how his/her situation is perceived by others. An individual may join a group(s) in order to make new claims and/or support old claims or simply to reap the benefits involved, i.e. to be a free-rider and/or to fight subordination. When the individual makes a choice, he/she will not be able to predict the benefits of various memberships to her/himself and society at large since the actions of others are unknown (Folbre 1994:5) and actions may have unintended effects.

Societal changes (economic, social and/or political) leading to growing contradictions between individuals/groups/countries will induce new collective actions that are in most cases a collective attempt outside established institutions to promote a common interest. Although the activities of the new collective action or social movements may be outside the establishment, they may promote their interest through formal channels (see Giddens 1993:642). The type of collective action will be the result of strategic calculations and is constrained by access to resources, other social blocks (domination and alliances) and social and political institutions (norms and rules). The strategic calculations are a continuous process of past actions that have both intended and unintended effects (see Regini 1995:35; Mósesdóttir 1995). Moreover, societal changes may also disrupt collective action. Social movements may either aim to bring about society change and/or the behaviour of people (see Giddens 1993:643). Alliances, compromises and patterns of domination within and among social groups are the result of individual and group dynamics, i.e. who has the right to make claims, choices and constraints faced by groups as well as co-operation and conflicts between groups (see Jenson 1990:18). Moreover, co-operation and conflicts between groups will be complicated by the multiple group identity of their members (Folbre 1994:82). After a stable system of social blocks has been built, it will only recognise new groups and social contexts or agency when the system can no longer by reproduced or regulated due to societal changes (see Jenson 1990:19).

Exclusion from Political Power

The social blocks governing in Sweden, Germany and the United States during the post war period will now be studied. The analysis will go beyond emphasis on the aggregate product of individual preferences. Instead social blocks involving alliances, compromises and patterns of domination among social groups will be examined. The focus will be on how women's political struggles have been constrained by and challenged established pressure groups, organised interest groups and political parties in the three countries.

It was not until the 1960s and 1970s that social blocks at the political level became more open for social identities other than class, religion, regionalism and nationalism. Hence, the female suffrage did not enable women in most West European and North American countries to exercise any dramatic impact on the political and policy processes. Women and the women's movements were induced to join other actors such as church groups as well as women's organisations within political parties and unions. Separate women's movements in politics that had in many instances struggled for female suffrage could therefore not be sustained during the early part of the post-war period. In many countries, the women's movement became a maternal and social reform movement concentrating on activities related to women's role as mothers and domestic workers. Hence, women's identity was linked to other social relations in a variety of ways. However, their gender identity still remained important (see Jenson 1990). Although women belonged to various groups, they were in most instances regarded as a homogenous group of citizens. The traditional division of work gave women this homogenous outlook. Most women were constrained to the sphere of reproduction. Women's engagement in the sphere of production was in most cases limited and discontinuous, confined to periods of lighter domestic activities. Men on the other hand were constrained to the sphere of production and assumed to be breadwinners. When men entered political process, their status was more heterogeneous as divisions along class, religion and regions were acknowledged as legitimate.

Assigned the Role of Mothers in the Swedish 'People's Home' [2]

The Swedish multi-party system consisting of five parties was already in place when Swedish women gained the national suffrage in 1921 and it was not until the 1980s that a new party entered the system (see Hancock 1993:413)[3]. In the 1920s and 1930s, women joined the political parties by entering separate women's organisations within four out of the five political parties (Oskarson and Wängnerud 1995:99)[4]. Women have seldom organised separately, outside of or across established parties or unions. In order to gain political power Swedish women have had to work through a political party, preferably combined with the women's organisation of the party but not through women's organisations alone (see Eduards 1991:175). Moreover, women in independent groups and organisations have always worked together with women in political parties in order to promote women's interests at the political level (see Oskarson and Wängnerud 1995:99). In addition, the centralised state system did not allow much space to groups outside the formal political system. The main federation of employers or the SAF (Svenska Arbetsgivareföreningen) and the largest federation of the industrial unions or the LO (Landsorganisationen i Sverige) built an alliance soon after women entered the electoral system that became the dominant social block in Sweden until the 1980s. The very strong and initially militant working class was able in 1938 to impose a national class compromise favourable to the labour movement as their right to centralised collective negotiations was recognised by employers[5]. The power of the labour movement was not only restricted to centralised bargaining. The LO was able to shape economic and social policies through its close links to the Social Democratic Party SAP that governed in Sweden during most of the post-war period (Regini 1995:38-39)[6]. The SAF that represents large firms in manufacturing, commerce and forestry has on the other hand aligned with the bourgeois parties, particularly the Conservative party (Moderata Samlingspartiet) (Hancock 1993:423). However, the Swedish business leaders have often expressed confidence in the competence and reliability of the SAP as a governmental party (see Therborn 1991:121).

The key to the success of the inter-war and the post-war SAP was its ability to pursue several cross-class alliances simultaneously. The SAP built alliances between workers, farmers and the domestic industry on the one hand and between employers and labour in the export sectors to curtail the wage demands of unions in sectors sheltered against international competition on the other hand (Pontusson 1994:40). Although the Social Democratic Women's League demanded in 1928 a role in the creation of the People's Home, radical changes of gender relations did not take place[7]. The historical compromise between employers and labour did not create opportunity for a transformation of gender relations. Women's maternal role was therefore emphasised and supported by family-oriented social polices that originated from the widespread concerns with the population growth. In the first half of the 1900s, around 25 per cent of Swedish women of childbearing age chose not to have children. The trade unions had acknowledged women's right to work in the 1930s and after the World War Two a third of Swedish women were in paid work. However, the unions did not promote women's labour force participation by demanding increased public expenditure on public child care. On the contrary, women's maternal role was actively supported during the 1930s and 1940s by free maternity care, a maternity allowance, child allowances and rental subsidies for families with children. Hence, women's role in the People's Home became the creation of the 'good home' where gender difference was recognised and even celebrated. The People's Home consisted therefore of mothers/housewives, farmers, workers and capitalists (Jenson and Mahon 1993:82-85 and 91; Bergqvist 1994:162).

It was not until 1918 that German women gained the right to vote in parliamentary elections (Bergqvist 1994:58). At the same time women were allowed to attend schools and universities. The German Union for Women's Suffrage (Der Deutsche Verband für Frauenstimmrecht) established in 1902 was one of the many women's groups and women's associations that sprung to life in the late 19th century and the early 20th century. After gaining entrance to electoral institutions, many feminist groups started to fight with some success for the decriminalisation of the abortion law or paragraph 218 of the Penal Code introduced in 1887[8]. When the Allies established the West German model of democracy in 1949, they disregarded the various women's associations and women's groups that had been an important social force during the Weimar Republic. Moreover, many of the 'misogynist' views and laws from the Nazi period remained until the 1960s and 1970s (see Kaplan 1992:104-109). The Allies only acknowledged divisions along class, religious and regional lines inducing German women to organise within post-war unions, political parties and religious groups. The suppression of feminist activities during the Nazi period and the neglect of the past activities created a total break in the history of the women's movement in Germany (1992:108). An umbrella organisation called the German Women's Council (Der Deutsche Frauenrat) was soon formed that was loosely linked to various women's organisations within the political parties and the unions. The German Women's Council fought along with other women's groups for the inclusion of the Equal Rights Clause into the West German Basic Law that was adopted in 1949. However, the potential power of the Equal Rights Clause was greatly impaired by another clause in the Basic Law which expressly committed the state to defend and preserve the family. The Constitutional Court resolved the potential conflict by ruling that functional difference in the family and in the paid employment could justify different treatment of women and men (Ferree 1995:97-98). Although, women's labour force share was 29 per cent in 1948 and many women were the main breadwinner after the war, limited efforts were made to build child care facilities, improve women's working conditions and to reduce the pay gap between men and women. When the 'Wirtschaftswunder' started in the 1950s, the unions became increasingly disinterested in promoting women's interests that they had started to see more as social issues rather than workers' issues. Moreover, the legal rights of the family and the ruling of the Constitutional Court concerning the Equal Rights Clause had strengthened the housewife-marriage. Women therefore started to see the full-time housewife role as an attractive alternative to paid employment (see Buchholz-Will 1995:185-190).

The Allies fragmented and dispersed the political power among a variety of institutions and elites in West Germany. The political parties were made quasi-state institutions in order to secure coherence in the policy making[9]. Moreover, a system of consultation between politicians, state elites and the leading representatives of interest groups was introduced to secure coherence and consensus (see Conradt 1993). The major interest groups in West Germany have been those of employers, labour, agriculture, the churches and professional organisations that are well organised at the local, state and national levels and work closely with the political parties and the state (1993:243)[10]. The German Trade Union Federation DGB (Der Deutscher Gewerkschaftsbund) became labour's main political force and has pursued a policy of 'business unionism' concentrating on wages and working conditions (1993:246-247)[11]. The Confederation of German Employers' Associations BDA (Die Bundesvereinigung der Deutschen Arbeitsgeberverbände) became the central organisation of the strongly united and disciplined body of employers (Smith 1994:276). Strong alignment between the main organisation of employers and labour on the one hand the political parties on the other hand was not established. Each major interest group maintained contact with all major parties. The labour unions have though had closer ties with the Social Democratic Party SPD (Die Socialdemokratische Partei Deutschlands) than the Christian Democratic Party CDU and its Bavarian partner Christian Social Union CSU (Die Christlich-Soziale Union) while employers have enjoyed warmer relations with the CDU/CSU than the SPD (Conradt 1993:243-244). The political position and influence of the churches have been strong[12]. The dominant political party from 1949 to 1969 was the CDU that emphasised Christian principles and thereby gained the support of the Catholic church. While in government, the CDU has been sensitive to issues such as state support of church schools and strict divorce and abortion laws stressed by the church. The SPD has, on the other hand, sought to have a normalised, less conflictual relationship with the church since the late 1950s (1993:203). The West German political system has been characterised by great stability

44

in terms of government formation as well as by coalition governments. The Free Democratic party FDP was the junior coalition partner with the CDU/CSU governments from 1949 to 1957 and again from 1961 to 1965 (1993:222)[13].

Acknowledging the Maternal Role of American Women

American women gained the national suffrage in 1920 after a long and bitter campaign (McDonagh 1990:46). The inclusion into the electoral system did not empower women politically as their maternal role had become the dominant identity in women's struggle for protective legislation in the workplace and for social welfare programmes. The male unionists regarded women as temporary workers who were subject to extraordinary exploitation due to their disadvantaged position in the labour market and lack of unionisation. Although an exception to the usual union practice of struggling for gains in the workplace, the unions demanded protective legislation for women (Jenson 1989:256). The Supreme Court granted in 1908 a special protection for women that justified differential treatment of women and men workers (1989:243)[14]. Moreover, the practice of 'marriage bars' involving an explicit rules against hiring married women or retraining women in their jobs after marriage was widely used in traditional female occupations until the 1950s (Drobnic and Wittig 1997:291). The only public social expenditure available across the United States until the 1930s was the mothers' pension that was pushed through by a group of women before women's franchising[15]. Hence, a certain group of American mothers could collect publicly founded social benefits while almost no American adult male worker could collect such benefits for either themselves or their dependants (Skocpol 1995:76). This maternal welfare programme laid the ground for the 'two-channel' welfare state established in the 1930s that addressed women and mothers and men as workers (Jenson 1989:241; Skocpol 1995:76). The emphasis on women's reproductive role located them outside the formal political system. Moreover, the political system was highly developed at the time of women's franchise, making it difficult for the suffragette movement to gain political power. Hence, the suffragette movement disintegrated and women became depoliticised (see McDonagh 1990:51; Katzenstein 1992:31). As a response to the long struggle for the vote, Congress established the Women's Bureau[16] by statute in 1920 that has basically pursued the interests of organised labour involving protective measures for women. Moreover, the Equal Rights Amendment ERA to the Constitution was first proposed to Congress in the early 1920s by women inside and outside the political and state organisations but without success (Sapiro 196:123; Stetson 1995:256 and 267).

The Democratic party took over from the Republican party as the majority party in the 1930s when it managed to build the so-called New Deal coalition consisting of the South, the unions, the big cities, ethnic groups and academics. The Republican party emerged after the Civil War as the party of national unity and it soon became dominated by the coalition of industrialists, bankers, Northern and Western farmers and some industrial workers. The decentralised (federalism) and divided government (Congress versus the presidency) fragmented the organisational structure of the two main parties, making them coalitions of interests of a number of social groups and regional interests instead of a political entity capable of countering interest group influences (McKay 1993:82-88; Piven 1991:236 and 244). The most important groups supporting the Democratic party at the outset of the New Deal period were the white Southerners, representing agricultural interests and the working class (Piven 1991:238)[17]. As a result of restricted franchise in the South, decentralisation as concerns representation to the Senate and the electoratal college and division of power between the presidency and Congress, the Southern agricultural interests were strong within the Democratic party and thereby Congress since the party had the majority of seats during most of the post-war period (1991:247; McKay 1993:82 and 135).

The electoral coalition of the white Southerners and the working class did, however, not last for long. The Southerners soon formed an alliance with the business-oriented Republicans in Congress who could join forces in an attempt to hinder the implementation of new social programmes and policies in favour of labour. This new alliance made certain that the legislative protections of the National Labour Relations Act won by mass strikes in the mid-1930s were eroded within a few years by giving the states the necessary autonomy to undermine this federal policy[18]. Moreover, the low turnout of working class voters and the growing susceptibility of Congress to business lobbyists and the lack of resistance by the Democratic presidents to the assault on the unions further alienated the unions from the Democratic party (Piven 1991:250). According to Piven, the Southern Democrats and business-oriented Republicans were able to ensure that the new national welfare state programmes introduced in the 1930s conformed to regional and sectoral diversified labour markets. Regional variations were safeguarded by granting the states and, in some instances the counties, part of the authority over the unemployment insurance programme and other 'categorical' welfare programmes, making certain that local employers were able to influence the conditions of eligibility and benefit levels[19]. Sectoral diversification was constituted by excluding many categories of low wage workers from the old age and unemployment insurance programmes. The domination of the Southen agricultural interests and the business-oriented Republicans in Congress forced the unions to return to the workplace where they bargained with employers for, for example, health insurance (1991:252-253)[20]. As concerns gender interests, there was no significant difference between men's and women's party and candidate voting in Congress and Presidential elections from the 1950s until the 1970s. Hence, women were not considered to be a group that required a special attention by the Democratic and Republican parties (Molitor 1991:103).

New Challenges and Shifts in the Balance of Power

The female suffrage did not enable women in Sweden, Germany and the United States to exercise any dramatic political and policy impact as social blocks at the political level were only open for social identities involving class, religion, regionalism and nationalism. From the 1960s until the 1980s, women moblised in mass numbers around the social identity of gender that cut across more established identities such as that of class. The women's movements were a part of the 'new' social movements organising around race/ethnicity, gender and generational divisions that challenged the governing social blocks.

The Case of Sweden

It was not until the mid-1950s that the Swedish People's Home started to develop but the name refers to social relations based on equality, consideration and co-operation. At this time, the system of centralised collective bargaining became a regular practice in Sweden and social expenditure expanded, especially in the area of social security. However, women were not satisfied with their maternal role (Jenson and Mahon

1993:84-:85; Bergqvist 1994:162)[21]. In the early 1960s, a largely female group of sociologists, economists and psychologists advocated the break-up of the sexual division of labour in the home and demanded policies of equal opportunities and affirmative action outside the home in the welfare state and in paid employment. Moreover, Swedish feminists campaigned during the 1960s actively in favour of mandatory separate taxation of spouses. The Social Democratic Women's League took up these ideas in 1964 and struggled for their acceptance within the SAP. As a result of growing pressure from the women's groups and other social movements demanding greater equality, the leadership of the SAP renewed during the 1960s its socialist commitment to equality of outcome in terms of both class and gender. The equality programme adopted by the SAP in 1969 was by no means a feminist declaration as ideas of 'sex' equality had been integrated into an equality programme that had something for everybody (Ginsburg 1992:32 and 50-51; Lyttkens 1992 quoted in Sundström 1997:275). Motivated by the labour shortage in the 1960s caused by export-led economic boom and the expansion in almost all fields of welfare provisions, the LO and the SAP started to incorporate women's issues into their class politics. The LO and the SAF agreed in the early 1960s to end a separate women's wage classifications and LO was committed to use the centralised wage agreements to reduce wage differentials or to achieve wage solidarity (Jenson and Mahon 1993:87-88).

Policy reforms stimulated by the 'sex' equality movement included the introduction of separate income tax assessment for wife and husband (1971), extensive statutory parental leave (1974), a liberation of the abortion law (1976), the Equal Status (jämställdhet) law (1979) and a great expansion in public expenditure on child care (Ginsburg 1992:51; Statistics Sweden 1995:6). Hence, women became identified as working mothers and women's equality was to be achieved through collective negotiations and not through legislature and state initiatives (see Elman 1995; Persson 1990:229). The measures undertaken by the SAP and the LO stimulated women's labour force participation that went from 59 per cent in the 1970 to 74 per cent in 1980 (Jenson and Mahon 1993:91). In order to cope with the double burden, around 47 per cent of women worked fewer than 32 hours or part-time in 1980 (see Sundström 1993:41). However, the majority of women did not identify with the SAP to the same extent as men during this period. From 1960 to 1979, women were more likely to support the bourgeois block or the Centre party (Centerpartiet), the Liberal party

(Folkpartiet) and the Conservative party than the socialist block (socialistiska blocket) or the Left party and the SAP (Oskarson and Wängnerud 1995:79-77)[22].

The class compromise achieved in 1938 started to breakdown during the 1970s and continued through the 1980s. The breakdown can be attributed to structural changes, growing internal divisions among labour, a shift in the balance of power, and to the fragmentation of the parliamentary party system. The Swedish industry experienced falling export demand and technological/organisational exhaustion from 1974 onwards (Ryner 1994:412). Hence, industrial employment contracted during the 1970s while employment in services expanded (OECD 1993:187). This development weakened the leading role of the Metalworkers Union (Svenska metallindustriarbetareförbundet) within the LO. Moreover, the wage policy which was based on the private sector blue-collar unions being the wage setters, became less acceptable to a growing number of public sector employees. The tensions within the labour movement were intensified by the organisational division between the unions of white collar workers (TCO and SACO)[23] and the union of blue collar workers or the LO (Ryner 1994:402; Mahon 1991:303). Moreover, women had more success in promoting their interests within the white collar unions than within the LO which was not willing to present itself as the largest women's organisation until the 1990s (Jenson and Mahon 1993:96-97).

The balance of power shifted towards employers during the 1970s and 1980s due to the ineffective wage-earner funds, breakdown of centralised collective bargaining and greater internationalisation of Swedish capital. In order to make wage restraint more acceptable to workers in high profit firms and to transfer capital ownership to employees, the LO adopted in 1976 a proposal for wage-earner funds, to be financed by the extra profits. However, the wage-earner funds did not appeal to all social groups as they excluded domestic workers and pensioners. Moreover, employers and the non-socialist government of 1976-1982 resisted their implementation. When the wage-earner funds were finally introduced in 1984, their functions had been changed so much that they could not reduce the growing concentration of capital ownership (Standing 1988:139-143). Moreover, employers in the engineering industry managed to split the fold of the LO in 1983 when it got the powerful Metalworkers Union to bargain separately in order to achieve higher wage (Ryner 1994:404). The decentralisation of the wage bargaining has led to growing wage dispersion

49

especially between the private and public sector and to widening gender wage gap but the unintended effect of the centralised bargaining was a contraction in the gender wage gap (see, for example, le Grand 1994:121). Finally, Swedish employers have in recent years weakened the power of the unions by becoming more mobile. After 1987, Swedish investment overseas rose sharply and by 1990 it exceeded 6 per cent, higher than any other developed economy (Wilks 1996:103).

The Breakdown of the Class Compromise

During the 1980s and early 1990s, the parliamentary party system in Sweden started to fragment, first on the left and then on the right. Moreover, the support for the SAP became more unreliable. It became increasingly apparent in the early 1980s that the SAP had not managed to incorporate all groups into its vision of the People's Home. Dissatisfaction was growing among environmentalists and women. Women were still underrepresented among the top level representatives within the LO and the SAP and experiencing gender inequalities in the labour market. Hence, women joined the new political movements such as the peace and environmental movements and organised feminist activities (see Oskarson and Wängnerud 1995:39 and 70). In 1985, the Women's Party was established and a Women's network (Stödstrumporna) operated secretly (Eduards 1992:87-89). In order to sustain its political support, the SAP sought during the 1980s to include into its policies some of the demands put forward by the new social movements. The number of female representatives was gradually increased and after the election in 1994 women constituted 48 per cent of the party representatives in the Riksdag (see Oskarson and Wängnerud 1995:101). However, the Environmentalist Party-the Greens (Miljöpartiet De Gröna) managed in 1988 to become the first new party to enter parliament in seventy years, appealing to the young electorate as well as to women (see Hancock 1993:411; Oskarson and Wängnerud 1995:78-79)[24]. Moreover, gender relations at the electoral level were changing. Women had since 1979 used their voting right to a greater extent than men[25] and they had also changed their party voting such that the socialist block had a female surplus and the bourgeois block had a male surplus after 1979. However, the difference or what has been termed the gender gap was only significant in the elections 1985 and 1988 and it almost disappeared in 1991 and 1994 (Oskarson and Wängnerud 1995:53 and 78-79)[26].

Although the SAP has been the largest party in Sweden since 1932, its electoral support has become more unstable as it has been unsuccessful in accommodating new and old social divisions such as class, gender and generational divisions[27]. The willingness of the SAP's leadership to lower welfare benefits and limit welfare service expansion have contributed to the party's loss of the electorate among blue collar workers and later women (Jenson and Mahon 1993:92-95). The ties with the LO have loosened in recent years due to tensions between public and private sector unions on the one hand and between party unionists (LO) and those advocating more party democracy on the other hand. The SAP has not been able to maintain women's support due to its contradictory policies, promoting on the one hand women's representation within the party and attacking, on the other hand, welfare rights that have enabled women to combine their roles as mothers and workers. By 1989, the fertility rate in Sweden was among the highest in the Western World[28]. The female surplus that the SAP had after the elections in 1979 changed in 1994 to a male surplus of 3 per cent as a result of an announcement made by the Social Democrats shortly before the election that they would reduce the number of paid sick days. After the election in 1991, the parliamentary party system showed further signs of fragmentation. The two new parties to enter the Riksdag were the New Democratic party (Ny Demokrati) and the Christian Democratic party (Kristdemokratiska Samhällspartiet) but the Environmentalist Party-the Greens lost their parliamentary mandate. After the election in 1994, the Greens re-entered the Riksdag but the New Democratic party lost its parliamentary mandate. Moreover, there existed a gender gap and a generation gap among electorates in the parliamentary elections in 1994. Women 45 years and younger were more likely to vote for the socialist block than men[29]. In addition, women 46 years and older voted to a greater extent for the bourgeois block than younger women. On the contrary, men 45 years and younger were more inclined to vote for the bourgeois block than older men (see Oskarson and Wängnerud 1995:78-79).

The Case of Germany

In the 1950s and 1960s, the family policy under the CDU aimed at strengthening the family, fostering self-sufficiency and protecting family privacy. Women were, for example, prohibited by law to take paid employment without their husband's permission (Chamberlayne 1994:174 and 179). In addition, the time pupils were required to spend in education and training was lengthened and the retirement age was lowered. Hence, women's labour force share fell slightly or from 31 per cent in 1950 to 30 per cent in 1970 and men's labour force share dropped during the same period from 63 per cent to 58 per cent (Molitor 1991:47-48). The dramatic fall in the number of children from 2 children in 1950 to 1 one child in 1970 for each marriage may, on the other hand, explain why the labour force share of married women increased from 25 per cent in 1950 to 36 per cent in 1970 (see 1991:48-51). The coalition of the CDU and the SDP from 1969 brought a more critical view of the family, seeing it as an obstacle to social equality and to the emancipation of both women and children. Women's aspirations and political preferences started to change during the 1970s as more women were engaged in paid work. At the end of 1970s, women's party voting had became more similar to that of men. During the 1950s and 1960s, a greater proportion of women had voted for the conservative parties (CDU/CSU) than men[30]. This gender difference in party voting has been attributed to women's position as housewives and their religious belief or Catholicism (Rudolph 1993:53; Molitor 1991:26).

The Marriage and Family Rights reform implemented in 1977 introduced the notion of partnership between husband and wife and equal worth between the wife's paid employment outside the home and her family roles as family caring became recognised in the pension law (Chamberlayne 1994:179-180). The federal parliament mandated in 1979 an equal treatment for women in paid employment. The drive behind the changes in women's employment status was the need to bring the West German law into compliance with the EU directives on equal pay (1975) that later developed into equal pay for work of equal value (1976). It was, however, not until 1986 that women's labour force participation started to show signs of continuous increase but the growth of the service sector started first after the mid-1980s in West Germany. Women's labour force participation has been relatively low in West Germany when compared with other countries in North America and Western Europe[31]. Limited availability of child care for working mothers and the splitting of the income of married couples introduced in 1958 that favours a home-based wife, has contributed to the limited growth in women's labour force participation. The principle of subsidiary advocated by the Catholic Church through the CDU forms the basis of the West German social welfare state (Sozialstaat). According to this principle, responsibility for welfare is held to lie with individuals and their families and the state is only to intervene as a last resort (Freeman and Clasen 1994:11). Hence, the principle of subsidiarity has served as a constraint on the expansion of public welfare services.

The 'new' women's movement in West Germany started in the early 1970s and was catalysed by the strict abortion law making abortion a punishable crime. The oppressive nature of the church and its influence on politics was also of concern to many women activists. The abortion issue was taken up by the political parties and drafts were prepared of an amendment and put to the test in Constitutional Court. The amendment was accepted with extensive restrictions in 1977 such that abortion was allowed in specific situations or in case of grave health reasons, eugenic and/or circumstantial problems (Kaplan 1992:114-117). The 'new' women's movement started in the early 1970s involving women organising outside the established political system in 'autonomous' groups as well as women working inside the established organisations as, for example, the church, unions and political parties. The 'autonomous' groups worked from time to time together with women inside the system in order to pursue certain issues (see Chamberlayne 1994:175). However, the West German governments have, during the years of active feminist movement, demonstrated that they do not allow special interest groups to interfere. The striving of many women's groups for autonomy from the political machinery was therefore not very successful. Hence, many women's groups became during the 1980s more willing to give up their autonomy in order to work with and through government institutions (see Kaplan 1992:143). In 1979, the Women's Party was formed (Frauenpartei) which has so far not been able to break through the 5 per cent of the vote threshold to get into the Bundestag. However, the women's movement entered parliamentary politics during the 1980s through political alternative movements like the Greens (Die Grüne Partei). In 1983, the Green Party was the first newly formed party to enter the Bundestag since the 1950s. The ecological and feminist considerations of the Green Party have attracted women but they have had to fight for a place within the party by creating their women's lists (1992:127; Conradt 1993:240). The success of the Greens in promoting women candidates and appealing to young women induced both the SPD and the CDU to increase the number of women candidates after the mid-1980s (Chapman 1993:237).

Since the elections in 1983, the CDU/CSU has once again had a greater number of women among its electorate, but the female surplus was smaller from 1983 to 1990 than from 1953 and 1969 (Molitor 1991:25-32; Statistisches Bundesamt)[32]. The pro-family stance of the Kohl governments involving child allowances and glorification of motherhood has found support among a certain fraction of the women's movement (Kaplan 1992:118). Many radical feminists have argued for difference to the point of a separation of roles between men and women. However, the CDU has claimed that they were promoting shared roles and equality between housewives and employed women (Chamberlayne 1994:182). Measures to achieve equality between housewives and employed women included the Parental leave Legislation from 1986 that gives a parent entitlement to a flat rate sum for two years while caring for a child as well as pension rights during the caring period. Another measure was the Long-Term Care Insurance (Soziale Pflegeversicherung) passed in 1995 that acknowledges care in the pension system by granting care receivers right to payments to pay care givers for their services. The Child Care Facility Act (Kindergartengesetz) passed in 1996 grants each child over three years access to child care which has led to some expansion of part time nursery places (see Ostner 1998). The parental leave legislation and the new care insurance provide incentives for women to interrupt their labour force participation while the child care provisions have institutionalised part time work among mothers with older child(ren).

Growing Tensions within the 'Consensus' Model

The West German consensus model has come under growing pressure due to fragmentation of the parliamentary party system and growing tensions between employers and labour. Moreover, unification has both enhanced social divisions and created conditions for changes that are no longer incremental. The vote for the SPD increased from the election in 1953 to the election in 1972 when it received 46.3 per cent of the votes. The SPD's attempts in the sixties and early 1970s to integrate the new generation were not very successful and the party started to lose voters that continued through the 1980s and until the elections in 1994. (Statistisches Bundesamt; von Baratta 1995:159). The cultural and generational revolt in the late sixties paved the way for the emergence of the Greens but many of its activists had worked within the SPD but had been unsuccessful in reforming the party (Padgett and Paterson 1994:113). The development of the Greens was soon marked by a battle between the pragmatic wing or the 'Realos' who were interested in co-operation with the SPD and the fundamentalist wing or the 'Fundis' who did not want any arrangement with the SPD as they would help the latter to absorb the Greens in the long run. The balance between the two has been shifting but the majority of party members have in fact been among the realist fraction (1994:111). The vote for CDU/CSU has been more stable than that of the SPD fluctuating from 43.3 in 1953 to 48.5 in 1983. In 1994, the party received 41.5 per cent of the total vote in Germany (Statistisches Bundesamt; van Baratta 1995:159).

It became apparent after the European parliament in 1989 that the CDU/CSU was not able to appeal to voters on the far right as the Republicans (Republikaner) received 7.1 per cent of the votes in the election (see Molitor 1991:121). However, the support for the Republicans declined after 1992 when the constitutional rule concerning asylum-seeker was made more strict and they failed to be re-elected to the European parliament (Gibowski 1995:31). Further fragmentation of the parliamentary party system took place after the all German election in 1990 when the East German based party, the old Communist Party PDS (Die Partei des Demokratischen Sozialismus) managed to enter the Bundestag (Conradt 1993:243). After the elections in 1994, the PDS was more strongly presented in Bundestag than in 1990. Like the Greens, the PDS did particularly well among younger female voters (Betz and Welsh 1995). The strong position of employers in West Germany strengthened during the 1980s. The return of the CDU/CSU to power in 1982 was supported by employers and the coalition government of the CDU/CSU and the FDP passed legislation in 1986 that weakened the trade unions' capacity to strike (Conradt 1993:246-248). The reduction in entitlements and levels of benefit in the areas of health, pension and social security that had started under Chancellor Schmidt in the late 1970s were intensified between 1982 and 1985 but stopped as a result of the CDU's poor performance in regional elections (Freeman and Clasen 1994:12).

During the unification process, the West German trade unions were readily accepted in the East and they soon became organised on an all-German basis (Smith 1992:202). The inclusion of East Germans reduced the imbalance between male and female membership but 49 per cent of the

East German labour force was female at the time of unification as compared to 38 per cent in the West (Lane 1994:194; Kolinsky 1992:265). Wages in West Germany were low in relation to the return of employers in the early 1990s due to the wage restraints implemented in the late 1980s. Hence, the unions demanded higher wages when the economy started to boom in the West after the unification and renewed their demand for a 35-hour week. Outbreaks of labour unrest took place in 1992 as the trade unions claimed that ordinary wage earners had been forced to bear the burnt of the unification. The West Germans have paid for the unification by running huge government deficits and by relaxing the contribution principle of social insurance programmes such as the unemployment insurance and pension insurance thereby granting many of the new entrees exceptionally 'cheap' admission to the system. After the strike of the public sector unions, wage increases beyond the inflation rate were accepted (Smith 1992:51 and 203; Ganssman 1993:85-87). The German unions have become more heterogeneous as the East and the West members do not share the same economic situation and industrial and political demands. The lack of cohesiveness within the unions has enabled employers to utilise these divisions (Lane 1994:194). Moreover, mass unemployment, especially in the East has weakened the unions in the mid-1990s and employers' demand of a reduction in workers' social benefits has become a feasible political measure to undertake.

The German unification has not only led to more extensive access to social insurance programmes but also to greater federal centralisation. As a result of social difficulties and financial weakness in the East, the federal government has in many cases been forced to move into areas traditionally the responsibility of the federal states. Moreover, the financial framework of the federal government that was originally planned as an instrument to fine-tune the economic convergence of the states has been transformed into extensive aid programmes for the East German states (Sturm 1992:127-131). The unification has been a great disappointment to many women as it has not involved extensive improvements in the area of child care and abortion. The most favourable development is women's greater access to the male-privileged social insurance programmes, for example, the pension system. Moreover, divisions between 'wives' and the 'careerists' deepened during the unification period and a new division was created between women in the East and West Germany. The unification has created more opportunities for those women willing and able to work, especially in the

West while family work has received greater recognition (cf. Long-Term Care Insurance and the Child Care Facility Act). At the time of the unification, the East German women were in most cases working mothers who wanted to achieve a West German standard of living. The East German women have had to pay a high price for unification as social services, social benefits and the right to an abortion have been eroded. Moreover, co-operation between feminists in the East and West Germany has not been without problems due to their different ideological background as well as social and economic situation (see Rosenberg 1991:18).

The Case of the United States

In the United States, the core New Deal social insurance programmes or the old-age insurance and unemployment insurance of the 1930s did not reach most blacks and many women since occupations in agriculture and the service sector were excluded from social insurance taxes and coverage. Women who were surviving dependants (1939) were covered by the old-age insurance or what is termed as Social Security. The poorer caretakers of children who were increasingly women outside wedlock were left to be helped by Aid to Families with Dependent Children AFDC or what Americans call 'welfare'[33]. Variations in benefits and eligibility in public assistance at the state level allowed state and local officials to exercise administrative discretion causing the blacks and poor women to be deprived of adequate welfare assistance (see Skocpol 1995:218-219 and 256). By the 1960s, blacks were pressing the federal government and the Democratic party to expand the few social programmes available and for new programmes to address their needs. The Democratic party responded to the demands made by the civil rights movement with the Great Society programmes involving War on Poverty. New layers of programmes especially targeted for both white and black poor were tacked onto the Social Security System (1995:220-221). Federal expenditures for cash and in-kind transfers directly targeted to the poor almost tripled from the end of the fiscal year 1969 through the fiscal year 1974. Most of the increase was not in cash assistance but in programmes such as Food Stamps, Medicaid[34], housing subsides and student aid (1995:257). One of the major achievements of the civil rights movement and women's movement was an expansion of the AFDC that had been a relatively minor part of the welfare state in the 1960s. Moreover, the expansion of paid employment in the

57

welfare state was the most important stimulus behind the greater economic mobility of women and minorities (Ginsburg 1992:108 and 111). In 1972, federal old age and other assistance programmes were nationalised in order to ensure more standardised benefits while the administration of the much larger AFDC remained decentralised (Skocpol 1995:14). When the real income of blue collar and middle income white collar workers and their families started to decline along with a rising tax burden, the support for the Democratic party and its anti-poverty policies started to fade (1995:258). The Great Society programmes became vulnerable to criticism as they were expensive and neither eliminated poverty nor benefited the white working class (Skocpol 1995:222; Thomson and Norris 1995:5).

The demands made by the civil rights movement influenced the women's movement during the 1960s and the 1970s. More and more women became mobilised around equal rights ideology and women on the left who wanted to hold on to special protective laws were pushed aside (Stetson 1995:262). In 1966, women frustrated with the unwillingness of the government to enforce anti-discrimination legislation in the area of gender, organised the first leadership group for the National Organisation for Women NOW (1995:256). The NOW became active in pursuing legal changes in the status of women as concerns education, paid employment and reproductive rights. Many other national, state and local organisations that struggled for related goals were formed in the following years. One of the best known organisations is the National Women's Political Caucus (NWPC) that is devoted to increasing the influence of women in government. Apart from these liberal feminist organisations, women activists were involved in the new social movements of the 1960s that organised more at the local level (Sapiro 1986:123). Women's issues in the post-war period were frustrated by the unresolved conflict between demands for equality defined in terms of non-discrimination supported by those in favour of the ERA on the one hand and demands to preserve and extend special protections for women in the workforce advocated by the unions and the Democratic party on the other hand. It was first in 1963 that the President's Commission on the Status of Women found common ground and Congress passed the Equal Pay Act in 1963 and amendment to the Civil Rights Act in 1967 prohibiting discrimination based on sex in paid employment (Stetson 1995:256). The Equal Pay Act now requires employers to provide equal pay for women and men doing substantially similar work (Hartmann and Aaronson 1994). The Civil Rights Act applies to private firms with 15 or more employees, educational institutions, state and local governments, employment agencies and unions. Moreover, special federal regulatory agencies enforce the rules and sanction those who have not complied (Badgett and Hartmann 1995). During the 1970s, the advocates for equality and non-discrimination were also successful in promoting equality at the federal level. Congress passed the ERA in 1972 and a very important victory was won when the Supreme Court (the Roe v. Wade case) effectively outlawed in 1973 all state laws that prohibited abortion during the first three months of pregnancy (see Stetson 1995:262; Sapiro 1986:126; McKay 1993:270)[35]. Instead of pursuing pregnancy discrimination as a form of protective labour law, liberal feminists argued that pregnancy was a temporary job-related disability. After a long battle at the federal level, advocates of the pregnancy disability leave managed to secure the passing of the Pregnancy Discrimination Act in Congress in 1978 (Stetson 1995:264)[36].

During the 1980s, the women's equal rights movement suffered two major setbacks. The narrow defeat of the ERA in 1982 after many years of campaigning by the women's movement was the first defeat. The second defeat was the weakening of the administration of the equal rights laws by cuts in funding and staffing for the regulatory agencies (Ginsburg 1992:112-113). At the same time, President Reagan (1981-1988) appointed more women to government positions than did his predecessors. For the first time, a woman became a Supreme Court judge and two women were appointed to government. However, the women appointed by Reagan to governmental positions were conservative and anti-feminists as they opposed the ERA and reproductive choice (Sapiro 1986:130-133; McKay 1993:255). These appointments enhanced divisions among women and many women's groups started to insist that their representatives pusued women's interests. By appointing more women to office, Reagan was responding to the 'gender gap' in voting. In the presidential elections in 1980, Reagan received 54 per cent of the male votes and only 46 per cent of the female vote. This gender gap in men's and women's voting behaviour continued to exist all through the 1980s and into the 1990s. In 1992, Clinton received 46 per cent of women's vote and only 41 per cent of men's vote. Younger, single women are most likely to vote Democratic. The gender gap has been contributed to the influences of the women's movement as an interest group, women's greater economic autonomy and professionalisation as well as the so-called war and peace issues (Molitor

1991:103-104; Katzenstein 1992:35; McKay 1993:125). Moreover, there has been a high and consistent support for the Democrats among the Black and some other minority voters (McKay 1993:126)[37].

Intensified Polarisation

A distinct feature of the American political system is that it has always had just two major parties competing for major offices. However, these parties have not always been the same two parties as they have consisted of different coalitions of interest groups (McKay 1993:80-81). During the 1960s and early 1970s, American blacks were finally fully mobilised into the Democratic party but the party was incapable of creating a coalition of workers, blacks and some middle class people due to its internal contradictions between the conservative Southerners and its urban members (see Skocpol 1995:246-247). Moreover, the party was unsuccessful in developing strong ties with the unions (see Piven 1995:111). The Republicans, on the other hand, managed to build a new coalition by 1980 consisting of a regional component (the West and South West), a religious/moral component and an economic/ideological component that appealed to the middle class (McKay 1993:82). The business groups and business money moved into the Republican party and electoral politics in the 1970s when it finally overcame its fractured interest group politics (Piven 1995:111-112).

Supported by the business community, the Reagan administration lowered taxes on business and on the better-off, accelerated deregulation and cut welfare state programmes (1991:261). Targeted public assistance programmes for low income people that account for less than 18 per cent of federal social spending were mainly attacked by the first Reagan administration (Skocpol 1995:266)[38]. By changing laws and administration of unemployment insurance at both the federal and state levels, the Reagan and Bush administrations managed to reduce the number of people receiving unemployment benefits (Mishel and Bernstein 1993:225)[39]. Moreover, the real value of the minimum wage fell considerably during the 1980s as it was frozen by the Reagan administrations from 1981 to 1989 (see Stoesz and Karger 1992:122)[40]. The unions suffered during the anti-labour policies of the Reagan administrations and the share of the workforce represented by unions contracted more rapidly in the 1980s than in the previous several decades (Mishel and Bernstein 1993:187)[41]. As a

60

result of lower unionisation and growth in service jobs, fewer workers were covered by health insurance and pension plans in the late 1980s than in the late 1970s[42].

Although Reagan supported women's maternal role, his administration increased tax credits for child care expenses (Sapiro 1986:133). The tax relief on child care expenses and the employer paid health insurance programmes which accompany most full-time and not part-time employment are important reasons for the predominance of full-time employment of women in the US. In order to support poor families, Reagan implemented the Earned Income Tax Credit EITC in 1986. During the Reagan era, the family policy was strengthened that included an ideology of privacy, self-sufficiency and the celebration of motherhood on the one hand and the availability of only essential services aimed at the poor and the radicalised minorities on the other hand (see Ginsburg 1992:113-119; Mishel et al. 1997). Hence nurseries are either profit organisations or non-profit organisations frequently receiving support from public funds (Ginsburg 1992:125). As a result of falling real hourly earnings since the 1977, women have increased their labour force participation in order to maintain the real value of family incomes. Women's participation rate rose, for example, from 58 per cent in 1977 to 70 per cent in 1992 (OECD 1994a:462-463). The growth in women's labour force participation and earnings were the main generator of the family income growth during the 1980s (Mishel and Bernstein 1993:15). The women's movement has become more decentralised during the 1980s and early 1990s consisting of many small groups working within enterprise, communities, professional associations, universities and religious groups (Katzentstein 1992:31).

Within the Republican party, the New Right intensified its attempts to move the party to the right threatening the coalition of the early 1980s (see Stoesz and Karger 1992:28). Moreover, the anti-labour policies led to growing polarisation of the American Society in the 1980s that contributed to the success of the Democrats under the leadership of Clinton in appealing to the old New Deal coalition consisting of workers, minorities, women and many middle class voters (see Piven 1991:258; McKay 1993:83). After President Clinton assumed office in January 1993, his administration started to rework America's social and economic policies. However, budgetary constraints imposed by the huge budget deficits of the Reagan and Bush administrations prevented at first the full implementation of the administration's plans to promote job training and welfare reform (see Skocpol 1995:4). For employed women, the American state, especially the federal government led by the Democratic party was regarded as a potential source of improvements as concerns health and child care provisions (see Ginsburg 1992:119). In 1993, Congress passed the Family and Medical leave legislation that had been a central element of Clinton's agenda and a top priority of congressional Democrats. The act requires that employers grant their employees unpaid family or medical leave of up to twelve weeks when requested (Campbell and Rockman 1996:100 and 267). The leave arrangements have not been as successful as initially hoped and the take-up rate has only been between two and four per cent (see Albelda et al.1997).

Since 1994, the Republicans have had the majority in Congress which has further constrained the reform efforts of the Clinton administration. The Republicans in Congress managed to get the Clinton administration to sign a new federal act in 1996 called the Temporary Assistance for Needy Families (TANF) designed to replace the AFCD. Clinton had promised during the first champaign for office to reform 'welfare' or the AFCD. The Republicans knew that the Clinton administration needed a 'welfare' reform before the second presidential election and they decided to include block grants for child care and job creation and training along with the TANF in order get Clinton to sign. The TANF meant, however, an institutionalisation of the 'waiver' system that Reagan administrations had implemented to give greater responsibility for welfare policy to the states. Under the TANF, states receive a block grant which they may use to finance their own assistance programmes for low income families with children. The main change from the AFCD is that the definition of a needy family is not limited to single parents. However, the eligibility criteria has become more difficult to fulfil as the states themselves define what means to be a needy family. In addition, at least one member of the family receiving assistance under the TANF is required to be involved in work activities within 2 years of receiving benefit. There exists also a life-time limit of 5 years for receiving benefits. The group hardest hit my the reform are legal immigrants who will lose entitlements to all means-tested welfare support. Critics claim that the TANF will push more unskilled workers into the low pay segment of the labour market which in turn will press wages in that segment further down and thereby increase the impoverishment of the poor (Bernstein 1997; Mishel and Schmitt 1997; Edelman 1997). Moreover, the child care and job and training block grants supplemented with the TANF are considered to be too small to secure a sufficient number of quality child care and training places for the working poor (Edelman 1997). The full impact of this radical change will take place in 2002 when the first welfare recipients have exceed their life-time of 5 years. However, it is already evident that the TANF will not lead to great improvements in the condition of the poor as the states are now given an opportunity to decrease their responsibilities for welfare recipients. If the poverty of the working poor increases, the TANF will intensify further divisions between low paid women and high paying women in the American labour market.

Institutional Constraints

The focus of our study will now shift from women's integration into the political system to institutional arrangements affecting women's position and political struggle in Sweden, Germany and the United States. The form of the state, policy formation and the implementation process will be compared across the three countries.

The Swedish Unitary State

The unitary state system, the highly institutionalised legislative process and the possibility of forming a minority government are institutional factors that have shaped women's political struggle and women's position in Sweden. Parliamentary politics are the most important level of struggle in a unitary state as the functions exercised by national and local institutions are constitutionally subordinated to the parliament and the central government (see Hancock 1993:398). Hence, women have been able to concentrate their efforts at one governmental level in their struggle for reforms and new initiatives. The strong position of the LO within the legislative process has enabled it to influence the content of and the boundaries between state legislation and collective bargaining. Moreover, the highly integrated participation of the public officials who have emphasised consensus and of the principal organised interest groups (employers and organised labour) in state commissions as well as the consultative procedure has made it difficult for women to enter the policy formulation without accommodating to class politics (see Elman 1995:239)[43]. The centralisation of the state has ensured that policies are implemented in a unified manner. The Swedish Constitution permits the formation of minority governments in the absence of a majority that has contributed to the success of the SAP in remaining the main governmental party during most of the post-war period[44]. Moreover, the party has been in favour of state intervention and public social policy to ensure fair redistribution (Marklund 1992:3). Hence, centralisation of the state, involvement of employers and labour in policy formation and the long periods of SAP in government which enjoyed close ties with labour, have ensured that welfare policies and labour market policies have been relatively coherent and complementary. Contradictions as concerns women's assumed role have therefore been comparatively few so that women constitute a rather homogeneous group of mothers until the 1960s and after that, a rather homogeneous group of working mothers.

The German Federal State

The institutional features affecting the political efforts of women and their position in Germany can be considered to be the federal state system, the judicial review power of the Constitutional Court, the fragmented social policy administration, the consensus policy formation process and the effective necessity of a government by a coalition. Germany is a federal state in which certain governmental functions are reserved to the constituent federal states (Länder) that in turn share responsibilities with the municipalities (Kommunen) to some extent. The national government is responsible to the Bundestag (the lower house of parliament) while the states are represented by the Bundesrat (the upper house)[45]. Public spending is shared between the federal, state and local governments[46]. This fragmented governmental structure has weakened women's political struggle as they have had to spread out their efforts. West Germany until the 1970s lagged behind other Western European countries in setting up formal policy channels to address women's concerns. Assistance at the federal level has, however, come from the European Union (EU). The federal parliament mandated in 1979 an equal treatment for women in paid employment to bring the West German law into compliance with the EU directives from 1975 and 1976 (Ferree 1995:98-99).

West German federalism has not resulted in great variations in the conditions of, for example, women across the country as there are at least three unifying mechanisms to ensure balanced development. First, the federal state governments and their bureaucracies are involved in the legislative process at the national level as members of the Bundesrat. Secondly, the laws and rules of procedure for state bureaucracies are unified. Finally, the constitution requires a 'unity of living standards' (Finanzausgleichung) throughout the republic (Conradt 1993:271)[47]. Moreover, the power of the Constitutional Court to engage in judicial review or to examine and strike down legislation if considered to be contrary to the constitution is another dimension of the federal structure that has had implications for women's struggle in the areas of equal rights and abortion. After the Christain Democrats had appealed to the Constitutional Court, the court overturned in 1974 and again in 1993 acts passed at the federal level to liberalise the abortion law. The reform legislation passed by the social-liberal coalition in 1974 allowing termination of a pregnancy in the first 12 weeks, provided the pregnant woman agreed and the termination was carried out by a doctor, never came into effect as the Constitutional Court ruled against it. The Constitutional Court rejected in 1993 large parts of the new Abortion Act from 1992 that involved a deterioration from the East German statute and a small improvement from the West German statute. According to the Abortion Act of 1992, abortion continued to be a criminal offence except if a women who was less than 12 weeks pregnant consulted a doctor in an emergency clinic three days before the abortion. A legal entitlement to a place at a kindergarten for all children above the age of three from 1996 was passed with the abortion law. According to the new abortion law, abortions on social grounds were no longer allowed within the first 12 weeks but women could no longer be prosecuted for their 'wrongful' doing. The court has stressed through its rulings that the protection of the unborn had priority over the women's right of self determination (see Maleck-Lewy 1995).

The German administration of social policies is even more fragmented than the governmental structure. The federal state guarantees and checks that social rights are fulfilled by other agencies including the Länder, municipalities, the social partners who control the social insurance funds as well as independent social service agencies[48]. It has been difficult for, for example, women to innovate or reform the social policy area as consensus must be established across many organisations, both service agencies and insurance funds. However, the support given by local, Land and federal authorities to voluntary organisations in the provision of social services has created scope for alternative initiatives in the area of, for example, child care and health care that women have made used of in the 1970s and 1980s (Freeman and Clasen 1994:11-13; Chamberlayne 1994:175). Moreover, the complicated consensus political bargaining involved in policy making at federal level has led to high levels of spending on existing programmes at the cost of policy innovation (Freeman and Clasen 1994:3)[49]. Hence, it has been difficult to press through policies that could modify the contradictions women face when trying to combine the role of wife and mother with a career. The privileges involved in being a 'standard worker' encourage women to pursue a career without having children while the welfare system has been the most supportive towards the unemployed married housewife (Chamberlayne 1994:176). In addition, the effective necessity to form a coalition government[50] has further impeded fundamental changes as the FDP that has been the main coalition partner of both the SPD and the CDU/CSU, has opposed policies involving redistribution of economic resources and power. The inability of the institutional framework to respond to innovation and reform initiatives has also frustrated attempts to reverse welfare rights (see Freeman and Clasen 1994:12; Conradt 1993:268-269).

The American Federal State

In the United States, federalism, the power of the Supreme Court to engage in judicial review, divided government, fragmented political parties and a complex policy formation and implementation process have affected women and gender politics. The federalism in the United States involves decentralisation of responsibilities between the federal, state and local governments[51]. The definition of federal and state roles has been left to judicial interpretation (McKay 1993:62). The states are important administrative and political units and each has its own separate legal and political system (1993:78). The American federalism is different from the German federalism as the American states do not have unified laws for divorce, bankruptcy or criminal offences (Conradt 1993:271). In addition, American federal laws often permit flexibility as concerns implementation at the state level[52]. Federal regulation and spending expanded from 1930 to 1950 as a result of a co-operative federalism as concerns intergovernmental relations that were facilitated by the economic difficulties of the 1930s and the external threat. However, the intergovernmental relations have became more fragmented as programmes and policies proliferated at all governmental levels (McKay 1993:66-76). The flexibility provided by federal regulation has increasingly become an opportunity for competition among states and for businesses playing one state off against another (Tarullo 1992:105). Hence, standards as concerns, for example, labour market policies and social assistance are not harmonised across the states, leading to considerable variations in the conditions of, for example, employed women as well as women on welfare across the United States. Hence, the poor in the poorest states receive the least due to the uneven standards of social assistance (Skocpol 1995:14). The AFDC programme was administrated by the states but subject to federal requirements. Hence, the states and local officials could exercise more administrative discretion in welfare programmes from which single (black) mothers benefited than in the federally administrated social security programmes from which (white) men have benefited as wage-earners and (white) women to a lesser extent as wives and widows (see Fraser 1989:150-151). In order to challenge laws passed by state and national legislatures together with all executive actions, women can appeal to the Supreme Court (McKay 1993:249). Hence, the Court is the final arbiter with respect to how women's role is formally interpreted. Moreover, the Court has affected the strategies of the civil rights and women's movements by chosen individual rights rather than collective rights of Blacks and other minorities who have sought redress for a pattern of past discrimination. In 1973, the Court outlawed all state laws prohibiting abortion during the first three months grounded on the individual rights of women (1993:270).

The federal government in the United States is divided between Congress and the presidency. The legislative power is vested in the House of Representatives and the Senate or Congress (McKay 1993:132)[53]. The Constitution assigns to the presidency the roles of chief executive and with time the president has become the 'chief' legislator[54]. Hence, the president frames most major laws, draws up the budget and has the responsibility for implementing all laws (1993:175 and 192). The federalism and the division of power have forced the women's movement to recognise various levels of subordination against which struggle has to be organised (Katzenstein 1992:29). Women have been able to make use of the federal structure but their struggle has also been impaired by that same structure. According to McDonagh (1990), women's success in gaining the vote was the result of their strategy designed to take advantage of the federal structure. The strategy involved putting pressure on the president and carrying out campaigns at the state level in order to ensure successful passage of the suffrage amendment through Congress. Women have not had the same success in getting the ERA through the federal system but their main strategy has been to fight for the amendment at the federal level or in Congress. Access to members of Congress is relatively easy but women and other lobby groups have not been able to count on the support of either of the two parties when lobbying for their interests in Congress as the parties have taken up issues of various groups (see McKay 1993:222).

The parties are constellations of different interest groups and their elected members are more dependent on the regional support for their candidature than the party support (see Oskarson and Wängnerud 1995:127). Hence, the interests of many localities and interest groups need to be brokered into most laws in Congress. As a result of the divisions at the federal level and between federal, state and local governments, thousands of different policies are at any one time being implemented, each with its own political, interest group and bureaucratic supporters (McKay 1993:72). The complicated policy formation and implementation make it difficult for women to reform policies without accommodating to the interests of various other groups. Hence, policy changes are only incremental and very seldom involve redistribution of economic resources and power. Until 1996, social welfare programmes treated women primarily as wives, and mothers (see Sapiro 1986:125). Since 1996, single mothers on welfare are expected to work but the assistance provided is considered to be too limited to lift them and their children out of poverty (Edelman 1997).The contradictions other women face when combining various roles have not been modified, although the majority of American women now need to combine the role of wife and mother with a career[55]. Moreover, public policies in the United States reinforce regional differences and labour market differentiation. Hence, American women are divided across class, ethnic/racial and family lines.

Conclusion

The focus of this chapter has been on women's struggles in Sweden, Germany and the United States in relation to other social and political relations. Moreover, the effects of the institutional arrangements of the state on strategies adopted by the women's movements have also been examined. As our analysis of the state as gendered social relations involved both political struggles and political strategies, we were able to capture the main historical developments in social relations at the state level (cf. Bonefeld 1993).

In our empirical analysis, women's political struggles in Sweden, Germany and the United States were studied in view of Regulationists' discussion of social blocks and Jenson's (1990) claim that the Canadian suffragette movement failed to enter into electoral institutions as the political system was not open to new actors. It appeared from our analysis that the female suffrage did not enable women in the three countries to exercise any dramatic political and policy impact as social blocks at the political level were only open for social identities involving class, religion, regionalism and nationalism. In Sweden, the class compromise established in 1938 did not create an opportunity to transfer gender relations. Moreover, women's maternal role was emphasised and supported by family-oriented social polices. After World War Two, women were excluded from the West German 'consensus' model but the Catholic Church became influential through its close ties with the CDU that remained in power until the 1960s. Hence, a clause was put into the West German Basic Law that committed the state to defend and preserve the family. This clause and the tax splitting introduced in 1958 contributed to the development of the male breadwinner family in West Germany. In the United States, unions and women's groups were successful in their struggles for a recognition of women as mothers in need of special protection. Moreover, the alliance between the Southern agricultural interests in the Democratic Party and the business-oriented reinforced women's maternal role by blocking all welfare reforms from the 1940s to the 1960s. To sum up, the exclusion of women from political power during the early part of this century prevented Swedish, German and American women from challenging their assigned role as mothers (Sweden and the United States) and wives (West Germany). Men, on the other hand, were considered to be a heterogeneous group of male breadwinners who were divided across class, regional and religious lines. Norms assigning the role of a mother or a wife to women and a male breadwinner to men became engraved in the norms and the institutional structure of the state during the early part of the welfare state's development.

The social blocks established during and after the Swedish, German and American women entered the electoral institutions started to disintegrate in the 1960s. Contributing to the disintegration was the greater access of groups located outside the boundaries of dominant social blocks to resources (paid work and/or public benefits and services as, for example, education) that enabled them to mobilise politically. Moreover, contradictions within and between social blocks were growing due to the decline of the mass-production system and the enhanced internationalisation and then globalization of capital and communities (mass-media). Hence, the balance of power started to shift and space was created for alternative movements, new alliances, compromises and systems of domination within and among social groups. From the 1960s until the 1980s, women moblised in mass numbers around the social identity of gender that cut across more established identities such as that of class. The women's movements were a part of the 'new' social movements organising around race/ethnicity, gender and generational divisions that challenged the governing social blocks. In Sweden, women's greater political mobilisation and labour market participation was followed by an erosion of the male breadwinner model. In West Germany the breadwinner wages still remain the norm and women's labour force participation lagged behind the other two countries until the mid-1980s when the gap started to narrow.

Women's groups and other social groups in Sweden demanded greater equality of outcome in terms of both class and gender in the 1960s. The SAP responded to these demands by integrating an equality programme that had something for everybody. Swedish women were integrated into the labour market as working mothers by extensive provision of social services. Moreover, equality in the labour market was to be achieved through collective agreements or wage solidarity. In Germany, the family was strengthened until the late 1960s. As more married women were engaged in paid work, women's aspirations and political preferences started to change. During the 1970s and 1980s, autonomous women's groups started to demand a greater say in decisions concerning abortion and whether or not to become housewives. Women's integration in the political party system and paid work was relatively slow in West Germany due in part to the resistance of the West German 'consensus' model to outside pressures and limited growth of the service sector. However, the main governmental party, the CDU, took on board demands made by the women's groups and implemented during the 1980s and early 1990s measures to achieve equality between housewives and employed women.

The civil rights movement in the United States strengthened those groups within the women's movement that advocated equality and non-discrimination. During the 1960s, these equality groups were successful in promoting women's individual rights at the federal level. Hence, American women were slowly integrated into the labour market as individuals, i.e. without any major increase in social services.

In Sweden, the class compromise has started to disintegrate as the balance of power shifted towards employers and the electoral support for SAP has become more unstable. Employers were able during the early 1980s to push through a breakdown of the centralised collective bargaining system which led to a greater gender pay gap. During the 1990s, there has been a retreat from the goal of class solidarity and full employment which has sharpened the gender and generational divisions in Sweden. Young people have had difficulties obtaining permanent employment in the labour market (OECD 1996a:111-114). The West German 'consensus' model has, on the other hand, come under growing pressure as a result of fragmentation of the parliamentary party system, growing tensions between capital and labour and the unification with East Germany. Women have become less supportive of the conservative political parties adhering to the traditional gender division of work. Greater engagement of women in paid work has intensified divisions between wives on the one hand and employed women on the other hand. In order to ease the tensions, the state has increased its support for care of children and the elderly in the family. At the same time, employers have demonstrated that they are no longer willing to support the male breadwinner wages. Employers' growing unwillingness to pay breadwinner wages and the persistent high level of unemployment has robbed many men of the opportunity to become male breadwinners.

The two main parties in American politics changed during the 1980s and 1990s. The Republican party managed to build a new coalition by 1980 consisting of regional, religious and business components that appealed to the middle class. The Republicans' anti-labour policies, freezing of the minimum wage, tax cuts for the rich and cuts in welfare programmes for the poor led to growing polarisation of American Society. Divisions among women intensified as the number of educated women entering good paying jobs increased at the same time as the impoverishment of unskilled women increased. Moreover, the lower and middle income families were hard hit by the rise in inequality during the

1980s (Mishel and Bernstein 1993:20). The falling wages of men and growing employment opportunities in the private sector stimulated women's labour force participation, such that dual breadwinner households became more common. The growing polarisation of the American society contributed to the success of the Democrats in 1992 in appealing to the old New Deal coalition consisting of workers, minorities, women and many middle class voters. Clinton's presidency has, however, not led to any radical reduction in the growing polarisation of American Society. Clinton's health reforms and the welfare reforms became watered-down compromises as they had to be negotiated with the Republicans who have since 1994 been the majority party in Congress. Although the passing of the unpaid parental leave measure was an important achievement for the women's movement, it has only assisted a very small group of women who want to reconcile work and family life.

Variations in the institutional arrangements of the state need to be acknowledged in order to explain why the strategies and success of the women's movements in Sweden, Germany and the United States differ. The institutional arrangements of the state vary across countries as the state is a product of past struggles that are to a large extent country-specific (see table 2.1). Hence, the state is more accessible to certain political strategies than others. The unitarian state in Sweden has enabled women to concentrate on one level of government when fighting subordination. The federal states in Germany and the United States on the contrary, have various levels of government forcing women to scatter their efforts, such that the women's struggle has been weakened.

Table 2.1 Institutional Arrangements Affecting Women's Political Struggles

	Sweden	Germany	United States
State:			
Structure	Unitary	federal	federal
Government	Minority	coalition	divided
Policies:			
formation	Institutional	consensus	bargaining
implementation	Unified	unified*	flexibility

*The administration of social policy is fragmented.

Laws and rules of procedure for state bureaucracies are unified in both Sweden and Germany ensuring that a policy formulated at the national level will be implemented in a unified manner. However, the social policy administration in Germany is a fragmented system that has in many cases enabled women to secure financial support for alternative arrangements in the provision of social services. In the United States, the states do not have unified laws in all areas and federal regulation allows some flexibility when introduced at the state level. The conditions of women in paid employment and on welfare differ therefore much more within the United States than within Sweden and Germany.

Factors contributing to women's homogeneity, first as mothers and then as working mothers, in Sweden are the centralisation of the state and the highly institutionalised policy formation within which the LO has had a strong position due to its close ties with the SAP. In addition, the possibility of forming a minority government has enabled the SAP to stay in power during most of the post-war period. German women on the contrary have found it difficult to press through policy reforms that could modify the contradictions women face when trying to combine the role of wife and mother with a career due to the consensus policy formation and the fragmented social policy administration, as well as the effective necessity to form a coalition government. The choice many German women have therefore had to make is between being a wife with interrupted labour force participation or to have a childless career. In the United States, public policies reinforce regional differences and labour market differentiation that have in turn have intensified divisions among American women across class, ethnic/racial and family lines. The decentralised (federalism) and divided government (Congress versus the presidency) has fragmented the organisational structure of the two main parties. The fragmented political parties and the complex policy formation and implementation process in the United States have prevented any major changes in the contradictions most women face when trying to combine the role of a wife and mother with a career. However, the Child Care block grant is an important recognition that poor families with children need support to be able to engage in paid work. The German Constitutional Court and the American Supreme Court are another dimension of the federal structure that has had implications for women's struggle for equal rights and abortion. In the United States, the Supreme Court has ensured legalisation of abortion within the first three months while the

Constitutional Court in Germany has rejected all governmental acts allowing abortion with the first 12 weeks of pregnancy.

We have now completed our discussion of the state as a site of gender struggles and strategies as well as a product of previous history of gender struggles. In the following chapter, the focus will be constrained to the state as a regulator of gender relations in the Swedish, German and the American labour markets. However, the interrelationship between the state and the labour market is considered to be relatively autonomous.

Notes

[1] As pointed out by Regini (1995), the reason for the neglect of the role of social and political institutions in the functioning of or in the dysfunctioning of the economic system lies in the sharp division of scientific work between, for example, economics, sociology and political science. The stringent division of work has created disincentives to engage in interdisciplinary studies as one runs the risk of being marginalised within the scientific communities.

[2] The People's Home is a metaphor created by the former Social Democratic leader Per Albin Hansson to describe the social democratic project. It drew a parallel between vision of the Social Democrats concerning the future and the 'good home' where relations are characterised by equality, consideration and co-operation (Jenson and Mahon 1993:77).

[3] These five parties are the Left party (Vänsterpartiet), the Social Democratic party (Socialdemokratiska Arbetarpartiet), the Liberal party (Folkpartiet), the Center party (Centerpartiet) and the Conservative party (Moderata Samlingpartiet).

[4] The Left party has not had a separate women's organisation as women's interests have been regarded to be inextricable from other interests (Elman 1995:253).

[5] The class compromise in 1938 involved an agreement between LO and the SAF that both parties would conduct centralised collective negotiations without the government intervention. Moreover, the LO agreed to recognise the 'management right to manage' (Regini 1995:38; Standing 1988:2).

[6] The LO and SAP have had an overlapping leadership and collective membership of most rank-and-file-union members in the party (Hancock 1993:414). Moreover, the TCO (Tjänstemannens Centralorganisation) that represents primarily white-collar workers in the public and private sectors has operated closely with LO and has therefore been more inclined to support policy initiatives made by the SAP than the bourgeois parties (1993:421-423).

[7] The Social Democratic Women's League made it clear at the party congress in 1928 that they did not want to be invited into the Peoples Home after its completion (Jenson and Mahon 1993:82).

[8]The penalty for abortion was changed in 1926 from imprisonment in high security prisons to imprisonment in low security prisons. Moreover, abortion was decriminalised by 1927 for cases in which women's life would be seriously endangered if she carried out the pregnancy (Kaplan 1992:106).

[9]The German constitution made the parties quasi-state institutions by assigning them fundamental responsibility for 'shaping the political will of the people'. This provision has been used to justify the extensive public financing of the parties. In addition, the parties have been able to ensure that the local state and national post-war bureaucracies were staffed, at least at the upper levels, by their supports (Conradt 1993:233).

[10]Small but important interest groups are the public servants (Beamte) and the farmers. Public servants receive a contract on appointment that specifies lifetime tenure and they enjoy guaranteed salary levels as well as generous non-contributory pension rights (Smith 1994:281-283). Farmers are the most protected and subsidised occupational groups in spite of their small size (around 5 per cent of the workforce) and limited contribution to the GNP (less than 3 per cent) (Conradt 1993:248).

[11]Instead of powerful central organisation, the trade unions were organised on an industrial basis such that each industry has its own trade union that bargains with the relevant employers' association (Smith 1994:14 and 276). Seventeen industrial unions make up the DGB and the most influential represents the metal workers (IG Metall). Freeman and Clasen argue that the unions are weak in the German industrial relation system reflected by the low unionisation, restrictive strike legislation and exclusion from the workplace in favour of the works councils (1994:7-9).

[12]Most Germans are 'born' into either the Roman Catholic or the Evangelical Protestant (Lutheran) church. Protestants and Catholics have been divided along regional lines. The churches have a close dependent relationship with the state as they are largely financed through a church tax (Conradt 1993:202-203).

[13]The CDU was the main governmental party from 1949 to 1969 and has remained in power since 1982. The SPD on the other hand was the main governmental party from 1969 to 1982. The SPD and CDU ruled together in what has been called the Grand Coalition formed in 1969. Both the CDU and SPD have preferred to build a coalition with the FDP rather than to form a Grand Coalition with the other party. Between 1969 and 1982, the FDP was in coalition with the SPD. The FDP changed partners again in 1982 when it turned again to the Christian Democrats (Conradt 1993:222 and 239).

[14]Protective legislation for women was passed in order to curtail exploitative work conditions so that women could carry out more effectively their roles as wives and mothers in the home (McDonagh 1990:53).

[15]The laws on mothers' pension were passed in 40 states from 1911 to 1920. The mothers' pensions were locally administered benefits intended to enable respectable impoverished widows and in some cases other categories of mothers or parents to care for children at home instead of being force to surrendering children to the custody of institutions or foster homes (Skocpol 1995:74 and 76).

[16]The Women's Bureau WB was placed in the Department of Labour. According to Stetson, the WB was the catalyst that enabled the compromises on the 1963 Equal Pay

Act. Moreover, WB provided the resources to the state commissions and created the space for the nucleus of the organised women's rights movement of the 1960s (1995:256).

[17]The alliance with the rural south was not an alliance with the family farmers as in the Scandinavian labour parties but with a quasi-feudal political formation. The southern system was protected from electoral challenges from below by the disenfranchising arrangements of the late 19th century that excluded poor whites and blacks from the electorate (Piven 1991:246-247).

[18]After President Roosevelt put his support behind the legislation, the unions broke with their traditional policy of abstaining from national politics and joined forces with the Democratic party. At the end of the World War Two, one-third of the workforce was unionised but it soon started to decline and it was around 16 per cent in 1989 (Piven 1991:246 and 249). Ethnic and racial divisions in the United States have in many instances constrained unions' possibilities of engage in class politics (see Skocpol 1995:103).

[19]Corporations have enormous influence at the state and local level and are therefore able to affect land, taxation, labour and public work policies (McKay 1993:231).

[20]The American Federation of Labour (AFL) and the Congress of Industrial Organisation (CIO) combined their forces in 1955 and have lobbied hard in Washington on whole range of public polices which affected worker and working conditions, union rights, social security, job training, vocational education, occupational health and safety, overseas trade relations and economic policy generally. Through its political organisation Committee on Political Education (COPE), AFL/CIO have become one of the most coherent and visible of the Washington lobbies. However, the union structures are highly decentralised and local and state units are often responsible for bargaining over wages and salaries (McKay 1993:234-235).

[21]According to a survey that was done in the early 1950s for the Social Democratic Women's League, over 60 per cent of housewives were dissatisfied with their lives whereas working women in general express satisfaction (G. Karlsson 1990 quoted in Jenson and Mahon 1993:84).

[22]Information concerning men's and women's party voting is only available after the election in 1956 when the proportion of women voting for the social block was higher than the proportion of men. At the same time, men were more likely to support the bourgeois block. This pattern turned around after the election in 1960 and remained unchanged until 1979 (Oskarson and Wängnerud 1995:76-77).

[23]TCO (Tjänstemännens Centralorganisation) refers to the Confederation of Professional Employees and SACO (Sveriges Akademikers Centralorgansation) is the Confederation of Academics in Sweden.

[24]The Environmentalist party has always had high proportion of female representatives or 45 per cent in 1988 and 44 per cent in 1994 (Oskarson and Wängnerud 1995:101 and 157; Statistics Sweden 1995:72).

[25]In 1994, 89.0 per cent of women voted while 87.6 of men voted (Oskarson and Wängnerud 1995:53).

[26]The term gender gap was first used after the presidential elections in the United States when Ronald Reagan was supported by significantly more men than women. In Sweden, the bourgeois block had a male surplus of 5 per cent in 1985 and it went up to 6 per cent in 1988. The socialist block on the other hand had a female surplus of 4 per cent in the elections 1985 and 1988 (Oskarson and Wängnerud 1995:76-79).

[27]The support for the SAP has fluctuated between a high of 50.1 per cent in 1968 to 37.6 per cent in 1991. The party received 45 per cent of the votes in 1994 (Hancock 1993:411-425; Nordic Council of Minsters 1995:378).

[28]The fertility rate peaked in 1965 when it was 2.5 and it was not until 1983 that the fall in the fertility rate halted. In 1989, the fertility rate had risen to 2.0 (Gustafsson 1991:510).

[29]The gender gap in party voting in 1994 was greatest among the age group 18 to 25 years. In this age group, the Left party and the Environmental party were twice as strong among women as. The Conservative party on the other hand was tree times as strong among men than women, a trend that started in 1979 (see Oskarson and Wängnerud 1995:78-79).

[30]The gender difference or the female surplus of the CDU/CSU went from 8 to 10 per cent from 1953 to 1969. Men on the other hand voted were more likely to vote for the SPD and the gender difference or the male surplus was between 5 and 8 per cent (Molitor 1991:24-27).

[31]In 1991, female labour force participation in West Germany was 58 per cent while it was 82 per cent in Sweden and 70 per cent in the Unites States (OECD 1994:463-489).

[32]Since the elections in 1983, the CDU/CSU has once again had a greater number of women among its electorates. However, the female surplus was only on average 2.3 per cent from 1983 to 1990 while it was 9.2 per cent from 1953 to 1969. The SPD's female-deficit increased again in 1987 and 1990 when it was 0.7 and 0.5 per cent respectively. As concerns other parties, the FDP has had on average around 1 per cent female deficit of women among its electorates. More men than women voted for the Green party until 1990. However, the difference was relatively small or around 1 per cent. In 1990, there was a very small 'female-surplus' in the votes for the Greens. Although the difference between men's and women's voting was small, other parties had a male surplus (Molitor 1991:25-32; Statistisches Bundesamt 1994:99). East German women's choice of parties was not significant different from that of East German men in the elections taken place during 1990 (Molitor 1991:190).

[33]The AFDC was first designed to provide relief for impoverished children and from 1950 for their caretakers in families in which one parent is absent, disabled or deceased (Miller 1983 quoted in Sapiro 1986:128).

[34]Medicaid is a non-contributory national health scheme for the poor (McKay 1993:68).

[35]The Supreme Court has declared that states may withhold public funding for abortions including those that are medically necessary. Feminists interpret this as being inconsistent with the logic of protecting women's individual rights as the rights of poor women are not protected (see Sapiro 1986:128).

[36]The Pregnancy Discrimination Act prohibits discrimination against pregnancy in employment and requires those employers who have disability policies to include pregnancy (Stetson 1995:264).

[37]In 1984, around 90 per cent of Blacks voted Democratic and in 1992, this number had fallen to 82 per cent (McKay 1993:126).

[38]The administration of conservative president Reagan had to postpone all plans in the early 1980s to cut Social Security when it discovered the widespread bipartisan popularity of the program and was confronted with the political opposition of the organised elderly constituencies (Skocpol 1995:3; Stoesz and Karger 1992:30).

[39]In 1991, only about 40 per cent of the unemployed received unemployment benefits as opposed to 67 per cent in 1976 (Mishel and Berstein 1993:225). Moreover, there is no means-tested assistance for the long term unemployed who have exhausted entitlement to unemployment benefit or for those not covered at all (Ginsburg 1992:110).

[40]The legislated increase in 1990 and 1991 raised the minimum wage but it still did not achieve 1979 level. Minorities and women are disproportionately represented among minimum wage workers (Mishel and Berstein 1993:195-197).

[41]In just two decades, the membership of American unions has fallen from about thirty-five million to fifteen million (Piven 1995:111). Except for college educated white women, women were in 1989 less likely than white men to be unionised and black men and black women were in most instances more likely to be unionised than white men and women (Mishel and Berstein 1993:191-193).

[42]In 1979, 68.5 per cent of the labour force was covered by health insurance and the coverage had dropped to 61.1 per cent in 1989. The greatest loss of health insurance was among men, Hispanics and workers with less than a college degree. The percentage of the private workforce covered by a pension plan dropped from 50 per cent in 1979 to 42.9 in 1989. Lower pension coverage has basically occurred among men. Women are still less likely than men to be covered by an employer's pension plan (Mishel and Berstein 1993:10 and 155-157).

[43]The unions and employer's organisations are represented on commissions of inquire into new policy proposals, consulted on proposed legislation before it goes to the Riksdag (the remiss procedure) and given entry to the Riksdag committees as well as being represented on the governing bodies of major executive agencies such as the Labour Market Board (AMS). After the voluntary withdrawal of business representatives in 1992, union representatives were expelled by the conservative government from most commissions, committees and agencies (Compston 1995:101-102).

[44]The SAP has been in government either alone or in formal or informal coalitions since 1932 except for the period 1976-1982 and the period 1991-1994 (see Hancock 1993:425-426). The Swedish constitutionalism makes the formation of a minority government possible in the absence of a majority by a single party or coalition of parties as a prime minister can be elected if not more than half of the parliamentary members vote against him (1993:398-406).

[45]The Bundesrat very seldom initiates legislative proposals and it concentrates on the administrative aspects of policy making. West Germany did not experience a form of divided government until 1970s when the Bundesrat started to oppose more often than in the past to government legislation but most legislation on major issues are subject to mandatory approval on the part of the Bundesrat (Conradt 1993:218; Schmidt 1995:11).

[46]Most federal spending goes to defence and social security transfer payments, most state spending is taken up by salary payments for staff in education and the police and a great part of local government spending involves public investment in health care, welfare, education and sewage and roads (Freeman and Clasen 1994:2-3).

[47]A system of tax redistribution or revenue sharing is used to make up for differences between resources and expenditures (Conradt 1993:271). However, considerable regional disparity has existed in the West due to the unequal size of the federal state and uneven development (Smith 1994:38 and 41).

[48]While the local, Land and federal authorities are responsible for ensuring that social service needs are met, they do so by supporting and promoting voluntary organisations. The more than sixty thousand freie Träger (free bearers) of social services are grouped into six associations: the Protestant, the Catholic, the union-sponsored, the Red Cross, the German Jewish community and a federation of small agencies (Freeman and Clasen 1994:11-12).

[49]In order to engage in successful policy making, an approval is needed from the main interest groups, extra parliamentary organisations of the governing parties, key members of parliament, the states, the courts, semi-public institutions such as the Bundesbank, the leadership of the health and social security system, the Federal Labour Institute administration and even the opposition parties through their chairmanship of various parliamentary committees and their representatives in the Bundesrat (see Conradt 1993:260).

[50]Legislative changes of the German constitution require two-thirds majority in the Bundestag and in the Bundesrat. Two-thirds majority requires in practice the formation of an oversized coalition or an all-inclusive coalition in general and co-operation between the major governing party and the major opposition party (Schmidt 1995:11).

[51]The responsibilities of the federal government are defence and foreign affairs together with some aspects of financial management. Domestic policies such as education, roads, welfare, the administration of justice are allocated to state and local governments (McKay 1993:62).

[52]This flexibility can be summarised into three patterns. First, the federal law may set minimum standards and permit states to enact higher standards within their own boundaries. Secondly, The Congress may implement pre-emption of an entire field of regulation. Thirdly, the federal regulatory system may leave opportunities for states to adjust the system in some fashion (Tarullo 1992:103-105).

[53]Congress has a power to appropriate money, to raise armies and to regulate interstate commerce as well as the right to declare wars and to ratify treaties. The Senate is empowered to ratify treaties, approve appointments by the president to the judiciary

and executive branch and the House can accuse executive officers for wrong-doing. Representatives are elected every two years and senators every six but with one third elected every two years (McKay 1993:132 and 134).

[54]Moreover, the president is commander in chief of the armed forces, chief diplomat, chief recruiting officer to the executive and courts and legislator (McKay 1993:175).

[55]Women on welfare have increasingly been assisted since 1988 to combine motherhood and work. However, those women able to find work do not necessarily earn enough to become economically self-sufficient (Stoesz and Karger 1992:64).

3 The Feminisation of the Labour Force and the Withdrawal of Men

The main labour market developments occurring during the post-war period are the continuing feminisation of the labour force and the withdrawal of many men from the labour force. The process stimulating the feminisation of the labour force has been attributed to demand and supply factors. Examples of demand factors contributing to the rise in women's paid employment are production growth, new technology, the expansion of the service sector and the rise in the education of women which has made them more attractive labour. The supply factors include among others more work orientated preferences, lower fertility rates, higher divorce rates, longer parental leave and greater availability of affordable child care services. More and more women have entered into education and the labour market in order to make use of newly acquired skills and job opportunities and to secure a certain consumption level for the family as well as to gain access to the social security system. The decline in male participation during the post-war period has been attributed to employment contraction in traditional male industries and greater substitution of female for male labour on the one hand and to rising real wages and greater availability of benefits that have enabled men to leave the labour market earlier than before on the other hand (see Jacobsen 1994:127-136). Although these labour force trends or the feminisation of the labour force and the withdrawal of many men appear to be common across the three countries, a closer examination reveals different patterns of integration and withdrawal across space. Although the population growth has been fastest in the United States, the fall in men's labour force participation rate has been slower than in the other two countries and the rise in women's participation rate has been the fastest. As compared with Germany and the United States, the labour force participation of Swedish women has become relatively equal to that of men. The greatest withdrawal of men has occurred in Germany followed closely by Sweden. The slow integration of German women into the labour market has, however, prevented the gender gap in participation rates narrowing to the same extent as in Sweden and the United States.

The aim of this chapter to analyse the forces behind the feminisation of the labour force and the withdrawal of many men from the labour market in Sweden, Germany and the United States. Moreover, explanations for divergent patterns of integration and withdrawal will be sought in order to uncover the importance of actors and institutional arrangements in shaping labour market trends. The focus will be on how demands for labour in the production sphere have given rise to supply responses on the one hand and on the role of the state in mediating between demand pressures and supply response on the other hand. Our main assertion is that the interrelationship between the household, the labour market and the state is relatively autonomous, such that there is no direct relationship between the nature of the welfare state and employment structures. Moreover, the interrelationship has been shaped by actors involved in power struggles which in turn have contributed to divergent labour market patterns across space. This contrasts with widely used neo-classical theories that assume a direct causal relationship between demand and supply for labour and universal patterns across competitive labour markets. In addition, the role of collective actors and the state in influencing the functioning of the labour market is ignored, except when a distortion from a competitive equilibrium needs to be explained.

In the first part of this chapter, theories used to explain labour market changes across time and space will be explored. The discussion will include theories reducing trends in paid employment to changes in variables on either the demand or the supply side on the one hand and theories explaining trends as the outcome of dynamic interactions between demand and supply that are conditioned by struggle and institutional arrangements on the other hand. The subsequent empirical analysis will start with an investigation of how the economic climate or changes in the aggregated demand since 1960 relate to changes in paid work in the three countries. A shift-share analysis of the changes in female and male employment will then be undertaken as it discloses how much can be accounted for by structural developments on the one hand and by employers' labour use strategies on the other hand. The results will be related to public-private division in the provision of services. Although the focus is on the demand side, we recognise that it has become difficult to isolate demand and supply pressures as the latter has increasingly come to condition the former. In the second part of the empirical analysis, responses on the supply-side will be analysed in view of the role of the state in altering the volume of the labour supply and in creating incentives/disincentives to participate in paid work. We will start our discussion by studying participation rates in more detail in order to draw forth gender and country differences in activity and inactivity as well as in full-time and part-time work. Variations in activity rates and part-time work of men will be related to early retirement paths and youth paid employment. In order to explain differences in women's activity rates, state policies concerning immigration, taxation, parental leave and child care will be studied. Moreover, different patterns of combining motherhood and work will be examined to explain variations in the levels of part-time and full-time work.

The Interaction of Demand and Supply

Neo-classical models (see, e.g. Becker 1965; Mincer 1962) on how households allocate their time have been extensively used to explain why women's labour force participation lags behind that of men. The basic assumptions of these models are that individuals within the household act rationally and seek to maximise the household's welfare when making decisions concerning the allocation of time between alternative activities. Women have according to Becker (1965), a comparative advantage in the area of unpaid work due to their 'intrinsic' nature that makes them more productive in household production. Hence, women will specialise in unpaid work and men in paid work. Becker's model of the household's allocation of time has been criticised for biological determinism and for assuming that the preferences of partners are identical (see, e.g. Arrow 1951; Humphries 1995). Moreover, Chippori (1992 quoted in Woolley 1993) has pointed out the inconsistency between the methodological individualism and the assumption that the preferences of household members are identical. In order to solve the problem of aggregating individual preferences into a collective preference, Becker (1981) has developed an alternative model in which one member of the household is altruistic or concerned with the welfare of others. This version has been criticised for being incoherent in its analysis by assuming altruism in the household and selfishness in the market (see Woolley 1993:491).

In spite of these methodological problems, the time allocation models have been dominant in research on changes in women's and men's labour force participation. The models are based on the assumption that an individual chooses hours of work by considering his/her real wage per unit time in relation to the value of their time in alternative activities. Hence, an individual chooses the combination of income/consumption of goods and leisure that maximise his/her utility. A rise in the real wage rate may induce an individual in paid work to increase his/her hours of work (substitution effect) and/or to reduce hours of work (income effect). Empirical evidence suggests that two effects cancel out almost exactly for men but the substitution effect dominates for women (Goldin 1990:124-125; Begg et al. 1994: 193). In other neo-classical models, individuals have 'tastes' that influence their choice of income/consumption of goods and leisure. Changes in tastes will result in a once in for all shifts in the labour supply. Tastes are treated as an exogenous variable or not related to changes in income and prices.

Other variables have been incorporated in order to enhance the explanatory power of, especially, the female labour supply model. These variables include fixed costs of working, non-labour income and the form (marriage, single parenthood) and the size of the family. Women's labour force participation will increase, when fixed costs of working such as, for example, child care costs fall. Non-labour income includes in the case of married women the earnings of other family members such as the husband. If men's earnings fall, women will increase their participation in paid work. Research based on the neo-classical models of the labour supply attributes the increase in the female labour force participation primarily to rising real wages and falling non-labour income of women (see Jacobsen 1994:128-135; Goldin 1990:125-126; Begg et al. 1994:193). The family size has proven to be problematic for the neo-classical models of the labour supply as it may be jointly determined with work decisions. Women may, for example, postpone having children as they desire to have a working career (see, e.g. Goldin 1990:125).

Neo-classical economists have focused primarily on the supply side when explaining women's integration into paid work, although empirical evidence points to the primacy of the demand side in affecting the female supply. Study of several countries during the post-war period suggests that the rise in the real earnings of women was of primary importance in the secular increase in women's labour force participation and in their hours of paid work and not a shift in their labour supply function (see Mincer 1962; Smith and Ward 1984; Mincer 1985). Neo-classical economists are more aware of the demand side when explaining men's withdrawal from the labour market. The decline in men's labour force participation has primarily been attributed to demand changes or to employment contraction in traditional male industries and greater substitution of female for male labour. Moreover, it is acknowledged that structural unemployment in traditional industries may lead to discouraged worker effect, especially among older workers. Those older workers who are not able to obtain new jobs matching, for example, their skills may become discouraged and retire from the labour market. As concerns the supply side, neo-classical theories have attributed men's withdrawal from the labour market to rising real wages (income effect) and greater availability of benefits such as early pension (see Jacobsen 1994:127-136; Begg et al. 1994:480).

Humphries and Rubery (1984) claim that neoclassical models fail to provide a satisfactory framework for analysing the labour supply as behaviours that cannot be accounted for by changes in incomes or prices are attributed to unexplained changes in tastes. As tastes develop independently of changes in incomes or prices but influence at the same time the behaviour of individuals within the family, social reproduction is treated as autonomous from the system of production. Moreover, Humphries and Rubery criticise time allocation models for studying the labour supply separately from the labour demand and for assuming that the behaviour of individuals within the family is identical to the behaviour of individuals in the economy which implies a functionalist/reductionist relation between social reproduction and the system of production. This method ignores the conflicts and complementarities between household members. For Humphries and Rubery, tastes are affected by the on-going interaction between social reproduction and the system of production. Moreover, social reproduction develops in response to changes in the productive system and the interaction of the two spheres is non-accommodating or relatively autonomous and evolves through time.

The framework offered by Humphries and Rubery (1984) is more satisfying than neo-classical models to analyse changes in behaviour over time and variations across space as it is non-deterministic and able to account for some of the complexities of real-life decision-making processes. When analysing changes in the behaviour of individuals over time, neo-classical models assume that these take place within a universal and stable system of behaviour. Individuals adjust their behaviour to changes in the relevant variables and the system shifts to a new location or a new equilibrium. For Humphries and Rubery, there is a continuous dynamic interaction between the demands of the production system and the responses of the social reproduction system, such that the two spheres cannot be studied in isolation. Working within this framework, Rubery (1988b:3-6) has identified three 'demand-side' pressures that may affect women's labour force participation. First, women may serve as a flexible reserve such that they are drawn into the labour market during booms and expelled during recessions. Secondly, the demand for female labour may be dependent on demand in female-dominated sectors if the labour market is characterised by rigid sex typing of occupations. Paid employment will then be related more to secular trends in sectoral and occupational structures than to cyclical developments. Thirdly, employers' search for cost-saving may induce substitution towards less expensive labour such as women. The demand for female labour will then intensify during recessions. The labour supply will increasingly condition these demand pressures as women's labour force participation becomes more permanent. A more stable female workforce may induce employers to offer longer hours in a wider range of occupations and industries.

A major drawback of neo-classical models when applied in comparative studies is their inability to explain variations in the labour market behaviour of individuals across space as they are reduced to different tastes that are exogenous to the models. In contrast, Rubery (1988d:253-254) claims that differences in women's paid employment across countries can only be understood by analysing the interrelationship between country-specific system of industrial, labour market and family organisations as well as the role of political and social values in maintaining the relationship. Rubery also asserts that the internationalisation of markets and production technologies put common pressures on the labour demand structure across countries and the growing importance of the state and decreased importance of the family has led to cross-national influences on the labour supply across countries. Although the framework offered by Humphries and Rubery (1984) and Rubery (1988) is more relevant than the neo-classical models to analyse changes over time and variations across space, it needs more theoretical work on what constitutes tastes and on role of the state in shaping labour supply and labour demand.

Hakim (1995) claims that women's work orientation is the 'hidden factor' determining their hours of work. Hence, women may either be committed to work or to marriage and child-rearing and the commitment is more and less independent of conditions in the labour market and in the family as well as of state policies. Various authors have criticised Hakim's interpretation of empirical evidence and her assumption that individual choice is free of constraints. Ginn et al. (1996) question Hakim's treatment of hours of work as an indicator of women's commitment to work. O'Reilly and Fagan (1998), point out that various comparative studies have not found that there exist a direct relationship between motherhood and part-time work across space. Moreover, Crompton and Harris (1998) criticise Hakim for reducing women's disadvantageous position in the labour market to a static 'voluntary choice' and for assuming that women's work orientation is heterogeneous at the same time as men's is homogeneous. For Crompton and Harris, men's and women's paid employment is shaped by both choice and context which do not remain constant over time. This discussion demonstrates the need for a more theoretical work on how tastes for work interrelate with demands of the system of production and responses of social reproduction.

The tastes of men and women are both exogenous and endogenous to demands of the production system reflected in, for example, real wages. Cultural traditions and social norms are examples of exogenous influences on tastes for work. Social norms or stereotypes have their origin in past struggles in the spheres of social reproduction and production and have become engraved into institutional arrangements such as the church. An example of social norms are those that describe the 'appropriate' division of work between men and women. However, social norms may become inconsistent with tastes as the latter are also influenced by conditions prevailing in the family and in the labour market. Although social norms assign the role of mothers to women, they

87

may be committed to paid work as men's wages are not sufficient to provide for a family (additional worker effect). Women's level of education will also influence their tastes for work. Tastes fluctuate as the conditions prevailing in the family and the labour market change over time. Hence, women with young children may have greater taste for part-time work than women with older children. Moreover, the structure of jobs may favour men's paid work over women's or the other way around. Women's and men's tastes for work may conflict with their actual hours of work as their behaviour is also affected by their income and job opportunities. The experience of gender discrimination in the labour market and/or the lack of job opportunities may induce women to 'prefer' part-time work and/or to leave the labour market (discouraged worker effect). The state structures tastes through its policies and institutional arrangements such as child care provisions. Men's and women's commitment to work may, for example, be affected by tax policy. Tax policy rewarding 'housewifery' creates an incentive for women to stay out of the labour market after children have left the home. To sum up, the choice of an individual to work is in continuous non-accommodating interaction with social norms, family structures, structures of paid employment and employers' policy as well as structures and policies of the state. The various influences may involve differentiation between men and women that will contribute to gendered tastes.

Brosnan et al. (1995:669) have developed a framework for analysing how the state shapes demand and supply for labour and their interaction. First, the state may regulate the labour supply through social security, education, training, child care and immigration. Secondly, the state may influence the demand for labour through fiscal and monetary stabilisation policies and as an employer. Finally, the state may regulate the interaction of actors in the labour market through the legal framework by implementing and enforcing rules concerning industrial relations and discrimination. A problem with this framework is that it lumps together policies creating incentives/disincentives to work and those increasing directly the volume of labour/jobs as these have different implications for the labour force. Social security, education and tax policy create incentives/disincentives for the working population to work while immigration of adults will increase directly the size of the working population. Moreover, higher levels of aggregated demand and public sector employment may affect the number of jobs. An additional problem with the framework of Brosnan et al. is, however, that it does not attempt to relate divergent labour market patterns across space to the nature of the state. The state has become an important source of variations in labour market outcomes across space as economic internationalisation and regional co-operation in the economic spheres is reducing variations accounted for by the structure and the functioning of the industrial system.

Esping-Andersen (1990) has analysed the role of the state in creating cross national difference in labour markets. According to Esping-Andersen, cross national differences in labour market behaviour may be attributed to the nature of welfare state regimes. Moreover, welfare state regimes and employment regimes tend to coincide (1990:159). The corporatist welfare regime in Germany encourages exit and reduced labour supply as it is committed to preservation of the family and labour market status differentials. The liberal welfare state in the United States is concerned with ensuring the free play of the market and therefore does little to stimulate either exit or female participation. The social democratic welfare state in Sweden promotes equality at the highest possible level. Hence, maximum labour supply and modest exit rates among older males are the goals of the Swedish welfare state. The structure of the welfare state explains therefore why women's labour force participation has been high in Sweden and low in Germany. However, the high labour force participation of American women despite the state offering little encouragement to participate is puzzling to Esping-Andersen's theory as it assumes a functional relationship between the welfare state policies and the participation in paid work. This contradicts with his rejection of a functional relationship between industrial development and the welfare state (1990:chapter 1).

The interrelationship between the welfare state, the household and the labour market is better described as being relatively autonomous as there is not necessarily a smooth accommodation between policies adopted by the state and participation pattern in the labour market. Moreover, the degree of relative autonomy will differ as responses are shaped by the dominant social blocks at the state level (see our analysis in chapter 2). In the United States, business interests have been successful at the political level in ensuring the free play of market forces involving a continuous flow of labour into the country which in turn has reduced the need for an active involvement of the state in social reproduction.

Moreover, the liberal ideology of the two main political parties ensured that the state did not intervene directly into the private sphere to enable women to work. Hence, the American state has adopted a more autonomous stance towards the household than the Swedish and German state. In Germany, the Catholic Church has enjoyed a warm relationship with the dominant political party, the CDU, and the state has been committed to support the family through tax policies and transfers instead of service provisions which corresponds to the Catholic principle of subsidiarity. According to this principle, the state should not engage in solving social problems before the family, the church and voluntary organisations have failed to solve the problems (Borchorst 1994). In Sweden, the commitment of the main federation of labour, the LO, to equality beyond the market and its strong position within the main governing party, the Social Democratic Party, has facilitated an extensive involvement of the state in social reproduction and production. Hence, the interrelationship between the different spheres or, for example, welfare policies and labour force participation has been much more functional in Sweden than in the other two countries.

In the following empirical analysis, the main changes in paid employment occurring since the 1960s in the Swedish, German and the American labour markets will be identified and analysed. In the first section, the economic climate and changes in paid employment since the 1960s in Sweden, Germany and the United States will now be studied. The aim is to examine the relation between changes in aggregated demand and trends in paid employment. Thereafter, participation rates will be studied in order to evaluate the feminisation of the labour force and the extent to which men have withdrawn from the labour market. Changes in female and male employment will then be decomposed by shift-share analysis as it shows how much can be accounted for by structural developments on the one hand and by changing shares of female and male labour within industries on the other hand. The results will be related to public-private division in the provision of services. In the second part of the empirical analysis, a comparison of activity and inactivity rates since the 1960s will be undertaken to highlight some of the divergences in men's and women's labour force participation across the three countries. Variations in labour market patterns will be analysed in view of the role of the state in altering the volume of the labour supply and in creating incentives/disincentives to engage in paid work. The responses of the state to the changes in paid work have been conditioned by social blocks in different ways across the three countries that has in turn contributed to divergent developments as concerns paid employment.

Demand Pressures and Trends in Paid Work

During the period 1960-1990, the Swedish, German and American economies expanded on average (see real GDP in table 3.1).

Table 3.1 Macro-economic Growth Rates During the Post-War Period

Average annual real growth rates	Period	Sweden	Germany*	United States
Real GDP	1960 -1970	4.65	4.46	3.84
	1970 -1980	1.97	2.74	2.72
	1980 -1990	2.01	2.19	2.72
	1990 -1995	0.43	1.17	2.31
Private consumption	1960 -1970	3.76	5.14	4.13
	1970 -1980	1.63	3.35	3.02
	1980 -1990	1.40	2.19	3.01
	1990 -1994	-0.44	1.37	2.44
Public consumption	1960 -1970	5.73	4.46	3.57
	1970 -1980	3.17	3.48	0.96
	1980 -1990	1.63	1.32	2.67
	1990 -1994	0.56	1.87	-0.32
Employment**	1960 -1970	0.79	0.31	1.76
	1970 -1980	0.99	0.22	2.42
	1980 -1990	0.5	0.84	1.53
	1990 -1994	-1.54	0.02	1.07

*West Germany until 1990 and unified Germany since 1991. The period 1990-1994 refers therefore always to 1991-1994 for unified Germany.
** The period for Sweden is 1962-1990.

Source: OECD 1973; 1985; 1994a; 1996b; 1997a.

If the expenditure side of the economy is considered, the source of growth differed across the three countries. In Sweden, public consumption grew faster from 1960 to 1990 than private consumption while the opposite occurred in the United States.

In West Germany, the growth rates for public and private consumption were similar. United States performed best in terms of growth in paid employment during the period 1960-1990, primarily due to the expansion of the private sector[1]. The average annual growth of employment was 1.9 per cent in the United States at the same time as real GDP grew on average 3.09 per cent per year. West Germany was the least successful in turning economic growth into growth in paid employment. In West Germany, employment rose on average only 0.4 per cent annually and real GDP increased 3.13 per cent. Paid employment in Sweden grew 0.76 per cent annually at the same time as the rise in real GDP was 2.88 per cent. The public sector in Sweden has been the main source of growth in paid employment since the early 1960s while the private sector has experienced very limited employment expansion (Rosen 1995:64).

Pronounced change occurred from the period 1960-1970 to the period 1970-1980 as concerns the annual average growth rates of real GDP, private consumption and public consumption in the three countries. The greatest reduction in the average growth rates of real GDP and private consumption took place in Sweden where real GDP fell by a factor of 2.36 or from 4.65 per cent to 1.97 per cent and private consumption by a factor of 2.31.

The reduction in public consumption was, however, greatest in the United States where it fell by a factor of 3.71. The turbulent economic situation during the 1970s had roots in the oil price rises in 1973/1974 and 1979/1980 that imparted major terms-of-trade shocks (see OECD 1994b:29). In spite of slower economic growth, paid employment in Sweden and the United States grew faster during the period 1970-1980 than in other periods. In West Germany, the fastest growth in paid employment occurred during the subsequent period 1980-1990. The annual average real GDP growth rates became more similar across the three countries in the 1980s that may be attributed to a more interrelated economic development as a result of greater reliance on international trade[2], freer movement of capital and/or expansion of global corporations. In the early 1990s, the annual average real growth rates of real GDP were relatively low for the three countries but the slowdown in growth rates was the most severe in Sweden where paid employment contracted for the first time since 1960.

To summarise, the economies of Sweden, West Germany and the United States expanded on average from 1960 to 1990. The similar economic growth rate across the three countries supports Rubery's claim that the internationalisation of markets and production technologies put similar pressures on labour demand across countries (1988d:254). However, the origin of the economic growth and the success of these economies in translating growth into paid employment differed. The economic growth in the United States occurred primarily in the private sector while the public sector was the main source of growth in Sweden. The United States was the most successful in transforming growth into growth in paid employment. Although less successful than the United States, Sweden's employment growth was also impressive. West Germany was the least successful in converting growth in the private and public sectors into growth in paid work. In all three countries, a rise in women's paid work accounted for most of the employment growth. We will now consider the feminisation of the labour force and the withdrawal of men by examining the development of participation rates across time and space.

Although the population growth from 1960 to 1995 in the United States was more than twice the growth in Sweden, the rise in women's participation rate was faster and the fall in men's labour force participation rate was also slower. The participation rates of women rose by 22.7 percentage points in Sweden, 29 percentage points in the United States at the same time as men's participation rates fell 12.9 percentage points and 4.7 percentage points respectively (see table 3.2).

It was, however, not until the 1990s, that the United States surpassed Sweden as the country with the most extensive growth in women's participation rates. The rates of female labour force participation in Sweden and the United States came closer in 1995 due to the differential rate of growth in the two countries. In Sweden, women's participation rates fell 6.3 percentage points at the same time as they increased 1.9 percentage points in the United States. The reduction in male participation rates in the United States was solely due to a decline in the armed forces and not to a drop in civil employment as was the case in Sweden and Germany. The largest fall in men's participation occurred during the period 1960-1990 in West Germany. However, women's integration was too slow to narrow the gender gap in participation rates to the same extent as in Sweden and the United States.

Table 3.2 The Labour Force Participation*

	1960	1970	1980	1990	1995	% points '60-'95
Sweden**						
Female	54.2	60.6	75.8	83.2	76.9	22.7
Male	95.0	90.6	89.8	88.4	82.1	-12.9
Gender gap(f/m)	0.57	0.67	0.84	0.94	0.94	
West Germany						
Female	49.3	48.1	52.8	57.0		7.7
Male	94.9	92.5	84.3	80.8		-14.1
Gender gap(f/m)	0.52	0.52	0.63	0.71		
United Germany**						
Female				61.1	61.0	-0.1
Male				82.0	80.1	-1.9
Gender gap(f/m)				0.75	0.76	
United States						
Female	42.6	50.4	61.5	69.7	71.6	29
Male	91.7	90.1	88.5	88.1	87.0	-4.7
Gender ratio(f/m)	0.45	0.56	0.70	0.79	0.82	

*Defined as the total labour force divided by the population aged 15-64.
** Participation rates refer to 1962 instead of 1960.
*** 1991 and 1995.

Source: OECD 1973 and 1997a.

In 1995, Germany had the largest gender gap in participation rates at the same time as Sweden remained the country with the smallest gender gap. Taken together, the trend since the 1960s in the three countries has been towards greater feminisation of the labour force and withdrawal of men from the labour market. The withdrawal of men from the labour market has, however, been less extensive and less uniform. Moreover, the extent of these changes in paid employment has varied across the three countries. The largest increase in women's labour force participation took place in the United States but men's participation rates fell more in West Germany than in the other two countries. Moreover, the gender gap has narrowed in the three countries but Sweden kept its position as the country with the most equal participation rates. Male participation rates were also more similar across the three countries than the female participation rates. Fluctuations in male participation rates have been greater in Sweden and West Germany than in the United States. The withdrawal of men has been at relatively low level in the United States while there have been large differences in the rate of withdrawal between periods in the other two countries. The largest reductions in male participation rates occurred in Sweden during the periods 1960-1970 and 1990-1995 while the most extensive fall took place from 1970 to 1980 in West Germany.

Decomposing Changes in Paid Work

Forces contributing to the feminisation of the labour force and the withdrawal of men will now be examined by applying shift-share analysis to data on civilian employment classified according to I.S.I.C major divisions (see OECD 1984 and 1996b). The major divisions include agriculture, hunting, forestry and fishing (1), mining and quarrying (2), manufacturing (3), electricity, gas and water (4), construction (5), wholesale and retail trade, restaurants and hotels (6), transport, storage and communication (7), financing, insurance, real estate, and business services (8) and community, social and personal services (9). In the shift-share analysis, a change in the number of men/women employed is attributed to changing structure of industry/occupation (industry effect), changing demand for men/women within industries/occupations (share effect) and interaction (interactive effect) between the two components (see Rubery 1988b; Rubery et al. 1996). Our shift-share analysis is based on annual changes in paid employment and shares which does not give the same results as when the analysis is based on changes between the starting year (1970) and the final year (1990) or period changes. The outcomes produced by the two methods are, however, not very different. The reason for the different results is that employment and shares are kept constant at their 1970 level when period changes are used while the variables kept constant change from year to year as they take on the value of the year before when annual changes are used. We have chosen to use annual changes in our calculations as the results are then not influenced by our choice of starting year which would be the case if periodical changes were be used. When comparing the three countries across time, we will primarily refer to the period 1970-1990 as the German unification involved a fundamental break in the time series on paid employment. In 1991, the working population of East Germany was added to the working population in West Germany such that information before and after 1991 are not comparable for Germany.

Women's Paid Employment

Our shift-share analysis of changes in female civilian employment for the period 1970-1990 discloses a similar pattern across Sweden, West Germany and the United States (see table 3.3). Across the three countries, shifts in the structure of industries (industry effect) accounted for a much higher share of total female employment change than changes in female share of employment within industries (share effect). The industry effect accounted for 80 per cent of the change in female employment in Sweden and the United States but for around 70 per cent in West Germany. Growing demand for female labour was mainly due to expansion of the industrial sector denoted *community, social and personal services* (9). In 1970, the share of women in this sector was 66 per cent in Sweden, 47 per cent in West Germany and 56 per cent in the United States. Hence, women benefited from a favourable employment trend in industrial sectors where women's share was close to or even higher than men's. Another expanding sector contributing to greater paid employment of women was *financing, insurance, real estate, and business services* (8) that had throughout the period fairly similar male and female shares across the three countries.

Table 3.3 Decomposition of the Change in Women's Paid Employment*
         (000s) each year

	Net change	Industry effect	Share effect	Interactive effect	Scale effect	Weight effect	Residual effect
Sweden							
1970-1980	386	320.01	64.74	1.24	160.14	158.59	1.27
1980-1990	230	175.12	56.44	-1.56	103.37	71.54	0.21
1990-1994	-225	-179.86	-46.17	1.03	-252.63	75.63	-2.86
1970-1990	616	495.13	121.19	-0.32	263.52	230.13	1.48
Germany**							
1970-1980	254	51.18	186.60	16.22	-137.81	191.93	-2.94
1980-1990	1652	1266.09	374.88	11.03	828.46	432.71	4.92
1991-1994	-428	-156.49	-288.96	17.45	-408.80	254.53	-2.22
1970-1990	1906	1317.27	561.48	27.25	690.65	624.64	1.98
United States							
1970-1980	12426	9189.16	3129.59	107.28	7976.28	1209.71	3.17
1980-1990	11362	9657.7	1677.08	27.21	8074.39	1569.31	14.01
1990-1994	3132	3161.48	-69.88	40.40	2322.12	840.52	-1.16
1970-1990	23788	18846.86	4806.65	134.49	16050.67	2779.01	17.17

* Civilian employment.
**West Germany until 1990 and unified Germany since 1991.

Source: OECD 1984 and 1996b.

Increased penetration of industrial sectors by women was especially evident in the United States. In the early 1990s, the industrial effect became negative in Sweden and Germany while it remained positive in the

United States. Female employment in Sweden declined across most sectors. Hard hit sectors were the male-dominated sector *manufacturing* (3) and the female-dominated sector *community, social and personal services* (9). In Germany, the largest contraction of female employment occurred in the mixed sector *agriculture, hunting, forestry and fishing* (1) and in the male-dominated sector *manufacturing* (3).

During the period 1970-1990, the share effect was positive in Sweden, West Germany and the United States. The largest share effect occurred in the industrial sector *community, social and personal services* (9) such that it became feminised or close to being feminised (West Germany). The share effect in the three countries was negative for the first time in the early 1990s which may indicate a turn-around in the employment situation of women who are no longer being substituted for men across most industries. In the United States, the change in female shares during the early 1990s was unfavourable in 3 out of 9 sectors and in 7 out of 9 in both Sweden and Germany. In Sweden, the largest part of the decline in female shares occurred in three sectors, i.e. the female-dominated sector *community, social and personal services* (9), the male-dominated sector *manufacturing* (3), and the mixed sector *financing, insurance, real estate, and business services* (8). The concentration of Swedish women in service sector industries appears to have become less effective in sheltering their paid employment during a period of recession. Public sector retrenchment and greater internationalisation/globalisation of the service sector, e.g. financial markets have contributed to greater employment insecurity among women in the Swedish labour market. In Germany, the largest reduction in female shares took place in *manufacturing* (3) but the unification process led to tremendous destruction of manufacturing jobs in East Germany (see Maier et al. 1996:table 1.3.1.1b). Greater concentration of German women in *community, social and personal services* (9) cancelled out some of the drop in the share of women in manufacturing. The largest part of the negative share effect occurred in two mixed sectors in the United States, i.e. *financing, insurance, real estate, and business services* (8) and *the wholesale and retail trade, restaurants and hotels* (6).

The industry effect can be decomposed into three components or the changing scale of employment with a constant structure of industry (the scale effect), the changing composition of industrial employment (the weight effect) and the remaining residual effect (Rubery 1988b; Rubery et al. 1996:92-97). A decomposition of the growth in female employment accounted for by the industrial effect during the period 1970-1990 reveals that the scale effect or expansion of employment opportunities was the largest component in all three countries (see table 3.3). However, the difference between the scale effect and the weight effect was much smaller in Sweden and West Germany than in the United States. In the former two countries, the scale effect accounted for around 53 per cent of the expansion in industrial employment while the equivalent ratio was 85 per cent in the United States. Women's employment opportunities expanded in all industrial sectors in the three countries and the compositional shift from agriculture and manufacturing to services was favourable for women.

Although the scale effect was negative in West Germany in the sub-period 1970-1980, indicating a contraction in employment opportunities for women, women's paid employment grew due to favourable changes in the composition of employment. In Sweden and Germany, the scale effect became negative in the early 1990s as both economies were hit by a recession or a slowdown in economic growth. The weight effect, on the other hand, remained positive during the whole period in the three countries. The weight effect or changing composition of employment was not large enough in Sweden and Germany to counteract the negative scale effect. Women's paid employment contracted across all industrial sectors in the two countries and those in *wholesale and retail trade, restaurants and hotels (6), manufacturing (3)* and *community, social and personal services (9)* were hardest hit.

As suggested by Rubery (1988b), the main demand pressures behind the feminisation of the labour force were the structural development and to lesser extent employers' greater use of female labour. The structural development involved both expanding employment opportunities and a shift towards female-dominated sectors. A closer look at the structural shift reveals that the community and personal services were more important in contributing to rise in women's paid employment in Sweden than in the other two countries.

Community and personal services have primarily been the responsibility of the public sector in Sweden but provided by the private sector in the United States. In Germany, on the other hand, independent social service agencies receive financial support from the state to provide welfare services (cf. discussion in chapter 2). The welfare services have not expanded to the same extent in West Germany as in the other two countries which has contributed to slower integration of German women into paid work. These findings support Esping-Andersen's claim that the growth in women's paid employment has been structured by the state in different ways across the three countries (1990:201). This does not, however, imply that there exists a functional relationship between the state and the labour market. The active role of the Swedish state in the labour market has made the interrelationship between the two spheres relatively functional, although non-accommodating. The American state, on the other hand, has not adopted an autonomous stance towards the labour market. The active enforcement of the equal rights laws through affirmative action programmes has contributed to the greater distribution of women across industrial sectors in the United States as compared with Sweden and Germany where such measures have been much more restricted (cf. chapter 2). Structural development and employers' labour use strategies have pulled German women into the labour market at the same time as the German state has actively discouraged women's paid work.

Men's Paid Employment

We have also applied shift-share analysis to data on male civilian employment in order to evaluate the forces behind men's withdrawal from the labour market in the three countries. If the results in table 3.4 and table 3.3 are compared, it appears that the male share effect is the inverse value of the female share effect. The share effect measures how much of the change in female/male employment can be attributed to changes in female/male shares keeping employment constant. As employers have a choice between employing either a man or a woman, a change in female shares will lead to corresponding inverse change in men's shares across industries. The male interactive effect is also the inverse value of the female interactive effect. The interactive effect estimates how much of the employment change can be accounted for by combined effect of changes in total employment and changes in shares across industries. The change in total employment takes on the same value for both men and women and the change in male shares will equal the inverse change in women's shares.

During the period 1970-1990, men's paid employment contracted in Sweden and West Germany while it expanded in the United States as civilian employment does not include the armed forces (see table 3.4).

Table 3.4 Decomposition of the Change in Men's Paid Employment*
(000s) each year

	Net change	Industry effect	Share effect	Interactive effect	Scale effect	Weight effect	Residual effect
Sweden							
1970-1980	-8	57.99	-64.74	-1.24	217.86	-158.59	-1.27
1980-1990	-18	36.88	-56.44	1.56	113.45	-76.37	-0.20
1990-1994	-296	-341.14	46.17	-1.03	-269.7	-74.34	2.89
1970-1990	-26	94.87	-121.19	0.32	331.30	-234.96	-1.47
Germany**							
1970-1980	-652	-449.18	-186.60	-16.22	-224.21	-230.60	5.63
1980-1990	565	950.91	-374.88	-11.03	1242.92	-291.42	-0.60
1991-1994	-599	-870.51	288.96	-17.45	-562.37	-310.96	2.81
1970-1990	-87	501.73	-561.48	-27.25	1018.72	-522.02	5.03
United States							
1970-1980	8196	11432.84	-3129.56	-107.28	12198.18	-777.24	11.91
1980-1990	7249	8953.3	-1677.08	-27.21	10207.23	-1248.42	-5.52
1990-1994	2017	1987.52	69.88	-40.40	2745.76	-761.84	3.6
1970-1990	15445	20386.14	-4806.65	-134.49	22405.41	-2025.66	6.39

*Civilian employment.
**Unified Germany since 1991.

Source: OECD 1984 and 1996b.

In Sweden and West Germany, unfavourable changes in the male share of employment within industries (share effect) more than cancelled out favourable changes in structures of industries (industry effect) such that men's paid employment fell. The share effect was also negative in the United States but the much larger industry effect ensured expansion in men's paid employment. Male shares within most industrial sectors fell indicating a less gender segregated labour market across the three countries.

The largest drop in male shares within industries was in *community, social and personal services* (9). In Sweden, the reduction in the share of men in this industrial sector reversed some of the favourable change in gender segregation as it was already female-dominated. The contraction in men's industrial employment in Sweden and West Germany was mainly in *agriculture, hunting, forestry and fishing* (1) and *manufacturing* (3). These sectors were male-dominated in 1970 except *agriculture, hunting, forestry and fishing* (1) which was a mixed sector in West Germany. The only industrial sector where men's employment fell in the United States was in *agriculture, hunting, forestry and fishing* (1). The greatest increase in male employment was in *community, social and personal services* (9) across the three countries. However, the increase was much smaller than for women. In the early 1990s, men's paid employment contracted in Sweden and Germany due to negative industry effect. The share effect was positive in both countries which had not been the case in earlier periods. Hence, women are now being replaced by men instead of vice versa.

A decomposition of the change in male paid employment accounted for by the industrial effect during the period 1970-1990 shows that the scale effect or expansion of employment opportunities was positive at the same time as the weight effect was negative (see table 3.4). The unfavourable compositional changes involving employment shift away from sectors such as *agriculture, hunting, forestry and fishing* (1), *mining and quarrying* (2) and *manufacturing* (3) were, however, smaller than the scale effect such that the industrial effect was positive. Sweden and Germany in the early 1990s had a negative industry effect due to unfavourable scale and weight effects which had adverse effects on men's paid employment. Men's employment opportunities contracted across all sectors in the two countries and those in *manufacturing* (3) and *community, social and personal services* (9) were the hardest hit.

As assumed by neo-classical theories, the withdrawal of men from the labour market in Sweden and West Germany was due to substitution of female for male labour and employment contraction in traditional male industries (see, e.g. Jacobsen 1994:127-136). Growing employment opportunities across all industries and the shift towards service industries as well as employers' increased use of female labour contributed to the feminisation of the labour force in Sweden and West Germany. However, women's paid employment expanded faster in Sweden than in West Germany as a result of greater expansion of welfare services. During the 1990s, women's paid employment dropped for the first time in Sweden and Germany due to both industrial restructuring and reduced use of women within industries. The economic recession during the early 1990s in Sweden led first to contraction in traditional male industries. The falling paid employment in the private sector (manufacturing and wholesale and retail trade) and the tax reform implemented in 1991 involving less progressive tax system had an adverse effect on the tax revenues of the Swedish state. In order to reduce the public deficit, many jobs within the public service sector were cut and contracted out (Mósesdóttir and Eydal forthcoming). Paid employment in manufacturing and agriculture contracted in Germany after unification without a corresponding expansion in the service industries. The largest destruction of both female and male manufacturing jobs occurred in East Germany. In the United States, industrial restructuring during the period 1970-1995 accounted for most of the growth in women's and men's paid employment. Manufacturing employment expanded until the early 1990s at the same time as there was a tremendous employment growth in the service industries. Hence, the civilian employment of American men expanded at the same time as the employment of Swedish and German men contracted slightly.

Supply Responses and the State

As revealed by our analysis, the withdrawal of Swedish and German men was primarily due to reduced use of men within industries. Industrial restructuring, on the other hand, accounted for most of the growth in women's paid employment in Sweden, West Germany and the United States. Moreover, men's civilian employment expanded slightly in the United States due to industrial restructuring. When participation rates are compared across countries they vary much more for women than men. As men's paid employment has so far not been affected by family responsibilities (see Maier 1994 and Fagan et al. 1995 quoted in Delsen 1998:67), the divergences in women's labour force participation must have their roots in different responses of households to demand pressures. However, the different fertility rates cannot explain divergences across the three countries. West Germany had the lowest fertility rate in 1990 as well as the lowest female labour force participation (see Tanda 1994:282). The German state, on the other hand, has created disincentives for women to work through the tax system at the same time as the Swedish state has stimulated women's labour force participation through the tax system and by extensive provision of public child care for pre-school and young school-children. Moreover, the state has also affected the use of male labour through its pension polices. As our shift-share analysis showed, contraction in employers' use of men across industries explained the contraction in men's paid employment in Sweden and West Germany. The availability of early retirement within the pension systems has enabled many men in these countries to leave the labour market. Moreover, retirement schemes have induced employers to create part-time work for older workers and/or to shift to female labour where there has been a shortage of male labour. Hence, demand pressures and the responses on the supply side cannot be studied in isolation from the state that has been an important source of gender and country divergences. However, it is not possible to read off supply responses from the state policies aimed at regulating the labour supply. State policies interact with other factors affecting the decision to work such as real wages, tastes and non-labour income and the interrelationship between the state, the labour market and the household is relatively autonomous. Moreover, the role actors have played in shaping the interrelationship between spheres needs to be considered as we would otherwise run the risk of assuming either a functional relationship (Sweden) or an autonomous relationship (the United States) between the state policies and employment patterns.

The following analysis will focus on the responses of social reproduction to the demand pressures. The main emphasis will be on the role of the state in affecting the volume of the labour supply and in creating incentives/disincentives to participate in paid work. We will start our discussion by studying participation rates in more details in order to draw forth gender and country differences in activity and inactivity as well as in full-time and part-time work. Although a distinction is made between demand pressures and supply responses, it has become increasingly difficult to isolate demand and supply pressures as the latter has increasingly come to condition the former. In our analysis, we will apply the framework of Brosnan et al. (1995) on the state's regulation of the labour supply. Hence, we will examine pension, education, taxation and child care policies aimed at creating incentives/disincentives as well as immigration policies affecting the volume of labour in order to explain gender and country differences in participation rates.

Activity and Inactivity

In our brief study of the activity status of working age population (15-64 years), we have chosen the year 1993 due to the availability of information on the division between full-time and part-time work in the three countries. It was only in Sweden that the female inactivity rates came close to approaching the level of male inactivity rates (see figure 3.1).

Figure 3.1 Activity Status of the Working Age Population (15-64 years) in 1993

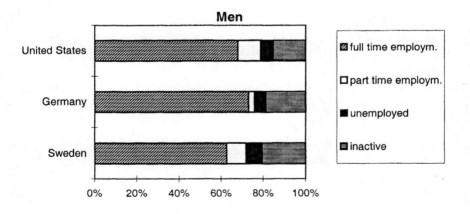

105

Figure 3.1 Continued

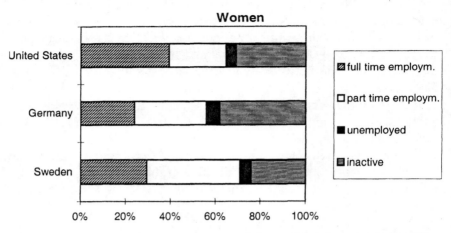

Unemployment is measured as a percentage of the working-age population. The conventional unemployment rate compares the number of unemployed to the labour force.

Source: OECD 1996a.

The high activity rates for Swedish women do not give an accurate picture of women's engagement in paid employment as their allocation of time to market work is less than full-time (between 20 and 34 hours) and they may be defined as being in the labour force although on temporary child care leave (Jonung and Persson 1993:262). Sweden stands out among the three countries as it had the highest part-time rate for women and the highest inactivity rate for men. Germany (unified), on the other hand, was the country with the highest inactivity rate for women and the highest full-time employment rate for men. East German women still engage in paid employment to a greater extent than West German women, although their participation rates have dropped since unification at the same time as they have increased in the West (see Maier et al. 1996:33). The greatest gender gap between the economically active (employed plus unemployed) and economically inactive was in Germany implying that degree of the utilisation of the female population was the least similar to that of men. In the United States, the male inactivity rate was lowest among the three countries while the part-time employment rate for men was the highest. Finally, women in the United States were more likely to work full-time than women in Sweden and Germany.

Withdrawal of Men

Variations in the pension and educational systems are important explanations for differences in men's inactivity rates and level of part-time work across the three countries. In Sweden, the state has employed various instruments to influence the demand and supply of older workers including sheltered jobs and subsidised employment, flexible retirement pension, partial pensions and financial incentives for firms to employ older workers[3]. These instruments have ensured high level of integration of the working age population during periods of labour shortages. During the recession of the early 1990s, these measures were used to enable many older workers to reduce their hours of work or to leave the labour market (Naschold et al. 1994a; Olafsson and Petersson 1994). Hence, men's inactivity and part-time work increased during the early 1990s (see Sundström 1997:273). Moreover, the dual pension system involving flat-rate benefits related to citizenship and compulsory supplementary pension payments (ATP) has enabled most older workers to maintain their life-style which in turn has reduced their incentive to engage in paid work after entering full-time retirement (Olafsson and Petersson 1994). If the labour force participation of those 15 to 24 years is compared across the three countries, Sweden has moved from having a high share of youth in paid employment in 1979 to having the lowest share among the three countries in 1994. During the 1980s, youth employment in Sweden was comparable to that of the United States. This unfavourable trend in Sweden was due to a tremendous increase during the early 1990s in youth unemployment (see OECD 1996a:111-114). Prior to the recession of the early 1990s, many students in Sweden combined work and studying in order to keep the amount of their student loans as low as possible (see Nätti 1995).

The low inactivity rate in the United States relative to Sweden and Germany may be attributed to limited pension coverage and insufficient replacement rates. Moreover, anti-age discrimination legislation has been implemented in the United States to encourage and protect the employment of older workers (Jacobs and Rein 1994). The

107

public social security system in the United States is designed to provide only a floor of social protection and it offers less coverage than in the public pension systems in Sweden and Germany. In the early 1990s, a higher ratio of persons over 60 years received public pension in Sweden and Germany than in the United States. The ratio for Sweden and Germany was around 88 per cent while it was 83 per cent in the United States (World Bank 1994:63). Moreover, only around half of the employees in the private sector have been covered by pension schemes and the share of those covered has been falling since the late 1970s (Mishel et al. 1997:160). In the United States, most private pensions are not indexed against inflation. In an inflationary period, the value of these pensions will erode forcing workers to re-enter work after spending some time out of the labour force simply because their pension is not adequate. The limited pension coverage and insufficient replacement rates have led to greater variations in the patterns of exit of older workers in the United States than in Sweden and Germany (see Jacobs and Rein 1994). People with higher incomes, especially private pension incomes tend to move directly from full-time to non-work while those with low income over the life-cycle are more likely to experience partial retirement. Moreover, American employers pursue a diversity of policies toward employment of older workers. Some employers discourage work by older people while others encourage it (Hutchens 1994). The state, on the other hand, has primarily been concerned with stimulating growth in order to ensure sufficient employment opportunities (Naschold et al. 1994a).

As concerns the high rate of part-time work among American men, there has been an increased tendency in the United States for older male workers to engage in part-time work (Hutchens 1994; Delsen 1998). Moreover, part-time employment among young men (15-25 years) is much more common in the United States than in Sweden and Germany (see OECD 1994c:85-86). One explanation is the widespread use of students and youth in part-time work (Rubery 1988d:263). The share of young persons attending school and engaging in work is greater in the United States than in, for example, Germany where the rate of part-time work among men was lowest. In 1994, 46.3 per cent of men and 45.6 per cent of women aged 18 in the United States were employed and attending school. The respective percentages for

Germany were 12 and 15.4 (OECD 1996a:132). One reason for the different engagement of German and American students in paid work is that the latter are expected to finance their studies themselves through work, loans and to lesser extent through scholarships. Parents in Germany with income above certain thresholds are excepted to support their children while in education. German parents still have a life-long obligation to support their children while other countries have an age limit signalling the majority of the child as in the Scandinavian countries (Scheiwe 1994:205).

A distinct feature of the participation status of German men is that they were most likely to engage in full-time work. Moreover, the inactivity rate in Germany was very similar to the rate in Sweden or 19.6 and 20.5 respectively (see figure 3.1). From the mid-1970s until the early 1990s, retirement in Germany was characterised by an acceleration of the full-time early-retirement process. The early retirement option meant that men remained in full-time employment until retirement (Naschold et al. 1994b). This pattern of full-employment until retirement was due to a low level of acceptance of opportunities for a staged transition to retirement and to the strict legal limits on pensioners wishing to top-up their transfer benefits with earned income. It was not until the mid-1990s, that part-time early retirement, combined with a replacement obligation was introduced and the full early retirement option was at the same time abolished (Delsen 1998:71).

To summarise, the states in Sweden, Germany and the United States have created incentives/disincentives for young and older men to participate in paid work. In Sweden, the state has been active in enhancing the integration of young and older workers into paid work during periods of labour shortage and encouraging externalisation or exit from the labour market during recession (Naschold et al. 1994a). The German state has stimulated the full-time employment pattern of men through the pension system that only allowed for full-time early retirement until the mid-1990s. Moreover, the opportunities for retired workers to top-up their pension payments were restricted. The life long obligation of parents to provide for their children which has been actively supported by the German state and the limited part-time employment opportunities have also contributed to low participation rates among young people. Hence, the German state has created disincentives for students to enter into paid work and incentives for older workers to exit employment on a full-time basis. The American state, on the other hand, has created incentives for the maximum integration into paid work by stimulating employment growth as well as by not ensuring universal pension coverage and high enough replacement rates for older workers to maintain their life-style. Moreover, the limited financial assistance to students and the relatively high costs of studying (tuition) has created incentives for American students to engage in paid work.

Feminisation of the Labour Force

In order to explain why women's activity rates vary much more across the three countries than men's we need to look at how the state has affected the labour supply as well as created incentives/disincentives for women to engage in paid work. Moreover, different patterns of combining motherhood and work will be studied in order uncover the reasons behind the variations in the levels of part-time[4] and full-time work. One way the state can directly affect the volume of the labour supply is through its immigration policies. The economic growth prevailing during the early post-war period induced employers to put pressure on the state to implement measures that would increase the supply of labour. The measures undertaken by the Swedish, German and the American state as a response to the demand pressures varied as they were formed by very different social blocks acting at the state level (cf. chapter 2). In Sweden, cross class alliances between labour and capital had been formed at the state level such that the state was committed to class and gender equality. Hence, the Swedish state responded to employers' growing demand for labour by implementing measures enabling women to reconcile work and family life. The German state, on the other hand, was influenced by the Catholic family ideology that committed the state to defend and preserve the family. Hence, employers' pressure for large labour force in West Germany was to a certain extent met by immigration which was allowed on a short-term basis. In the United States, business interests have been successful at the political level in

110

ensuring the free play of market forces involving a continuous flow of labour into the country. This inflow of immigrants reduced the pressure on the state to activate women's paid employment. Moreover, the liberal ideology of the two main political parties ensured that the state did not intervene directly into the private sphere to enable women to work. Instead the state ensured that the market provided incentives for women to participate in paid work.

In West Germany and the United States, the state used its immigration policies to increase the supply of (male) labour which reduced the need during the early part of the post-war period to activate the large reserve of female labour. In Sweden, on the other hand, immigration was not used as an instrument to affect the volume of the labour supply. Hence, women's paid employment expanded faster until the 1990s in Sweden than in West Germany and the United States (see table 3.2). However, immigration policy cannot explain all the difference in activity rates across the three countries. Immigration in the United States has always been on a much larger scale than in West Germany at the same time as women's paid employment has expanded faster in the former country. We therefore need to examine other state policies creating directly and indirectly incentives/disincentives for women to participate in paid work across the three countries. The role of these measures in creating divergent employment patterns will now be studied and compared across the three countries. Although the state has affected the labour force participation of men and women, it has not achieved equalisation between supply and demand. Moreover, men's and women's decision to work is not only influenced by demand for labour and state policies but also by other factors such as family size and social norms.

Creating Incentives/Disincentives

Individual taxation, generous statutory leave of absence for parenthood and extensive availability of subsidised public child services for pre-school children in Sweden have enabled Swedish women to attain similar participation rates to those of men. Moreover, women's real pay rose due to measures undertaken to narrow the gender pay gap, improve the position of the low pay and to reduce dispersion across

111

sectors (see Löfström 1995:43; Sundström 1997:275). In Sweden, separate taxation of spouses was introduced in 1971 that lowered the tax burden of families with two earners[5]. The introduction of separate taxation provided a strong incentive for married women to engage in paid work as the tax rates were highly progressive. During the 1980s, women's involvement in full-time work expanded as marginal tax rates for full-time workers were reduced stepwise and those of part-time workers were raised (Sundström 1997). Sweden was also the first country to introduce paid parental leave in 1974 which amounted to six months of paid leave and could be taken on a part-time basis until the child reached 8 years. The parental leave served as an incentive for women to participate in paid work as employment prior to birth gave rights to benefit payments related to former market earnings, i.e. 90 per cent income replacement (see Sundström 1993:139; Jonung and Persson 1993:272; Sundström 1997:275). In 1979, parents of pre-school children who had completed their parental leave were given the (unpaid) right to reduce their working to 75 per cent of full-time hours with the right to go back to full-time work again when the child reached 8 years. Finally, public child care facilities for pre-school and young school-children expanded rapidly during the 1970s and 1980s (Sundström 1997:275).

In Sweden, the length the parental leave in 1997 was until the child reaches 18 months and the parental benefit was earnings-related except for those not in the labour force who received a minimum-level benefit[6]. One month is reserved for the father and another for the mother. The parental leave may be taken partially, i.e. reduced by one quarter or by half with the corresponding reduction in the benefit level. (Bettio et al. 1998: National 'Assessment Tables': Sweden: Oláh 1998:61). In the pension system, leave for caring is treated as a period of normal insurance contribution. The parental leave scheme gives women strong incentives to work prior to child birth. Today, most Swedish women work full-time up to and after the birth of their first child and thus remain classified as full-time. After completing the parental leave, most mothers shift to part-time work until the youngest child enters school at the age of 7 years. Among the mothers shifting to part-time work are those making use of their right to reduced hours until the child is 8 years old. Women with higher level of education are more likely to continue to work full-time after returning from parental leave (see Gonäs and Spånt 1996:29; Sundström 1998). Extensive provision of public child care for pre-school and young school children whose parents study or work at least 20 hours a week has also contributed to the continuous labour force participation of Swedish women (Oláh 1998:53). In 1997, 75 per cent of children aged 1 to 6 years were in child care (Bettio et al. 1998: National 'Assessment Tables': Sweden).

In Germany and the United States, the state has actively supported the male-breadwinner model or a home-working housewife through the policies of joint taxation involving splitting of the income and derived rights of married women to pension benefits. The tax system in Germany (since 1958) favours married couples consisting of a home-working wife. The progressivity of taxing is reduced by allowing income-splitting between marriage partners (Buchholz-Will 1992:59-65; Nelson 1991:16-17). The marriage benefit (since 1948) in the United States has been curbed considerably since its introduction while it has remained more or less unchanged in Germany. However, Reagan implemented in 1986 the Earned Income Tax Credit EITC designed to assist low income families by refunding some proportion of the income taxes. The EITC which is based on a family system was expanded by the Clinton administration shortly after he entered the presidency (cf. chapter 2). In Germany, the tax splitting punishes dual full-time earner marriages and rewards women's non-work. Moreover, it is more favourable to work part-time than full-time, if women want to work (Blossfeld and Rohwer 1998:169). Contrary to Sweden, the tax system, especially in Germany, and pension rights granted on the basis of husbands' pension contributions have served as disincentives for both German and American women to participate in paid work.

In the United States, the right to parental leave and the availability of subsidised child care has been relatively limited. It was not until 1993 that a parental leave or the Family and Medical leave was passed in the United States on a national basis involving 12 weeks of unpaid leave. Moreover, child care services for the poor or disabled children are semi-public while child care services providing care for other children are basically private. Federal funds are used to finance private organisation and local government agencies that provide care for disabled or poor children. A minority of public and private enterprises provide child care services for their employees. In addition, there are various tax-provisions subsiding child care costs of families. However, many low income and minority families cannot afford private child care (Goodman 1995; Mishel and Bernstein 1993:11). In 1990, around 57 per cent of American families with children under five were paying for child care services (Goodman 1995).

The tax system, parental leave and subsidised child care have not been used to the same extent in the United States as in Sweden to encourage labour force participation and continuous paid employment. The tremendous rise since the 1960s in women's paid employment in the United States is therefore surprising (see table 3.2). However, if the rise in women's paid employment is examined more closely it appears that the increase is due to higher rates of re-entry after marriage and/or child birth and child rearing. Younger cohorts of women are re-entering the labour market sooner and on a larger scale (Goldin 1990; Drobnic and Wittig 1997). In 1996, 60 per cent of women with a child 1 year or younger were in the labour force (U.S. Department of Commerce 1997:404). Moreover, women employed full-time continue to interrupt their paid work when their marital and family situation changes but they are more likely to re-enter into full-time work than women with lower education as well as older women. Since the mid-1960s, women of all generations have increasingly entered the full-time work after a period of non-employment (Drobnic and Wittig 1997).

In the United States, the positive trends in women's pay relative to men and the fall in women's non-labour income (the income of the husband) have contributed to greater participation and continuity of their labour force participation (see Mishel and Berstein 1993:79). The federal government enforced anti-discrimination legislation during the early 1960s that led to a modest reduction in male-female pay gaps, especially during the 1970 (see Blau 1993:88). Moreover, the gender pay gap narrowed during the 1980s as a result of both improvements in the real hourly pay for women and real pay reduction for men. The federal government allowed pay of low paid workers to fall during the 1980s by freezing the nominal value of the minimum wage that was partially reversed by the Clinton administration (Mishel et al. 1997:205; Layard 1997). Moreover, a dramatic rise in the income gap between high and low income families occurred during the 1980s and early 1990s in the United States which may be attributed to the drop in

114

the value of minimum wage, deunionsation and expansion of paid employment in the low pay service sector (Mishel et al. 1997: 132-133 and 147). Hence, the state in the United States has stimulated the labour force participation of women indirectly by restricting the scope for gender discrimination in pay and by allowing real wages of low paid men to fall such that women's non-labour income has decreased.

The traditional work pattern of German women is paid employment, marriage, withdrawal when children are born and then re-entry six or more years later. When women re-enter paid employment they generally enter into part-time work (Maier et al. 1996:29). Only educated women appear to be able to make the transition from housewife status to part-time and then to full-time work (see Blossfeld and Rohwer 1997). The traditional employment pattern has been institutionalised through universal parental leave provisions encouraging parents to care for their children at home for a relatively long period of time, very limited availability of subsidised child care until children are 3 years and restricted opening hours of nurseries for those children 3 to 6 years. The universal parental leave provision was first implemented in 1986 for all mothers but has since then been extended. In 1997, the maximum parental leave period in Germany was until the child reached 3 years. The parental benefit was independent of prior paid employment and was flat-rate for the first 6 months and then income-tested for 18 months but the last year was unpaid (Bettio et al. 1998: National 'Assessment Tables': Germany). Moreover, the care of children is recognised to a certain degree as years of paid employment in the pension system (Maier et al. 1996:73). After completing the parental leave, only about 50 per cent of West German women and 60 per cent of East German women re-enter paid employment successfully. Mothers who work full or part-time also have the right to maternity leave that may start 6 weeks before birth and extend to 8 weeks after birth. The benefit paid during the maternity leave is average net income earned before pregnancy (Bettio et al. 1998: National 'Assessment Tables': Germany). In 1996, every child older than three years was given a legal entitlement to a place in publicly funded child care. The motive behind this legal entitlement was not so much to enable women to reconcile work and family life but rather to create employment opportunities for the unemployed and to bring West and East German provisions closer together during the process of unification (see Rubery et al. 1996:244).

Child care arrangements in Germany are supported by the state and operated by private organisation. It is almost impossible to find a place in subsidised child care arrangements for a child younger than 3 years. In 1994, the ratio of those under 3 years in child care was 7.8 per cent in Germany[7]. The ratio of those 3-8 years old in nurseries was on the other 72.2 per cent in Germany. However, only 33.8 per cent of the nurseries schools had full-time opening hours (Ostner 1998; Bettio et al. 1998: National 'Assessment Tables': Germany). In 1995, a new statutory care insurance scheme was established for long term care. Hence, the entire population has been compulsorily insured against the risk of long-term care and people receiving home or institutional care are entitled to cash to pay for the services and/or the services themselves (Ostner 1998). The parental leave and the long term care provisions have introduced the principle of universal coverage into a welfare state system that was grounded on the insurance principle including only those who make earnings-related contributions. The recognition of care work in the social insurance system does not, however, compensate German women fully for their loss of earnings as is the case with other insured risks. The care insurance only grants basic flat rate benefits for different care levels (Ostner 1998). Moreover, parental leave is evaluated at a very basic level in the calculation of pension benefits and the period covered for child care is three years while the average mother interrupts her paid employment for six years (see Maier et al. 1996). East German women, on the other hand, return to work after shorter periods of parental leave, often for economic reasons (Engelbrech 1997 quoted in Ostner 1998).

To sum up, Sweden has achieved relatively high activity rates among men and women by refraining from using immigration as a mean to satisfy employers demand for greater supply of labour. Moreover, state policies such as individual taxation, generous statutory leave of absence for parenthood and extensive availability of subsidised public child services for young children in Sweden have enabled Swedish women to attain similar participation rates to those of men. At the same time, Sweden has had the highest incident of (long) part-time work among women which may be attributed to parents' rights to reduced hours as well as to early retirement schemes enabling

116

part-time work. Hence, part-time work is most common among women with young children and among older women. Employed persons aged 60-65 who reduce their working hours can get a 65 per cent compensation for loss of income (Sundström 1998). Contrary to Sweden, Germany had the highest level of inactivity among women (see figure 3.1). Committed to preserving the family, the German state has actively encouraged women's non-working or part-time work through its immigration policy, tax splitting, parental leave provisions, encouraging long term care within the family and limited child care provisions. However, the state has started to acknowledge women's unpaid work by enabling them to interrupt work for care without losing pension credits and by paying for care work within the family, although at low rates.

In the United States, women were more likely to work full-time than women in Sweden and Germany (see figure 3.1). Various factors has contributed to the rise in women's full-time employment in the United States. First, part-time work in the United States has primarily been provided by the private sector to cut costs (see Drobnic and Wittig 1997). Hence, those working part-time in the United States have lower pay, less skilled jobs, poor chances of promotion, less job security, inferior benefits such as vacation, health insurance and pension (Mishel et al. 1997:257). In Sweden and Germany, part-time work has mainly been created in the public sector to recruit women and to enhance flexibility (see O'Reilly 1995; Blossfeld and Rohwer 1997; Delsen 1998). Contrary to employers in the United States who are allowed to discriminate on the basis of hours, employers in Sweden and Germany are prohibited from discriminating against part-time workers by European Union Directive (97/81) on part-time work. However, Sweden and Germany still restrict their benefit entitlements to certain thresholds of hours. Persons working fewer than 17 hours in Sweden are not entitled to all benefits and part-timers in Germany working fewer than 15 hours or having earnings below certain thresholds are not entitled to health and pension insurance (Olafsson and Petersson 1994; Büchtemann and Quack 1990:322). Secondly, Dex and Shaw (1986) underline the importance of child care tax allowances and the escalating costs of health care in facilitating women's full-time work in the United States but employers pay for health insurance for full-time workers but not for part-time employees. In 1994, 20 per cent of part-time workers in the United States stated that they were working part-time due to child care problems and family/personal reasons, another 20 per cent said their reason was schooling or training and 15 per cent gave economic reasons for working part-time (U.S. Department of Commerce 1995:409). Thirdly, marriage increasingly fails to provide life-long economic security for women but the divorce rate in the United States is twice the rate in Sweden and Germany[8]. The greater likelihood of a marital breakdown in United States is an incentive for women to engage in full-time work. Until the welfare reform in 1996, poor unmarried women could simply not afford to work part-time and risk losing Medicaid benefits. They therefore either remained on welfare and out of the labour force or find a full-time job with sufficient wages and social benefits to pull them and their children out of poverty (Drobnic and Wittig 1997). Hence, the state has created incentives for women to either stay at home if they are single mothers or can afford it on the one hand or to engage in full-time work on the other hand. After the welfare reform in 1996, it has become more difficult for mothers on welfare to reject jobs.

Contrary to Hakim (1995), it is not possible to divided Swedish, German and American women into three groups according to their working-hours. In all three countries, hours of work change over women's life-cycle. Full-time work is most common prior to the birth of the first child (Sweden and Germany) and marriage (United States). Most women in Sweden and Germany return to part-time work while they are more likely to return to full-time work in the United States. The different ways of combining motherhood and work in the three countries are more related to the nature of part-time work in terms of pay and employment rights as well as to the availability of subsidised child care than to preferences. In the United States, high child care costs as well as low pay and inferior benefits associated with part-time jobs have contributed to high level of full-time work among women. Moreover, the fall in the men's real-wages during the 1980s has meant that fewer women can afford to work part-time. In Germany, mothers' choice between part-time and full-time work is constrained by the lack of child care for children under three and the limited opening-hours of nurseries and schools for older children. Swedish women work long part-time hours as they are more likely than men to make use of parents' right to reduced hours. Moreover, part-time work in Sweden is not only associated with care responsibilities as older women combine part-time work and retirement.

Conclusion

In this chapter, we have analysed the forces behind the feminisation of the labour force and the withdrawal of men from the labour market in Sweden, Germany and the United States. Our analysis has demonstrated that changes in paid employment cannot be reduced to changes in a finite number of variables affecting either the decision of individuals to work or the decision of employers to employ workers (cf. neo-classical theories). On the contrary, employment changes are the outcome of a dynamic interaction between demand pressures and supply responses that is conditioned by collective actors and institutional arrangements. The state has become an important source of variations in labour market outcomes across space as economic internationalisation and regional co-operation in the economic spheres has reduced variations accounted for by the structure and the functioning of the industrial system. Hence, demand pressures and the responses on the supply side cannot be studied in isolation from the state that has been an important source of gender and country divergences. However, it is not possible to read off supply responses from the state policies aimed at regulating the labour supply. State policies interact with other factors affecting the decision to work such as real wages, tastes and non-labour income and the interrelationship between the state, the labour market and the household is relatively autonomous. The responses of the state to employment changes are conditioned by collective actors whose struggles are country-specific such that the relative autonomy will differ in degrees. Hence, the role actors have played in shaping the interrelationship between spheres needs to be considered as we would otherwise run the risk of assuming either a functional relationship (Sweden) or an autonomous relationship (the United States) between the state policies and employment patterns.

Women are not born with the dislike or like for marriage, motherhood or work (cf. Hakim 1995). The decisions of women and men to be inactive or active part-time or full-time in the labour market are in continuous non-accommodating interaction with social norms, family structures, structures of paid employment and employers' policy as well as structures and policies of the state. Moreover, the state has been active in adjusting the behaviour of women and men by creating incentives/disincentives that are based on certain norms about men's and women's roles, i.e. male-breadwinner and housewife or additional earner. However, the state has made greater efforts to influence women's paid employment than men's paid employment. Most men still have continuous full-time employment patterns while the employment pattern of women is more divergent. Family-obligations have prevented employers' demand pressures stimulating women's paid work to the same extent as men's paid work. The employment growth and shortage of male workers put pressure on the state to implemented various incentives to influence women's decision on paid work.

In order to achieve its goal of gender equality, the Swedish state has expanded welfare rights and welfare services to ensure maximum integration of women into the labour market. Most Swedish women combine work and motherhood by engaging in part time work until children reach school-age. Many older women, on the other hand, combine work and retirement through partial retirement schemes. Moreover, the state has created a flexible reserve of older and younger workers who enter during booms and exit during recessions. Committed to preserving the family, the German state has actively encouraged women's non-working or part-time work through its immigration policy, tax splitting, parental leave provisions encouraging long term care within the family and limited child care provisions. Most German women interrupt their paid employment at the birth of their first child and then return seven years later on a part-time basis. The state has started to acknowledge women's unpaid work by enabling them to interrupt work for care without loosing pension credits and by paying for care work within the family, although at low rates. Moreover, the German state sought until the mid-1990s to limit the size of the labour force by facilitating late entry of young workers and early full-time exit of older workers. During booms, temporary immigration has been allowed to meet pressures for more workers. In recent years, the state has started to give some support for part-time work as a means to reduce unemployment and costs of early full-time retirement.

Guided by the liberal ideology of the two main parties, the state in the United States has intensified its support for maximum integration of women and men into paid work by stimulating employment growth involving many new jobs without pension and health benefits and by allowing the real pay of men to fall. Moreover, the transition into work for young workers is relatively long in the United States which has led to a high incidence of part-time work among young men. The state has indirectly structured the supply of female labour by restricting the scope for pay discrimination which contributed to favourable change in women's real wages. Moreover, the state allowed real wages to fall during the 1980s such that the non-labour income of married women declined. Moreover, the support the tax system gave the male-breadwinner has been moderated at the same time as tax reductions for child care costs have been introduced. However, most women still interrupt work at marriage and/or as a result of child birth and rearing but return soon thereafter to full time work. The growing number of poor families and families headed by women has, however, led to renewed support for families within the tax system. The tax system gives support to poor families with children through Earned Income Credits. Moreover, women are still able to obtain access to public pension or social security as wives through their husbands contributions (see Meyer 1996).

In the following chapter, we will analyse the extent to which the Swedish, German and the American labour markets are gender segregated. Gender segregation is of interest as it demonstrates how the division of work between men and women has been altered by the integration of women into paid work.

Notes

[1]Whalen (1996 quoted in Ginsburg et al.1997:24) claims, however, that the newly created jobs in the United States have not been as good as the old jobs being destroyed since they pay on average less.
[2]International trade during the post-war period has grown at a faster rate than production. The World Bank estimated in 1995 that international trade is about one-fifth of the world output (Ginsburg et al. 1997:15).
[3]Part-time pension schemes were established in 1976 that enabled those between 60-65 years of age to exit part-time. A work requirement is set at a

minimum of 17 years but a reduction of at least five hours is needed to qualify (Olafsson and Petersson 1994:200).

[4]The three countries vary in their definition of part time work. In Germany, part timers are those persons who declare themselves to be on part time work. Part timers in Sweden are those who work less than 35 hours a week. In the United States, part timers include those who usually work a total of less than 35 hours a week for all jobs. Unpaid family workers working less than 15 hours a week are not considered employed.

[5]Before the tax reform was introduced, the earnings of the wife were taxed on top of her husband's that implied low net earnings due to the highly progressive Swedish tax system (Sundström 1993:139).

[6]The parental benefit in 1997 amounted to 80 per cent of previous earnings for 360 days; 90 additional paid at the guarantee level of pay, i.e. 6.8 ECUs per day) (Bettio 1998:Sweden).

[7]Per hundred children in the age group.

[8]The divorce rate is calculated as the annual number of divorces per 1000 inhabitants. In Germany, the divorce rate went from 1.26 in 1970 to 2.04 in 1990. The respective numbers for Sweden were 1.61 and 2.22 . In the United States, the divorce rate was 3.46 in 1970 and 4.70 in 1990 (Tanda 1994:284).

4 Gender Segregation in the Swedish, German and the American Labour Markets

If the Swedish, German and the American labour markets are compared, it appears that men and women are employed in different sectors/occupations. There are, however, important variations in the extent and the form of what appears to be a common labour market outcome. Studies of labour market segregation in these countries have found that Sweden has a relatively high level of occupational segregation and high concentration of women in public sector occupations (see Jonung 1984). In West Germany and the United States, on the other, occupational segregation has been lower and with greater concentration of female and male employment in private sector jobs (OECD 1988:209; Schmid and Ziegler 1992, Charles and Grusky 1995). The purpose of this chapter is to analyse gender segregation in the Swedish, German and the American labour market. There are two reasons why we are interested in gender segregation. First, gender segregation reveals how the division of work between men and women has been altered by the integration of women into paid work. Secondly, gender segregation is an important source of pay inequalities between men and women. Hirdman (1990) claims that gender segregation reveals how close women are to the essence of the gender system, i.e. challenging men's norms which assign women to 'female' areas which are subordinated to 'male' areas in terms of, for example, pay. Rubery et al. (1997), on the other hand, suggest that differences in pay structures and practices result in greater differences in gender outcomes than gender segregation. It will, however, be difficult to study gender pay gaps in Sweden and Germany without having information on gender segregation as pay in these countries is tied to the ranking of jobs. In the United States, on the other hand, there exists a weak relation between job grading and pay as there is no national system of vocational training providing basis for the grading of jobs (Rubery et al. 1997; Mósesdóttir and Eydal forthcoming). Hence, the scope for pay differentiation is greater in the United States than in the other two countries. The main emphasis in this chapter will be on gender segregation and its implications for the gender pay gap. Our discussion will include pay determination systems and vocational training systems in the three countries as these determine the scope for the overall wage inequality which in turn affects the gender pay gap.

We will start our analysis of gender segregation by discussing theoretical explanations developed to uncover the processes underlying gender segregation. The theoretical explanations range from blaming women themselves for their disadvantages to seeing gender segregation as the outcome of dynamic interaction between various parts of the social structures that are country-specific. Social structures refer to relations of reproduction, production relations and to the social and political framework involving collective actors, the state as well as ideology and social norms (see Wilkinson 1983 and Rubery 1989). Thereafter, an empirical investigation of the level of occupational segregation among men and women since the 1960s will be undertaken. Gender segregation will be measured by the Index of Dissimilarity (ID) and the Index of Segregation (IS) but these indices give some indication of whether the three countries are converging around a more desegregated labour market. Forces underlying changes in gender segregation will then be analysed, as they are not captured by the indices. Changes in occupational segregation may be attributed to structural changes, shifts in sex composition and to the interaction of these two factors. Moreover, the size of the labour force will influence how much power employers have over the segmentation processes. Immigration also affects the composition of the labour force and thereby the scope for segregation. When the working population consists of more than one race, differences between men and women become infused with race. Hence, gender segregation is likely to be low in countries with a relatively high proportion of immigrant or minority workers as the subordination of these workers to white men places them in jobs with female workers. Moreover, immigration may also contribute to a fall in gender segregation over time.

After discussing the forces behind changes in the level of gender segregation in the three countries, more disaggregated national data will then be studied in order to obtain some insights into men's and women's concentration in certain occupations. Occupations with a high level of concentration and gender-domination reveal the extent to which labour market segmentation is based on sex or reflects social norms about men's and women's perceived abilities. Thereafter, gender segregation will be related to variations in the vocational training systems and to the different nature of

124

service sector employment in order to uncover the role of the labour unions and the state in the segmentation processes. In Sweden, welfare services in the public sector have been the main source of growth in paid employment and women have became ghettoized in 'care' occupations that were previously performed in the household. Hence, gender segregation is higher in Sweden than in countries were these tasks are performed by women outside of the formal occupational structure of the labour market. Finally, the implications of gender segregation for the gender pay gap will be studied. The relationship between gender segregation and the gender pay gap differs across the three countries as it is shaped by the national system of pay determination as well as by the national vocational training system. In Sweden, the labour unions have ensured the development of a compressed wage structure such that the highly segregated labour market has a narrow gender pay gap. Moreover, the state finances partly the cost of vocational training in Sweden and Germany while American employers pass the cost of on-the-job training to young workers in the form of lower pay. Hence, the overall wage inequality is greater in the United States. The greater the overall wage inequality, the wider the gender pay gap (Rowthorn 1992; Blau and Kahn 1996).

Explaining Gender Segregation

Neo-classical theories and segmentation theories[1] have been used to explain labour market outcomes such as gender segregation and the gender pay gap. Neo-classical and segmentation theories are at the opposite end of the spectrum as concerns their methodological emphases. The main focus of neo-classical theories is the autonomous individual/household who behaves rationally by maximising utility/profit in perfectly competitive labour markets. The market mechanism achieves an equilibrium and an efficient allocation of resources. The main methodological interests of theories of segmentation are the social structures and regulatory processes that produce non-competitive productive systems or segmented labour markets. Moreover, the allocation of scarce jobs among abundant labour is the main source of conflict (see Craig et al. 1985; Wilkinson 1983; Rubery 1988).

Neo-classical theories explain gender segregation by referring to either women's tastes or preferences for certain kind of jobs or employers' tastes for certain type of employees (Anker 1998:14). Becker's (1964) human capital theory has been extensively used to explain the concentration of men and women in different industries and occupations. According to the human capital theory, women anticipate interrupting their labour force participation to bear and raise children and they therefore choose lower levels of education than men. As education signals different levels of productivity, employers will not hire men and women into the same occupations. Polachek (1980) has modified the human capital theory by claiming that women choose jobs with the greatest return to human capital given their anticipated shorter lifetime work. These explanations for gender segregation have been widely criticised for circularity. Women invest less in human capital or choose a less demanding job because they expect to spend less time than their spouse in the labour market - but they spend less time in the labour market as their earnings are lower (Humphries 1995:76). For Becker (1957), employers' taste for discrimination is the cause of the inequality remaining after differences in personal characteristics have been accounted for. Employers who have taste for discrimination will employ higher ratios of men to women than non-discriminating employers that may drive men's wages up and thereby production costs. Discriminating employers will therefore earn lower profits than non-discriminating employers such that the former will be driven out of business in the long run. Humphries (1995:55) points out that these explanations of gender differences in the labour market serve to justify unchanged gender relations since either women themselves are blamed for their disadvantages or employers who will not survive competition from non-discriminating employers.

In Sweden and the United States, the difference in men's and women's level of human capital is disappearing. In 1990, the number of years of schooling completed by the population 25 years and older was 12.2 years for men and 12.4 years for women in the United States. In Sweden, the number of years of schooling for men and women was equal, i.e. 11.1 years. The gender difference in education was, however, greater in West Germany than the other two countries. The number of years completed by German men was 11.7 years while German women only finished 10.6 years (Anker 1998:140). In Sweden, the difference in men's and women's educational level no longer reflects women's anticipation of motherhood, as women in the younger age groups are more likely than men to have university education (Statistics Sweden 1997:115). This educational difference in the younger age groups may in fact be a sign of women's greater lack of employment opportunities resulting from employers' discrimination against women. A research conducted among young people (19-25 years) in Sweden revealed that the reason why more women than men study is that young women have greater difficulties in finding a part-time and/or full-time job (Olofsson 1998:A4)[2]. This may, especially, be the case during periods of high unemployment as is now the case in Sweden. Hence, the main gender difference in education is not in terms of years of schooling. Rather the subjects men and women choose are different and the type of vocational training they receive varies (Anker 1998:140). Finally, the types of occupations 'chosen' by Swedish women have not changed radically, although they have stopped interrupting their labour force participation as a result of care responsibilities. Hence, there does not appear to be a direct relationship between women's anticipation of interrupted work and choice of subject.

Seiz, Ferber and Nelson as well as Folbre (cited in Seiz 1995:112) criticise neo-classical theories for placing too much emphasis on individual choice, thereby neglecting the social construction of tastes and the systematic differences in perceived options. Moreover, neo-classical theories do not capture the complex institutional contexts in which economic outcomes are determined. Although neo-classical explanations are reductionist, they contribute to our understanding of the processes behind gender segregation. Tastes draw our attention to social norms that may influence people's choice of subjects and occupations and employers' use of labour. Social norms often involve stereo-types about the role of men and women in society as well as their abilities. Walby (1990:90) claims that ideas about masculinity and femininity are important factors contributing to certain patriarchal structures. An example of social norms applied to men is that they are providers and able to work in physically demanding jobs. Traditional social norms assign the role of a care-taker to women and they are believed to be best fit to work monotonous and repetitive work (see Ellingsæter 1995:240). Anker (1998) has found that the characteristics of female occupations correspond to typical stereotypes of women and their supposed abilities. Examples of stereo-typed female characteristics are; caring-nature, skill at household-related work, greater manual dexterity, greater honesty and attractive physical appearance. Anker claims that these characteristics were used to 'typify' female jobs as low pay, flexible and low status. Moreover, masculine stereo-types also play a role in determining what are 'male' occupations. Typical male occupations are considered to be engineer, truck driver, police officer and construction worker (1998:23-27).

Individual tastes are not the only determinants of gender segregation. Gender segregation is the outcome of a dynamic interaction between social structures and individual tastes. Hence, we need more theoretical insights into the role of actors and institutions in the segmentation processes. According to segmentation theories, labour markets are characterised by non-competing groups and the interaction of economic, social and political institutions creates segmentation processes involving differentiated treatment of comparable groups of workers as concerns jobs and rewards (Craig et al. 1985:107; Brosnan et al. 1995:667). The demand side of the labour market is, however, the site where structures of jobs as well as the level and form of demand are determined (Rubery 1992:246). The processes of segmentation are common to most countries but the interaction of country-specific social structures produces non-equilibrium and variations in outcomes across space (see Wilkinson 1983; Rubery 1992).

The discussion of non-equilibrium and variations in outcomes across space needs to be expanded in order to explain why gender segregation varies across countries. Employers and the state are able to affect the size of the labour force by appealing to groups outside the labour market such as women as well as through immigration. Immigration may move the labour market from a non-equilibrium point where there is unsatisfied demand for labour to another non-equilibrium point where there exists over-supply of labour. There is, however, a continuous tension between labour and capital over the size of the labour force and working conditions. During periods of tight labour markets, labour unions are able to exercise strong control over pay and working conditions which in turn will intensify employers' demand for a greater supply of labour. Whether an economy remains in the non-equilibrium conditions of unsatisfied demand or over-supply will depend on the technological progress, the outcome of capital-labour struggles and the role of the state in mediating between the conflicting interests. The outcome of the tensions over the size of the labour force has important implications for employers' ability to differentiate between various groups in the labour market. The size of the labour force will influence how much power employers have over the segmentation processes. In addition, immigration affects the composition of the labour force. When the working population consists of more than one race, differences between men and women become infused with race. Hence, labour markets with relatively high shares of minority workers may be less gender segregated as these disadvantaged workers may be given jobs at lower levels in the job hierarchy where many women are also situated. Employers' scope for discrimination will, however, be constrained by laws on equal pay and equal access to jobs as well as unions' pay settlements.

In Sweden, employers' demand for labour was not met with immigration (see discussion in chapter 3)[3]. The strong position of labour unions and its close ties with the main governing party has led to active involvement of the unions in the segmentation processes. Hence, the unions have exerted a strong influence on the matching of jobs and labour as well as on the grading of jobs in terms of pay. Employers' continuous need for a larger labour force and the unions' commitment to equality and full employment created pressures on the state to mobilise the large reserve of female workers. The state provided services to enable women to work which in turn generated new employment opportunities for women. When paid employment in manufacturing contracted during the 1970s, women went from skilled jobs in manufacturing to temporary jobs in the service industries. These service jobs were mainly in the public sector in occupations such as cleaners or care assistants (Gonäs and Lehto 1997:58). Hence, the Swedish labour market has become divided into female-dominated public sector and male-dominated private sector. Employers were constrained by the centralised bargaining system in using this division of the labour force to differentiate between men and women.

In the United States, employers have been able to ensure a continuous inflow of immigrants which in turn has weakened the influences of the labour unions over the segmentation processes[4]. The unions have therefore played a very limited role in the matching of jobs and labour as well as on the grading of jobs by pay level. Hence, there exists no national system of grading jobs in terms of pay which has led to great variations in the level of pay across occupations. The over-supply of labour has enabled the state to limit its intervention into the segmentation processes to legal rules prohibiting, for example, race and gender discrimination. Legal rules act as a constraint on employers' decision concerning the matching of jobs and labour. Moreover, immigration has reduced the need to activate the female labour reserve. Hence, the state has primarily been concerned with securing a sufficient flow of labour into the labour market and stimulating employment growth in the private sector. During the 1980s, the state also implemented measures that indirectly stimulated women's paid work (cf. chapter 3). Gender divisions in the labour market have therefore become infused with racial divisions. In West Germany, immigration was also allowed but on a temporary basis[5]. The unions were able to ensure that it was only temporary and that the immigrant workers did not pose a threat to male-breadwinner jobs. Hence, the immigrant workers were employed below their level of skill and in badly-paid jobs (Maier et al. 1996:35). Moreover, the unions managed to resist all forms of non-standard employment in industries (Blossfeld and Rohwer 1997:169). Hence, there existed a limited need for activating the large female reserve and the state continued to supported women's non-involvement in paid work and then increasingly women's part-time work. When the service sector finally expanded during the 1980s, a more flexible labour force was needed. Employers recruited women who wanted to work during periods of lighter domestic activities.

Gender segregation does not only vary across space but changes over time. Reskin and Roos (1990) have developed valuable insights into the complex processes of segregation and desegregation over time. As in segmentation theories, Reskin and Roos emphasis the importance of the demand side in their job queue model of occupational segregation. In the job queue model, the labour market consists of labour queues (employers' ranking of potential workers) and job queues (workers' ranking of potential jobs) and occupational segregation is the result of the matching process between the two. There is no difference in the way men and women rank jobs. Underlying the queuing processes is a power struggle between groups with contradictory interest in shaping the composition of occupations. Labour queues function as gender queues as some employers (who are in most case men) and some male employees have the power to structure paid employment and find it beneficial to exclude women. Moreover, occupational segregation is not static and changes when (1) the relative distributions of workers/jobs change (2) employers re-rank workers or workers re-rank jobs or (3) workers' and employers' tastes for or against certain elements shift (1990:307-309). The processes of change involve first desegregation or feminisation of occupations that may either lead to ghettoization or resegregation. Ghettoization takes place when women and men hold the same occupational title but work in different specialities in an occupation. Resegregation on the other hand occurs when a major occupation switches from being systematically male-dominated to female-dominated (1990:87-88).

In the following empirical analysis, gender segregation will be measured in order to evaluate the extent to which it differs across Sweden, Germany and the United States. Persistent gender segregation violates assumptions

130

about competitive labour markets that ensure universal outcomes across space. Forces contributing to desegregated labour markets will then be analysed, as they are not captured by indices of segregation. As argued by Reskin and Roos (1990), occupational segregation changes when the relative distribution of jobs and workers shifts, employers re-rank workers or workers re-rank jobs or when workers' and employers' tastes for or against certain elements shift. Our main emphasis will be on changes in the distribution of jobs and workers as our data set does not allow inferences about employers' and workers' tastes. Thereafter, the concentration of men and women in certain occupations will be examined in order to evaluate to what extent the gender division of work corresponds to gender stereo-types. Moreover, changes in female and male occupational concentration give some information on desegregation and resegregation (see Reskin and Roos 1990). Gender segregation will then be related to variations in the vocational training systems and to the different nature of service sector employment in order to uncover the role of the labour unions and the state in the segmentation processes. Finally, the relationship between gender segregation and the gender pay gap will be studied in view of the national system of pay determination and the national vocational training system in the three countries.

Measuring Occupational Segregation

In comparative studies, aggregated classifications of occupations are used to measure gender segregation due to lack of comparable information at a more detailed level. These studies reveal significant levels of gender segregation across countries. More detailed analyses of occupational structures in a single country indicate even higher levels of segregation and less change over time. The most common measure of occupational segregation along gender lines is the Index of Dissimilarity (ID) that is defined as:

$$D = \sum_{j=1}^{J} |(F_j/F) - (M_j/M)| \times 100 \times 1/2$$

In this formula developed by Duncan and Duncan (1955), J refers to total number of occupations, Mj and Fj stand for the number of men and women in the jth occupation and M and F refer to the number of men and women in the labour force as a whole. The ID measures the sum of the minimum proportion of women plus the minimum proportion of men who would have to change their occupation in order for the proportion female to be identical in all occupations (Anker 1998:75).

This formula will now be applied to occupation data set collected by the International Labour Office (ILO) and classified into occupations according to International Standard Classification of Occupations (ISCO-1968). ILO classifies employment by occupations into the following major occupations: (1) professional, technical and related workers, (2) administrative and managerial workers, (3) clerical and related workers, (4) sales workers, (5) service workers, (6) agricultural, animal husbandry and forestry workers and fisherman and hunters production and (7-9) production and related workers and transport equipment operators and labourers.

During the period 1960-1990, the highest level of dissimilarity between the distributions of economically active men and women across occupations was in Sweden (see table 4.1). A study made by Jonung (1993 quoted in Gonäs and Spånt 1996:38) of gender segregation in Sweden since the 1960s disclosed similar level of segregation at the 1. digit level until the 1990s and greater level of segregation when 2. and 3. digit occupational data was used which indicates a high degree of ghettoization within occupations. In Sweden, West Germany and the United States, the value of the indices fell during the period under consideration, indicating a reduction in the overall segregation or a desegregation. The decline in gender segregation was, however, not continuous in West Germany. The largest reduction in the ID occurred in Sweden where it fell 13.9 percentage points from 1960 to 1995[6]. In the United States, the decline in gender segregation was 6.1 percentage points. The change over time was the least dramatic in West Germany where the ID fell 2.2 percentage points. The ID for unified Germany is not comparable to the other ID values as it is based on ISCO-88 which is slightly more disaggregated than ISCO-68 and gives therefore higher absolute value[7]. It is, however, apparent that the process of unification resulted in an increasingly segregated labour market.

Table 4.1 Gender Segregation Measured by Index of Dissimilarity

1. digit occupation groups ISCO-68
Percentages

	1960	1970	1980	1990	1995
Sweden	49.18	45.65	42.96	37.51	35.32
West Germany*	37.67	32.44	36.03	35.45	
Unified Germany**				42.52	43.46
United States	39.88	37.87	36.62	35.38	33.76

The score of 0 indicates no segregation and the distribution of women is identical. A score of 100 per cent indicates total segregation with men and women in completely different occupations.

*The years for West Germany are 1961, 1970, 1980 and 1991.
**The years for Unified Germany are 1993 and 1996 and the calculation is based on ISCO-88.

Sources: ILO, 1990, 1996 and 1997.

There are flaws with the use of the ID when comparing changes between countries and over time. The ID has been found to be sensitive to the structure of occupations or the relative sizes of occupational categories such as 'female' and 'male' categories and to the share of the female labour force. In order to 'solve' these problems, new indices have been proposed and a method to decompose the change in the ID has been developed. Blackburn et al. (1991) have proposed an index of segregation (IS) which is also termed the marginal matching index. The IS measures changes over time in occupational segregation by sex resulting exclusively from changes in the sex composition of occupations (see Rubery and Fagan 1993:131-132; Anker 1998:78). The formula for the IS can be denoted as:

$$D = \sum_{j=1}^{n} \left| (Ff_j/F - Mf_j/M) \right| \times 100$$

The $j = 1...n$ is those occupations where women are over-represented. When the ID is calculated the concentration of men in each occupation is subtracted from the concentration of women in each occupation derived

133

from $(F_j/F - M_j/M)$. The IS calculation starts with ranking of occupations according to the share of women in the occupational labour force. Then workers are cumulated starting with the occupation having the lowest (or highest) per cent female. The dividing line between 'female' and 'male' occupations is then made at the point where total numbers of workers employed in female occupations equal the total number of women in the labour force. The index of segregation is an index of association measured by the difference of proportions $(F^f/F - M^f/M)$; that is the share of female labour force employed in female occupations minus the share of men employed in female occupations (see Rubery and Fagan 1993:132).

Since the share of female labour force and structure of occupations varies between Germany, Sweden and the United States, gender segregation in the three countries will also be measured by the IS (see table 4.2). The ranking of the three countries does not change when segregation is measured with the IS but the level of segregation is in most cases lower.

Table 4.2 Gender Segregation Measured by the Index of Segregation

1. digit occupation groups (ISCO-68)
Percentages

	1960	1970	1980	1990	1995
Sweden	44.01	40.32	41.61	37.19	35.32
West Germany*	32.66	32.44	32.56	32.87	
Unified Germany**				38.60	39.32
United States	39.31	35.58	36.62	33.41	32.08

At zero per cent, the gender composition of each occupation is the same as the gender composition of the labour force.
At 100 per cent, all women would be employed in occupations where the workforces were 100 per cent female and all men would be employed in occupations where the workforces were 100 per cent male.

*West Germany. The years are 1961, 1970, 1980 and 1991.
**Unified Germany. The years are 1993 and 1996. ISCO-88 used.

Source: ILO 1990, 1996 and 1996.

The IS also manifests a fall in gender segregation over time but it is less dramatic than that recorded by the ID. Both ID and IS give a similar picture for West Germany and they suggest that little change has happened since the 1960s. This pattern has also been established by Anker (1998) and Rubery and Fagan (1993). The difference between the ID and IS across the three countries has narrowed since the 1960. Hence, inferences made from the values of the indices are not strongly dependent on the choice of indices of segregation.

Sources of Change in Gender Segregation

One of the main problems with the ID is that it does not allow inferences about changes in gender segregation over time. An observed change in the index could indicate either a change in the occupational structure being studied and/or a change in the proportion of women/men in one or more occupational categories, i.e. a sex composition change. A decline in, for example, paid employment in predominately male occupations would cause a decline in the index, although segregation within occupation remained unchanged. A standardised procedure can be used to identify sources of change in the indices between two points in time (see Blau and Hendricks 1979; Jonung 1984; Rubery 1988b). In the formulas below, D_S denotes the change resulting solely from the development of the occupational structure holding the proportion of women and men in each occupation constant. D_C is the value the ID takes as a result of compositional change holding total employment in each occupation constant. Finally, there is a change caused by the interaction between changing occupational structure and changing proportion of men and women in occupations.

The relative importance of shifts in the occupational structure and in sex composition within occupations in producing the observed changes in the index is estimated in table 4.3. During the period 1960-1970, the ID fell in Sweden, West Germany and the United States. This reduction in gender segregation was due to negative structural and sex composition effects, the latter being stronger across the three countries. In Sweden, the interaction effect had a significant effect in reversing some of the decline in segregation caused by the structural and composition effects. Gender segregation increased from 1970 to 1980 in West Germany while it fell in Sweden and the United States.

Structural effect ($D_s - D_{1960}$)

$$D_c = \tfrac{1}{2}\sum_i \left| \frac{(F_{i60}/T_{i60})T_{i70}}{\sum((F_{i60}/T_{i60})T_{i70}} - \frac{(M_{i60}/T_{i60})T_{i70}}{\sum((M_{i70}/T_{i70})T_{i60}} \right| \cdot 100$$

Sex composition effect ($D_c - D_{1960}$)

$$D_c = \tfrac{1}{2}\sum_i \left| \frac{(F_{i70}/T_{i70})T_{i60}}{\sum((F_{i70}/T_{i70})T_{i60}} - \frac{(M_{i70}/T_{i70})T_{i60}}{\sum((M_{i70}/T_{i70})T_{i60}} \right| \cdot 100$$

Interaction effect (R):

$$D_{70} - D_{60} = (D_s - D_{60}) + (D_c - D_{60}) + R$$

In the latter two countries, the effect of increased segregation by sex was reversed by a more favourable development in the occupational employment. In West Germany, on the other hand, gender segregation increased due to more uneven distribution of male and female workers across occupations and unfavourable occupational employment. Gender segregation fell for all three countries from 1980 to 1990. In Sweden, both the structural and the composition effects put a downward pressure on gender segregation. More uneven distribution of men and women across occupations in West Germany cancelled out a large part of the negative structural effect. In the United States, the negative interaction term prevented gender segregation from increasing[8]. During the period 1990 to 1995, gender segregation in Sweden and the United States continued to fall. The reduction was the result of negative structural and sex compositional effects, the former being stronger. In unified Germany, both the structural and the sex compositional effects put a small upward pressure on the ID.

In Sweden and the United States, the structural effect was negative for the four periods. Hence, growth in paid employment in these countries led to desegregation. The employment growth mainly took place in the female-dominated occupational category 3 that covers clerical and related workers. In Sweden, the sex composition effect was also negative except for the period 1970-1980. More unequal sex composition in occupational category 7-9 explains partly the positive sex composition effect for 1970-1980.

Table 4.3 Sources of Change in the Index of Dissimilarity

	Actual index change*	Structural effect**	Composition effect***	Interaction effect***
1960-1970				
Sweden	-3.53	-2.68	-3.03	2.17
West Germany****	-5.23	-1.4	-2.88	-0.95
United States	-2.02	-0.27	-0.55	-1.20
1970-1980				
Sweden	-2.69	-3.91	1.15	0.07
West Germany****	3.59	1.51	2.71	-0.63
United States	-1.25	-1.82	0.71	-0.15
1980-1990				
Sweden	-5.45	-3.34	-3.07	0.96
West Germany****	-0.58	-2.29	1.99	-0.28
United States	-1.23	-0.53	1.82	-2.52
1990-1995				
Sweden	-2.19	-2.16	-0.21	0.18
Unified	0.95	0.17	0.76	0.03
United States	-1.62	-1.29	-0.28	-0.06

* estimated as D1970 - D1960 and respectively for each period.
** estimated as Ds - D1960 and respectively for each period.
*** the interaction effect is the result of the interaction between structural and composition effects.
****West Germany for the year 1961, 1970,1980 and 1991. Unified Germany 1993 and 1996.

Source: Calculated using ILO employment by main occupations (1990, 1996 & 1997).

If the whole period is taken together, then male and female workers became more evenly distributed across occupations in Sweden. Swedish women moved into the predominately male-dominated occupational group *professional, technical and related workers* (1) and a process of desegregation and then resegregation took place as this occupational category became predominately female (cf. Reskin and Roos 1990). Men, on the other hand, moved into the female-dominated occupational group *service workers* (5) making it a mixed occupation (40 per cent - 60 per cent sex share). In the United States, the sex composition effect fluctuated between being positive and negative. The overall effect was, however, a more uneven distribution of men and women across occupations. The concentration of women within the female-dominated occupational group *Clerical and related workers* (3) increased at the same time as male-dominated occupational category 7-9 including production and related workers, transport equipment operators and labourers continued to have a high share of male workers. In West Germany, the structural effect put an overall downward pressure on the value of the ID as women's employment opportunities expanded in the female-dominated occupational category 3 and men's employment opportunities contracted in the male-dominated occupational category 7-9. The sex composition of occupations became, however, more uneven in West Germany but it was not enough to cancel out the favourable structural and interaction effects such that gender segregation declined slightly during the period 1960-1990. West German men increased their share in the male-dominated occupational group *administrative and managerial workers* (1) and *production and related workers, transport equipment operators and labourers* (7-9).

The analysis has so far highlighted cross-national differences in gender segregation as well as trends over time using ILOs 1. digit occupational data. As 1. digit data is very aggregated with only around 10 occupational categories, a great deal of occupational segregation by sex is hidden as compared to more disaggregated classifications (see Anker 1998:96). Women classified into the professional and technical occupational group (group 1) are primarily only working in two occupations (teachers and medical workers). Hence, a more disaggregated data would reveal considerably more occupational segregation. Anker (1998:chapter 9) has calculated the value of the ID for the Sweden, West Germany and the United States using more disaggregated data or 75 non-agricultural occupational categories but our calculations include agricultural occupations. Anker has adjusted the national classification systems such that each country has 75 comparable non-agricultural occupations as the value of the ID is influenced by the number of occupations included. Anker's calculations of the adjusted ID for the year 1991 using 75 occupational groups give higher level of segregation than our measures that are based on only 10 occupational groups (see table 4.1). The adjusted ID was 52.3 per cent in West Germany (1989), 63 per cent in Sweden and 46.3 per cent in the United States. The use of a more disaggregated occupational classification system has, however, not altered the ranking of the three countries as Sweden still scores highest followed by West Germany and then the United States.

Placing Gender Segregation into Context

According to neo-classical theories, gender segregation which involves restricting women's access to higher paying jobs will not prevail in the long run as discriminating employers will be driven out of business by the market forces. During the period 1960-1995, gender segregation has been a permanent feature of the Swedish, German and the American labour markets. The endurance of gender segregation supports claims made by the segmentation theories that labour is not free to compete for all jobs but neo-classical theories assume that labour markets are competitive. The variations in the level of gender segregation since the 1960 in Sweden, Germany and the United States were sufficient to suggest that country-specific social structures play an important role in shaping gender segregation as predicted by the societal effect approaches (see Rubery 1992). However, the level of gender segregation fell in all three countries indicating convergence around more desegregated labour markets. The growing share of immigrants and/or people granted asylmn in the population of the three countries may have contributed to the desegregation[9]. Moreover, the desegregation may only be the beginning of a process leading to resegregation (see Reskin and Roos 1990). Desegregation was the result of growth in paid employment and employers' decisions to employ more women. In Sweden, where immigration was not used to increase the size of the labour force, women's employment opportunities expanded due to both employment growth (structural effect) and greater use of female labour across occupations. In other words, Swedish women benefited from the shortage of male labour. In the United States, employment growth led also to desegregation in the labour market but the sex compositional effect was weak. Continuous flow of immigrant male workers into the labour market in the United States reduced employers'

139

interest in utilising female workers as the shortage of male workers could be met by immigrant workers. The distribution of men and women in the German labour market became more uneven during the period 1960-1990. Temporary flows of immigrant workers may have contributed to this unfavourable trend. In addition, women increased their share in female-dominated occupations at the same time as men increased their share in male-dominated occupations.

Reskin and Roos (1990) describe the processes of change as involving first desegregation which then may lead to women's ghettoization or resegregation. The processes of change in Sweden, Germany and the United States involved desegregation and in some cases resegregation. The occupational categories used so far were too aggregated to evaluate whether women became more ghettoized or held the same occupational title as men but worked in different specialities in an occupation. The greatest reduction in gender segregation occurred in Sweden and the smallest decline was in West Germany. In Sweden, the relatively large reduction in gender segregation was mainly due to structures of jobs and to a lesser extent to the level and the form of demand. A process of resegregation took place in the occupational group *professional, technical and related workers* (1) as it went from being primarily male-dominated to being mainly female-dominated. Gender segregation in West Germany changed little during the period as unfavourable sex composition of occupations cancelled out the positive development in the occupational structure. West German men increased their share in the male-dominated occupational group *administrative and managerial workers* (1) and *production and related workers, transport equipment operators and labourers* (7-9). The fall in gender segregation in the United States was reduced by unfavourable demand leading to more uneven sex composition of occupations. The concentration of women within the female-dominated occupational group *Clerical and related workers* (3) increased at the same time as male-dominated occupational category 7-9 including production and related workers, transport equipment operators and labourers continued to have a high share of male workers.

Occupational Concentration

The ID gives very limited information about the distribution of men and women across occupations as the variations in the distribution are combined into one index number for each year. In order to get some insights into men's and women's concentration in certain occupations, we will now study national occupational data at the 2. digit level for Sweden, Germany and the United States[10]. Our focus will be on the crowding of men and women into narrow range of occupations or employment concentration. In contrast, the ID looks at the distribution of female and male paid employment across all occupations while the IS gives information about the concentration of women's paid employment in female-dominated occupations. We will also examine the gender share within those occupations with the highest level employment concentration in order to draw forth the level of competition between men and women. Occupations with a high level of employment concentration and gender-domination are of interest as they denote the extent to which labour market segmentation is based on sex or reflects social norms about men's and women's perceived abilities.

The 2. digit occupational data used for the three countries are not completely comparable, as they rely on different systems of occupational classifications (NYK, BA and SOC)[11] and include different numbers of categories. However, the occupational data for Germany and the United States are more comparable than the Swedish data. In addition, the years covered are 1982 and 1992 for Sweden and the United States but 1980 and 1990 for West Germany. Occupational categories for Sweden are 35 while they are 67 for West Germany and 50 for the United States. Unfortunately, a more detailed occupational information for Sweden was only available for 1992. In order to get a more comparable information on Sweden, 2. digit occupational data with 53 categories for 1992 will also be used. An important occupational group is excluded from the West German data. This occupational group is 'Beamte' which refers to civil servants in central and local government, police, customs and significant group of teachers in university and secondary school education (Grimshaw and Rubery 1998:4). These deficiencies of the occupational data make inferences difficult to make but give some indications of the country-specific occupational concentration.

In table 4.4, occupations in Sweden, West Germany and the United States are ranked according to the proportion of women/men employed as a share of total female/male paid employment. In other words, occupations are ranked by concentration of female workers on the one hand and male workers on the other hand. The occupations with the highest share of, for example, total female employment are ranked first and only the first ten occupations are listed for each country. It is clear from table 4.4 that the largest part of women's paid employment can be accounted for by ten occupations. If Swedish women were in 1982 evenly distributed across the 35 occupations, then the ten occupations would account for 28.5 per cent of total female employment instead of around 80 per cent.

Even distribution in West Germany would mean that in 1980 the top-ten occupations accounted for 14.9 per cent of the total female employment instead of around 73 per cent. In the United States, 20 per cent would indicate an even distribution in 1982 across the top-ten occupations instead of around 64 per cent. One reason for the high concentration of female employment in Sweden among the top-ten occupations is that a relatively large number of female occupations are included among the top ten occupations as, for example, teachers and care workers are grouped together in one group (3). If we look at the more detailed occupational data for 1992 which divides category 3 into four categories (3,4,13,14), then the top-ten occupations accounted only for 69 per cent of total female employment. During the period under consideration, the concentration of female employment rose and male employment concentration declined in Sweden and Germany such that there was an increase in women's share of paid employment among the top-ten occupations in the two countries.

In the United States on the other hand, female employment among the top-ten occupations dropped while men's employment among the top-ten remained almost unchanged. The increased weight of the female-dominated occupational groups *health service occupations* (2) and *book keepers, cashiers & counter clerks* (21) contributed to the rise in female concentration in Sweden. The reduction in the level of female concentration in the United States was partly due to greater desegregation of the female-dominated occupational categories *other sales occupations* (22) and *food service occupations* (29), and *financial records processing occupations (25)*. During the early 1990s, men's paid employment in the three countries was less concentrated among the top-ten occupations than women's paid employment, indicating that men have greater occupational choice than women. The top-ten occupations in West Germany accounted for around 55 per cent of total male employment while the corresponding ratios were 51 per cent for the United States and 55 per cent in Sweden.

Table 4.4 Top-Ten Occupational Groups in Sweden, West Germany and the United States

Sweden - Female		All workers		Part time workers	
1982	NYK	Female		Female	
Occupations	code	concentr.	Fi/Ti	concentr.	FPTi/Fi
Health service occupations	2	16.2	91.1	8.2	50.4
Other clerical work	23	13.4	76.1	5.5	40.8
Housekeeping workers. beauticians and related	92	12.4	90.9	6.1	48.9
Teachers in nurseries. schools and play centres	3	8.2	66.1	3.3	40.2
Sales occupations	31-32	6.9	68.7	4.1	60.0
Fast food service occup. and cleaners	93	6.8	70.9	5.1	75.2
Artists. Journalists. reigious profess. librarians	5	5.6	43.1	1.9	34.2
Book keepers. cashiers and counter clerks	21	4.3	82.8	2.2	51.2
Secretaries. stenographers. typists	22	3.9	98.1	1.7	44.2
Hotel. Restaurant and other service work	94	3.3	72.7	1.9	58.0
Top-ten		81.0		40.0	49.4
Total		100		100	46.7

Sweden - Female		All workers		Part time workers	
1992	NYK	Female		Female	
Occupations	code	concentr.	Fi/Ti	concentr.	FPTi/Fi
Health service occupations	2	29.4	87.7	14.4	48.9
Book keepers. cashiers and counter clerks	21	13.7	91.4	4.9	35.9
Teachers in nurseries. schools and play centres	3	9.4	68.6	2.7	28.4
Sales occupations	31-32	6.6	71.5	4.1	61.8
Hotel. Restaurant and other service work	94	5.7	76.4	2.9	50.1
Fast food service occup. and cleaners	93	5.2	62.4	3.2	62.2
Administrative professionals	10	3.9	38.9	0.7	18.3
Other clerical work	23	3.3	52.3	1.0	29.1
Other transport and communication occupations	62	2.7	57.0	1.1	40.1
Technical. chemical and laboratorian occupations	1	2.7	16.8	0.7	27.6
Top-ten		82.6		35.7	42.7
Total		100		100	40.8

Sweden - Female		All workers		Part time workers	
1992	NYK	Female		Female	
Occupations	code	concentr.	Fi/Ti	concentr.	FPTi/Fi
Book keepers. cashiers and counter clerks	22	13.7	91.4	4.9	35.9
Health service occupations	10	11.8	85.9	6.0	51.3
Social work occupations	13	8.4	89.4	5.1	60.4
Sales occupations	31	6.6	71.5	4.1	61.8
Teachers	3	6.3	61.0	1.7	27.5
Hotel. Restaurant and other service work	91	5.7	76.4	2.9	50.1
Child care occupations	14	5.1	97.1	1.6	31.4
Cleaners	93	5.0	85.2	3.1	62.9
Other administrative occupations	25	3.3	52.3	1.0	29.1
Teachers in nurseries and play centres	4	3.1	92.2	0.9	30.4
Top-ten		69.0		31.3	45.4
Total		100		100	40.8

Table 4.4 Continued

Sweden - Male	1982	NYK code	All workers		Full time workers	
			Male concentr.	Male share	Male concentr.	MFTi/Mi
Occupations						
Constructin and related plant workers		74	13.4	90.2	12.9	95.8
Technical. chemical and laboratorian occupations		1	11.2	87.0	10.7	95.9
Artists. Journalists. reigious profess. librarians		5	6.3	56.9	5.7	89.4
Other hand-craft workers		82	5.3	68.1	4.9	92.8
Other sales occupations		34	4.9	81.3	4.7	94.9
Wood producers and treaters		76	4.7	95.1	4.5	95.3
Transport occupations		61	4.5	93.2	4.2	92.8
Agricultural forstry workers and hunters		41	4.4	78.4	3.9	88.9
Electrician		75	4.0	87.6	3.9	97.0
Other transport and communication occupations.		62	3.8	60.1	3.4	88.8
Top-ten			62.5		58.8	93.8
Total			100		100	92.5

Sweden - Male	1992	NYK code	All workers		Full time workers	
			Male concentr.	Male share	Male concentr.	MFTi/Mi
Occupations						
Technical. chemical and laboratorian occupations		1	12.3	83.2	11.9	96.5
Construction and related plant workers		74	11.2	88.2	10.7	95.2
Other sales occupations		34	6.0	74.1	5.6	93.8
Transport occupations		61	5.9	89.9	5.5	93.2
Administrative professionals		10	5.7	61.1	5.5	95.2
Building material production workers		78	5.1	99.8	4.9	95.8
Electrician		75	4.1	87.3	3.9	96.5
Nursery and school teachers		3	4.1	31.4	3.6	87.5
Health service occupations		2	3.9	12.3	3.3	85.5
Fast food service occup. and cleaners		93	3.0	37.6	2.4	81.9
Top-ten			61.3		57.3	93.5
Total			100		100	91.8

Sweden - Male	1992	NYK code	All workers		Full time workers	
			Male concentr.	Male share	Male concentr.	MFTi/Mi
Occupations						
Technical occupations		1	11.8	89.5	11.3	96.2
Plant and metal workers		73	10.6	89.3	10.1	95.2
Other sales occupations		32	6.0	74.1	5.6	93.8
Administrative professional occupations		20	5.3	64.6	5.0	95.1
Construction workers		78	5.1	99.7	4.9	95.8
Transportation (on land)		61	4.6	91.7	4.3	93.3
Teachers		3	3.8	39.0	3.3	87.4
Other administrative occupations		25	2.8	47.7	2.7	95.1
Agricultural and forstry workers		40	2.5	75.6	2.3	91.0
Electrician		74	2.5	95.4	2.4	96.3
Top-ten			55.0		51.9	94.4
Total			100		100	91.8

Table 4.4 Continued

West Germany - Female

1980 Occupations	BA code	All workers Female concentr.	Fi/Ti	Part time workers Female concentr.	FPTi/Fi
Clerical and secretarial workers	78	26.5	71.2	5.2	19.5
Sales occupations	68	12.3	63.4	3.3	27.0
Nursing professionals	85	7.6	90.0	1.0	13.7
Cleaners	93	7.2	80.1	4.0	55.6
Textile workers	34-36	3.7	79.8	0.6	16.4
Other assemblers and metal workers	32	3.6	52.2	0.3	8.3
Financial institution officers	69	3.4	46.9	0.4	12.7
Finance and computer associate prof.	77	3.3	53.7	0.9	26.3
Food processing worekrs	39-43	3.0	45.9	0.4	14.9
Quality inspetcors and packers	52	2.7	48.1	0.5	17.1
Top-ten		73.3		16.6	22.7
Total		100		100	21.2

West Germany - Female

1990 Occupations	BA code	All workers Female concentr.	Fi/Ti	Part time workers Female concentr.	FPTi/Fi
Clerical and secretarial workers	78	26.8	74.6	6.5	24.2
Sales occupations	68	12.4	64.4	4.0	32.5
Nursing professionals	85	9.8	89.7	2.1	21.2
Cleaners	93	6.2	78.6	3.9	63.2
Social work associate profession	86	3.8	80.5	1.1	28.1
Financial institution officers	69	3.7	48.6	0.6	17.4
Other assemblers and metal workers	32	3.1	46.8	0.3	8.5
Finance and computer associate	77	3.1	49.3	1.0	32.8
Food processing workers	39-43	2.8	43.4	0.6	20.5
Textile workers	34-36	2.3	77.3	0.4	19.3
Top-ten		74.0		20.5	27.7
Total		100		100	25.8

Table 4.4 Continued

West Germany - Male		**All workers**		**Full time workers**	
1980	BA	Male	Male	Male	
Occupations	code	concentr.	share	concentr.	MFTi/Mi
Fitters	26-27	7.6	99.2	7.6	99.7
Building trades workers	44-47	7.6	99.6	7.6	99.8
Clerical and secretarial workers	78	6.8	28.8	6.7	98.7
Physical and engineering science ass.	62-63	6.7	86.2	6.7	99.6
Metal workers and moniders	19-24	5.7	88.8	5.7	99.9
Road transportation operators	71	5.6	98.0	5.6	99.3
Transport workers and storekeepers	74	4.9	83.7	4.8	98.5
Sales occupations	68	4.5	36.6	4.5	99.2
Electrician	31	4.0	92.3	4.0	99.7
Engineers	60	2.9	97.5	2.9	99.7
Top-ten		56.3		56.1	99.4
Total		100		100	99.1

West Germany - Male		**All workers**		**Full time workers**	
1990	BA	Male	Male	Male	
Occupations	code	concentr.	share	concentr.	MFTi/Mi
Fitters	26-27	7.7	99.0	7.7	99.8
Physical and engineering science ass.	62-63	7.1	82.8	7.1	99.4
Clerical and secretarial workers	78	6.2	25.4	6.1	98.7
Building trades workers	44-47	6.1	99.4	6.1	99.6
Road transportation operators	71	5.1	96.8	5.1	98.7
Metal workers and moniders	19-24	5.0	89.5	5.0	99.8
Transport workers and storekeepers	74	4.7	83.0	4.6	98.1
Sales occupations	68	4.6	35.6	4.6	98.9
Electrician	31	4.4	92.7	4.4	99.7
Engineers	60	3.7	95.4	3.7	99.5
Top-ten		54.6		54.4	99.3
Total		100		100	98.8

Table 4.4 Continued

USA - Female

1982 Occupations	SOC code	All workers Female concentr.	Fi/Ti	Part time workers Female concentr.	FPTi/Fi
Other admin. support. including clerical	26	12.6	66.3	3.5	27.8
Secretaries, stenographers, typists	24	10.5	98.2	2.2	21.3
Other sales occupations	22	9.3	71.0	5.5	59.4
Food service occupations	29	7.9	63.8	4.7	59.2
Machine operators. Tenders.	43	5.7	44.8	0.9	16.3
Teachers. except post-secondary	15	5.6	71.2	1.5	27.9
Financial records processing occupat.	25	5.0	90.4	1.3	26.4
Manager, salaried	03	4.0	29.6	0.6	13.9
Health service occupations	30	3.5	87.8	1.1	32.1
Personal service occupations	32	3.3	78.2	1.7	51.0
Top-ten		67.4		23.0	34.3
Total		100		100	29.9

USA - Female

1992 Occupations	SOC code	All workers Female concentr.	Fi/Ti	Part time workers Female concentr.	FPTi/Fi
Other admin. support, including clerical	26	14.4	69.7	3.7	20.8
Other sales occupations	22	8.3	65.8	4.9	59.2
Secretaries, stenographers, typists	24	7.3	98.4	1.5	20.8
Food service occupations	29	6.7	58.2	4.0	59.7
Manager, salaried	03	6.4	38.4	0.7	11.0
Teachers, except post-secondary	15	5.9	75.2	1.4	23.0
Personal service occupations	32	3.8	80.6	1.7	43.6
Machine operators, tenders.	43	3.7	41.2	0.4	11.7
Health service occupations	30	3.6	88.4	1.1	30.6
Financial records processing occupat.	25	3.6	89.1	1.0	28.1
Top-ten		63.7		20.4	32.0
Total		100		100	29.9

Table 4.4 Continued

USA - Male			All workers		Full time workers	
1982	SOC	Male	Male	Male		
Occupations	code	concentr.	share	concentr.	MFTi/Mi
Manager, salaried	3	7.3	70.4	7.1	96.5
Mechanics and repairers	37	7.0	97.6	6.6	93.6
Construct. trades and extractive occup.	38	6.1	98.1	5.4	87.3
Machine operators, tenders.	43	5.4	55.2	5.0	92.9
Transportation occupations	46	5.3	91.3	4.6	86.7
Other admin. support. including clerical	26	4.9	33.7	4.2	84.4
Sales repr., commod. and finance	21	3.9	73.9	3.6	92.6
Supervisors and proprietors, sales	20	3.4	70.8	3.3	95.9
Food service occupations	29	3.4	36.2	1.7	48.2
Other profess., secialty occupations	16	3.4	62.4	2.9	84.9
Top-ten		50.1		44.4	87.9
Total		100		100	86.2

USA - Male			All workers		Full time workers	
1992	SOC	Male	Male	Male		
Occupations	code	concentr.	share	concentr.	MFTi/Mi
Manager, salaried	3	8.7	61.6	8.3	95.6
Mechanics and repairers	37	6.1	96.7	5.7	95.5
Construct. trades and extractive occup.	38	5.8	97.8	5.3	63.6
Transportation occupations	46	5.3	88.5	4.7	87.6
Other admin. support. including clerical	26	5.3	30.3	4.4	84.0
Machine operators, tenders.	43	4.4	58.9	4.2	93.9
Food service occupations	29	4.1	41.8	2.2	54.4
Supervisors and proprietors, sales	20	3.8	63.5	3.6	94.5
Sales repr., commod. and finance	21	3.7	65.9	3.5	62.4
Other sales occupations	22	3.6	34.3	2.4	64.7
Top-ten		50.8		44.3	86.7
Total		100		100	85.2

Fi: Female employment in each occupation; Mi: Male employment in each occupation
Ti: Total employment in each occupation; FPTi: Female part timer in each occupation
MFTi: Male full timer in each occupation

In West Germany, men were much more likely to be in exclusively male-dominated occupations (around 90 per cent male) than women in exclusively female-dominated occupations. West German women were more likely than men to be in mixed occupations (40 - 60 per cent). In the United States, on the other hand, the number of female/male-dominated and mixed occupations among the top-ten occupations did not differ much for men and women. In Sweden, only one occupation among the female top-ten in 1992 had a female share of less than 60 per cent while the male-dominated top-ten occupations had two occupations with a male share of 60 per cent or less. Although occupational classifications differ across the three countries, it is possible to identify three occupations in the early 1990s that employed a large share of women. These were secretarial and clerical occupations, health service occupations and sales occupations. In Sweden, these occupations provided 32.1 per cent of total female employment, 49 per cent in West Germany and 33.6 per cent in the United States. Women were over-represented in each of these occupational groups in all three countries.

Those occupations employing a large share of men were more diverse than for women. However, construction workers appeared among the top-three across the three countries. Few occupational groups were on both top-ten lists for men and women across the three countries. In the United States four occupational groups provided in 1992 a high level of female and male paid employment. These were *manager, salaried* (3), *other sales occupations* (22), *food service occupations* (29), *machine operators, tenders, except precision* (43). These occupational categories were male-dominated (3), mixed (29 and 43) and female-dominated (22). Among the top-ten occupations in Sweden for both men and women were *teachers* (3) and *other administrative occupations* (25). Teachers were close to being a mixed occupational group or with female/male share between 40 - 60 per cent while other administrative occupational group was mixed. On both top-ten occupational lists in West Germany were the female-dominated occupations *clerical and secretarial workers (78) and sales occupations* (68).

If the top-ten occupations in the early 1990s are ranked according to the female share within occupations, the list of the top-three occupations looks rather different for Sweden and West Germany. The two methods of ranking produce one common occupation in Sweden and West Germany and two common occupations in the United States. The three most female-dominated occupations in Sweden with a female share of more than 90 per cent were child care occupations (97 per cent), teachers in nurseries and play centers (92 per cent) and the secretarial and clerical occupation (91 per cent). These female-dominated occupations accounted for 22 per cent of women's paid employment. The top three occupations in terms of female-domination in West Germany were health service occupations or nursing (90 per cent), social work (81 per cent) and cleaners (79 per cent) and these occupations employed 14.5 per cent of female workers. The most female-dominated occupations in the United States were secretarial and clerical occupations (98 per cent), financial record processors (89 per cent) and health service occupations (88 per cent) that accounted for 19.8 per cent of women's paid employment. Hence, the reason for the relatively high level of gender segregation in Sweden is the unusually high proportion of workers in female-dominated occupations (see also Anker 1998:409).

When men's top-ten occupations are ranked according to their male-domination, construction workers and transport occupations appear on the lists for Sweden, West Germany and the United States. It should, however, be kept in mind that the occupational groups are not strictly comparable across the three countries. The share of men within these two occupational groups is very high even when compared with female-dominated occupations. In Sweden, construction workers (99.7 per cent), transport occupations (92 per cent) and electricians (95 per cent) accounted for 12.2 per cent of men's paid employment. In West Germany, building workers (99 per cent), fitters (99 per cent) and transport occupations (97 per cent) constituted 18.9 per cent of men's paid employment. Construction workers (98 per cent), mechanics and repairers (97 per cent) and transportation occupations (89 per cent) accounted for 17.2 per cent of men's paid employment. To sum up, there appears to be more diversity among the top-ten occupational groups for men than for women across the three countries. Hence, women's occupational choices are more restricted than men's. However, it is also possible that the classification of typical male occupations are more desegregated than typical female occupation. In addition, occupations with very high share of men (90 per cent and more) are more common than occupations with very high share of women across the three countries. Hence, women in female-dominated occupations face greater competition from men than men in male-dominated occupations.

We will now compare women's and men's concentration in occupations with social norms about men's and women's abilities. Anker's list of common stereo-typed characteristics of women appears to be well suited to describe the occupations with the highest employment concentration in the three countries (1998:table 2.1 and 251). The three occupations employing a large share of women during the early 1990s were secretarial and clerical occupations, health service occupations and sales occupations. Women's concentration in health occupations such as nursing is not surprising as women are often assumed to have a caring-nature. Moreover, women are also believed to be better sales persons and secretaries due to their attractive physical appearance and honesty as concerns handling money. The high concentration of male employment in construction work is often explained by referring to men's physical strength. The most female-dominated occupations among the top-ten occupations in each country also relate to norms about women's caring nature, i.e. child care and teaching in Sweden, social work and nursing in West Germany and health workers in the United States. In West Germany, cleaning is primarily done by women which is a household-related occupation. The female-dominated occupation, financial records processing, in the United States does not fit the belief that men are better at maths but may reflect employers' emphasis on honesty. Among the top-ten occupations with the highest concentration of men are transport workers but men are often considered to be more willing to travel than women.

Concentration and Hours of Work

Part-time work is one mechanism available to employers to segregate women into certain areas. The definitions of part-time work differ somewhat across the three countries. Part-time work in Sweden and the United States includes workers with less than 35 hours a week. In West Germany, on the other hand, part-time work is based on self-assessment. In addition, part-time workers in West Germany are underrepresented as the data only covers socially insured persons or excludes those with fewer than 15 hours a week. In Sweden and the United States, the contribution of part-time work to women's concentration among the top-ten occupations declined from 1982 to 1992. Part-time concentration is measured as the share of female part-time work in each occupation as a share of total female employment. This reflects a growing importance of full-time employment among women that was stimulated by less progressive tax in Sweden and falling real wages of men in the United States (see discussion in chapter 3). The share of part-time employment within the top-ten occupations rose, on the other hand, in West Germany at the same time as the share of full-time work contracted. Hence, German women have become more concentrated in occupations offering part-time work.

Across the three countries, occupations such as secretarial and clerical occupations, health service occupations and sales occupations have a high share of total female employment as well as part-time employment measured as the proportion of total women's paid employment. In the early 1990s, part-time work in these occupations accounted for 15 per cent of total female employment in Sweden, 12.6 per cent in West Germany and 11.2 per cent in the United States. In Sweden, the female-dominated occupations *social work occupations* (13), *sales occupations* (31) and *cleaners* (93) had in 1992 the highest share of part-time employment measured as a proportion of women's paid employment within each occupation. In the United States, two occupations had a high part-time share within an occupation or the female-dominated occupational group *other sales occupations* (22) and the mixed occupational group *food service occupations* (29). In West Germany, the female-dominated occupational group *cleaners* (93) had by far the highest share of part-time work measured as a proportion of women's employment within an occupation.

Full-time work among men is also a dimension of segregation in the labour market. The contribution of full-time work to men's concentration among the top-ten occupations declined in Sweden and West Germany from the early 1980s to the early 1990s while it remained almost unchanged in the United States. In Sweden and West Germany, part-time employment among men grew faster than full-time employment that may be attributed to more extensive use of part-time retirement schemes (see chapter 3). In Sweden, men's full-time employment actually contracted during the period under consideration. In the United States, on the other hand, the growth in men's full-time and part-time employment was about the same. In the early 1990s, German and Swedish men worked almost exclusively full-time within each of the top-ten occupations. The picture is more mixed for the United States where the share of full-time work within occupational group *food service occupations* (29) was only 54.4 per cent and 62.4 per cent in *sales representatives, commodities and finance* (21) reflecting a relatively high level of part-time work among men within these occupations. One explanation for the high level of part-time in these occupations is the widespread use of students and youth in part-time work (see Rubery 1988d:263).

Constructed Choices and the Gender Pay Gap

The more disaggregated data disclosed considerable differences in occupational patterns across Sweden, Germany and the United States. Divergences in gender segregation across space may be attributed to the interaction of country-specific social structures and individual tastes creating segmentation processes. Variations in the age structure may also affect the occupational structure. Health service occupations including nurses were among the top-three in Sweden and West Germany while this occupational category barely made it to the top-ten in the United States. Different age structures of the population in the three countries is one reason why the relative importance of health service workers varies. In 1990, the share of those 65 years and older were 18.3 per cent of the population in Sweden, 15.3 per cent in West Germany and only 12.5 per cent in the United States. Differences in vocational training systems and the different nature of service sector employment are examples of social structures that have affected the form gender segregation has taken in a particular country.

From the 1980s to the 1990s, the concentration of female employment among the top-ten occupations changed little in West Germany, increased slightly in Sweden and declined in the United States. According to Maier (1995) and Maier et al. (1996), women's segregation in the German labour market can be attributed to the traditional work pattern of women involving withdrawal and then re-entry on the one hand and to the vocational training system on the other hand. When women re-enter the labour market after years of child rearing, they are likely to be employed in low paid jobs that are below their level of skills and do not offer possibilities for advancements. The German vocational system which combines training in firms with education in vocational schools, creates gender divisions between and within major occupational groups. The vocational system in Germany has crowded women into limited number of occupations and those women who have been able to enter the vocational system have in most cases been directed into training for occupations offering fewer employment opportunities than typical male occupations. In the labour market, vocational qualifications are the main source of division between the unskilled, skilled (vocationally-trained manual and non-manual workers) and professional jobs. Mobility between these jobs is limited, such that upward mobility and employment careers are restricted to the initial job categorisation of a person.

In Sweden, a dual secondary school system of vocational and theoretical secondary schools existed until 1970 when the two systems were combined into one system of Secondary Schools for young people aged 16 to 20 years. Students attending the Secondary Schools can choose from 16 national programme of which 14 are vocational programme (Mósesdóttir and Eydal forthcoming). The abolition of the dual system, however, did not alter the crowding of young women into a narrow range of subjects. In 1995, 50 per cent of Swedish men trained for technical and natural science occupations while the corresponding ratio was 6 per cent for women (Statistics Sweden 1997:116). In the United States, training takes place on-the-job and it covers a much smaller share of the youth labour force than in Sweden and Germany (see Gitter and Scheuer 1997; OECD 1996a). Hence, vocational training in the United States does not play the same role in directing young people into certain career-paths as in Sweden and Germany.

The occupational groups on the top-ten lists for women across the three countries differ. In Sweden, occupational groups such as child care as well as nursery and school teachers accounted for a relatively large fraction of female employment in 1992 or 14.5 per cent. In addition, manufacturing occupations do not appear among the top-ten female occupational groups in Sweden while occupations such as other *assemblers and metal workers* (32), *food processing workers* (39-43) and *textile workers* (34-36) account for 8.2 per cent of the total female employment in West Germany. In the United States, on the other hand, manufacturing occupational groups such as *food service occupations* (29) and *machine operators, tenders, except precision* (43) account for 10.4 per cent. If the service sector employment as a percentage of total paid employment is compared across the three countries, it appears that the service sector in the United States has been the largest since at least the 1960s followed by Sweden and then by Germany. Hence, variations in the size of the service sector cannot explain why Swedish women are concentrated in service occupations while German and American women are to a greater extent in manufacturing occupations. The reason for the difference is found rather in the nature of services across the three countries. In Sweden, welfare services in the public sector have been the main source of employment growth. Hence, the care of children, elderly and the sick has been moved from the household to the public sphere. This expansion of care occupations in the public sector appealed to women who have traditionally been assigned the role of care-takers. Hence, women became ghettoized in occupations previously performed in the household. Gender segregation is, therefore, higher in Sweden than in countries where these tasks are performed by women outside of the formal occupational structure of the labour market. The main source of employment growth in the United States was the private sector where jobs in business-related services were created. Instead of expanding its welfare services, the German state has developed its transfer system (see chapter 3). When the service sector finally started to expand in the mid-1980s, German employers recruited women who wanted to work during periods of lighter domestic activities. The labour unions who were almost completely controlled by men did not interfere much with the expansion of the service sector. Hence, the private sector became less regulated in terms of grading of jobs as compared with the manufacturing sector (see Maier et al. 1993).

Implications of Segregation for Women's Pay

Gender segregation in the labour market is linked to the gender pay gap in each country or women's location in lower paying industries and occupations. Grimshaw and Rubery (1998) found in their study of the concentration of women's paid employment and relative occupational pay in Norway, Australia, United Kingdom, United States, West Germany, Canada and France that countries with a narrow gender pay gap had only a small widening of the wage penalty caused by patterns of female employment concentration. In West Germany, where the overall gender pay gap was wider than in the United States, the wage penalty was 31 per cent while it was 20 per cent in the United States. The wage penalty refers here to the difference between on the one hand the relative level of female hourly pay (full and part-timers) within the five most female concentrated occupations as a proportion of average male full-time hourly earnings for all occupations and on the other hand the gender pay gap in all the remaining occupations (1998:16-17). Moreover, women working as sales assistants in the United States earned the least while cleaners in West

Germany were by far the lowest paid. Unfortunately, it was not possible get comparable information on occupational earnings of women in Sweden. We know, however, that Swedish women are to a greater extent than men concentrated in low pay occupations. Typical low pay occupations for Swedish women in the private sector are *secretarial* and *clerical occupations* as well as *cleaning*. Low pay occupations in the public sector are occupations involving care-work and teaching in nurseries and play centres (Statistics Sweden 1997:119-129).

Comparable cross-country information on gender earnings is difficult to obtain and only available for the male-dominated manufacturing sector until 1990. As can be seen from table 4.5, women's share of men's wages in the manufacturing industry in 1990 was the lowest in the United States where gender segregation was relatively low. Sweden, on the other hand, had the highest level of gender segregation and the smallest gender pay gap.

Table 4.5 Women's Average Wages in Manufacturing as a Percentage of Men's*

	1970	1980	1990
Sweden	80	90	89
Germany**	70	73	73
United States			68

*Based on information from ILO and Statistics Sweden.
**West Germany.

Source: United Nations 1995:128.

Hence, men and women in Sweden are separate but equal as compared with the United States where men and women are in closer proximity but relatively unequal in terms of pay. The small gender pay gap in Sweden that has a rather high level of gender segregation and female concentration points to the importance of social structures in shaping labour market outcomes. A more desegregated labour market such as in the United States should according to neo-classical theories involve greater competition and thereby lower wage differentials than in the more segregated Swedish labour market. There are two important divergences as concerns the labour markets in Sweden and the United States. First, a larger share of the

American labour force is subject to market-determined wages than in Sweden. In 1994, trade union density or the share of the employed population in trade unions was 16 per cent in the United States and 91 per cent in Sweden (OECD 1997b:71). Secondly, the incidence of low pay is much higher in the United States than in Sweden. In 1994, the incidence of low pay among full time workers was 25 per cent in the United States and only 5.2 per cent in Sweden (OECD 1996a:74)[12]. Moreover, women and young people under 25 years in the United States were much more likely to be in low paying jobs than in Sweden. Hence, the labour unions in Sweden have had a much greater control over the setting of pay than their counterparts in United States. In addition, the Swedish labour unions have been relatively successful in achieving a compressed wage structure which has especially benefited women. Hence, the limited overall wage inequality in Sweden has ensured a narrow gender pay gap (Rowthorn 1992; Blau and Kahn 1996).

The scope for overall wage inequality is not only affected by the national pay determination system but also by the national job training system. Job training is a part of the school-system in Sweden but takes place on the job in the United States. In Germany where the incidence of low pay among young people under 25 years was 50.4 per cent in 1994, the training system involves education in vocational schools and training in firms. Hence, the state in Germany and Sweden finances partly the cost of vocational training while American employers pass the cost of on-the-job training to young workers in the form of lower pay. Although unions in Germany and Sweden have agreed on lower pay to trainees, the scope for low pay in the United States is greater since a smaller share of the labour force is protected by union wages. The share of the employed population in trade unions in 1994 was 16 per cent in the United States, 29 per cent in Germany and 91 per cent in Sweden (OECD 1997b:71). Moreover, the national systems of vocational training in Sweden and Germany provide basis for the grading of jobs while employers in the United States are only constrained by the minimum wage set by the federal government.

Conclusion

Our analysis of gender segregation in the Swedish, German and the American labour markets disclosed that the integration of women into paid work did not change fundamentally the division of work between men and women. Occupations with a high level of female employment correspond to stereo-typed characteristics of female workers. The three occupations in the early 1990s that employed a large share of women were secretarial and clerical occupations, health service occupations and sales occupations. Women's concentration in health occupations such as nursing is not surprising as women are often assumed to have a caring nature. Moreover, women are also believed to be better sales persons and secretaries due to their attractive physical appearance and honesty in handling money. Men were highly concentrated in construction work but this type of work is believed to require physical strength. Hence, women have moved from the private sphere to the public sphere without challenging men's subordination of women's work.

Women themselves cannot take on all the blame for their disadvantaged position in the labour market, as their level of education is approaching that of men. The problem is rather the difference in men's and women's 'choices' of subjects and occupations that are influenced by social norms and stereo-types. Individual tastes are, however, not the only determinants of gender segregation. Gender segregation is the outcome of a dynamic interaction between country-specific social structures and individual tastes that creates processes of segmentation involving different treatment of men and women. In Sweden, the state and the labour unions have been active in shaping employers' opportunities for differential treatment of men and women through immigration policies and the centralised bargaining system. Restricted immigration created a shortage of male workers and women were able to make use of the new employment opportunities in the public sector. The strong control of the labour unions over the pay determination system and their commitment to equality ensured a narrow gender pay gap across sectors. Hence, Swedish men and women are separate but relatively equal.

In the United States, continuous immigration has affected the size and the composition of the labour force and weakened the labour unions. American employers have been able to differentiate on the basis of race and gender, such that differences between men and women have become infused with race. Hence, gender segregation is relatively low as the subordination of minority workers places them in jobs with female workers. In other words, the lower end of men's job hierarchy combines with women's job hierarchy. Moreover, the weak position of the labour unions in grading of jobs and the reluctance of the federal government to rise the minimum wage during the 1980s created opportunities for considerable pay inequalities. In West Germany, the labour unions ensured that immigration was only temporary and did not pose a threat to male-breadwinner jobs. Immigrant workers are, therefore, often found at the lower end of the job hierarchy where women are also placed. This fusion of gender and race was much more limited in West Germany than in the United States as immigration was much more limited in scope in the former country. The German labour unions have been able to ensure that vocational qualifications are the main source of division between the unskilled, skilled and professional jobs. This *status system* has allowed greater pay dispersion than in Sweden but smaller than in the United States where employers are only constrained by the minimum wage.

In the following chapter, we will analyse from a more historical perspective how gender relations or the hierarchical relations between men and women have been transformed and reproduced during the post-war period. The main focus will be on the interaction of the industrial system and the industrial relations system as well as on the role of the state in mediating between competing interests.

Notes

[1] There does not exist a single model of segmentation as the theories have been taken up and developed within variety of cultural and intellectual traditions in Europe (Rubery 1992:246). Segmentation theories in the context of this chapter refer to theoretical insights developed by members of the Cambridge Labour Studies Groups and the International Working Party on Labour Market Segmentation.

[2] Around 56 per cent of the men aged 19-25 had a full-time job while the ratio for women was only 26 per cent. If part-time and full-time work is combined, the ratio for men was 61 per cent and 42 per cent for men. This research is only an indication for the situation in the whole of Sweden as it only covered one community or in Halmstad (Olofsson 1998:A4).

[3] The share of the foreign population in Sweden went from 2.5 per cent in 1960 to 10.1 per cent in 1990. The largest increased occurred during the 1980s and involved refugees and not immigrant workers (Nordic Council of Ministers).

[4] The population in the United States consists of various ethnic/racial groups and those designated as Whites are the largest group. The share of whites in the population has fallen. In 1960, the whites constituted 88.6 per cent of the population but in 1990 their share was down to 77 per cent. The share of Blacks and others (Hispanic, Asian and

others) was 11.4 per cent in 1960 and 23 per cent in 1990 (U.S. Department of Commerce 1995:14).

[5]In West Germany, the share of foreigners in the population went from 1.2 per cent in 1961 to 8.4 per cent in 1990 (Statistisches Bundesamt 1995:66). However, the size of the immigrant group is larger than 8.4 per cent of the population as immigrants of 'German' origin are not included among those counted as foreigners.

[6]The percentage changes from year to year are not very reliable measures on the real change in gender segregation as they are also due to alterations in the definitions of occupations.

[7]Occupational groups according to ISCO-88 are: (1) *legislators, senior officials and managers*, (2) *professionals*, (3) *technicians and associate professionals*, (4) *clerks*, (5) *service workers and shop and market sales workers*, (6) *skilled agricultural and fishery workers*, (7) *craft and related trade workers*, (8) *plant and machine operators and assemblers*, (9) *elementary occupations*, (0) *armed forces*.

[8]The high value of the interaction term is partly due to the occupational category x including undefined occupations until 1990. In 1990 and 1995, this category was zero as an effort had been made to define these occupations among the other occupational groups.

[9]The share of the foreign population in Sweden went from 2.5 per cent in 1960 to 10.1 per cent in 1990. During the 1980s, Sweden was the leading country among the Nordic countries in granting asylums. (Nordic Council of Ministers 1994:46). In West Germany, the share of foreigners in the population went from 1.2 per cent in 1961 to 8.4 per cent in 1990 (Statistisches Bundesamt 1995:66). However, the size of the immigrant group is larger than 8.4 per cent of the population as immigrants of 'German' origin are not included among those counted as foreigners. In the United States, the share of whites in the population has fallen. In 1960, the whites constituted 88.6 per cent of the population but in 1990 their share was down to 77 per cent. The share of Blacks and others (Hispanic, Asian and others) was 11.4 per cent in 1960 and 23 per cent in 1990 (U.S. Department of Commerce 1995:14).

[10]Damian Grimshaw and Jill Rubery have kindly provided me with the 2-digit occupational data for West Germany and the United States. Jack Hansson and Christine Osterberg at Statistics Sweden provided me with the 2-digit occupational data for Sweden. A similar analysis of Norway, Australia, United Kingdom, United States, West Germany, Canada and France can be found in the article 'The concentration of women's employment and relative occupational pay' written by Grimshaw and Rubery for the OECD.

[11]In Sweden, occupations are coded according to NYK 58 for 1982 and 1992. The more detailed occupational grouping for 1992 is coded according to NYK83. In West Germany, the occupational coding structure is given by the 'Bundesanstalt für Arbeit' (BA).

[12]Low pay is defined as less than two-thirds of median earnings of full-time workers (OECD 1996a:74).

5 The Shift from the Male Breadwinner Model towards the Dual Breadwinner Model

As stated in chapter 3, one of the main changes occurring during the post-war period is the feminisation of the labour force. Women's labour force participation has become a more permanent feature across the Swedish, German and the American labour markets. Moreover, the labour force participation of women is no longer constrained to those women whose husbands are not able to earn male breadwinner wages but involves the majority of women. The feminisation of the labour force was driven by greater availability of job opportunities and a rise in women's real wages (see chapter 3) and it has contributed to a shift from the male breadwinner household model to the dual breadwinner household model. At the same time, divorces have become more common in the three countries which may be the start of a shift towards a one-headed household model involving either female-headed or male-headed households with or without children (see Tanda 1994). However, female-headed families are more prone to poverty than male-headed families and many women have no choice but to stay in a marriage or to remarry in order to avoid means-tested social assistance. Hence, we are seeing a move from the male breadwinner household model towards the dual breadwinner household model at the same time as there are signs that the dual breadwinner household has started to shift towards one-headed households. In other words, the development over time has not been linear involving a move from one model to another but rather an overlapping development with more than one model existing at the same time. Moreover, the shift to the dual breadwinner model has diverged across space. Sweden was, for example, among the first to establish the dual breadwinner model while Germany is only slowly moving away from the male breadwinner model. The United States is positioned between the other two countries. In addition, the establishment of a dual breadwinner model has not necessarily involved greater gender equality as women are still extensively segregated in jobs that are low paid (see chapter 4). Hence, the growing importance of the dual breadwinner model during the post-war period has also involved the reproduction of gender inequalities.

In this chapter, we will analyse changes affecting gender relations over time and across space by focusing on developments within the production sphere. In chapter three, we studied the interaction between the sphere of production and sphere of reproduction and the role of the state in mediating between demand pressures and supply response. A more detailed analysis of the production sphere is, however, needed as it has increasingly become the site where the hierarchical relationships between men and women are determined. In our analysis of the production sphere, we will study the interaction of the industrial system and the industrial relations system and the role of the state in mediating between competing interests in order to explain overlapping trends over time and multi-linear development across space.

In the first part of the book, approaches used to explain changes over time will be discussed. Very few analyses have been undertaken to explain changes in gender relations or in the hierarchical relations between men and women across time and space. Insights from theories explaining changes as evolutionary processes passing through stages will be used to analyse the development of gender relations across time and space as they capture some of the complexities involved in change and allow for overlapping trends and divergent patterns across space. In the second part, we will analyse how the interaction of the industrial system and industrial relations system has shaped the feminisation of the labour force and the conditions under which men and women are employed. The feminisation of the labour force has generated a move from the male breadwinner household model towards the dual household model. In recent years, decentralisation and international regionalisation has occurred in the three countries. These developments have further strengthened the dual breadwinner model in Sweden and the move towards the dual breadwinner model in the United States and Germany. International regionalism has also exacerbated differences between the United States on the one hand and Sweden and Germany on the other hand. Examples of regionalisation are the European Union, the EU, and the North American Free Trade Association (NAFTA).

Explaining Changes Through Time

Approaches that can be used to analyse processes behind changes over time can be divided into two groups, i.e. theories based on individualism on the one hand and holism on the other hand (see figure 5.1). In the first group are neo-classical theories and new institutional theories. These theories are based on methodological individualism but vary in their time span. Neo-classical theories regard change as a movement from one equilibrium to another or a steady-state growth that is caused by spontaneous aggregation of individual actions. The invisible hand ensures that self-interested individuals act in the interest of the society as a whole. The outcomes will be unintended and universal (assuming all factors are equal) as individuals are not able to affect the change. In new institutional theories change is in most cases viewed as a process designed by actors acting strategically such that outcomes are intended (for example, game theories involving co-operation, property right theories, transaction cost theories and public choice theories). Change refers in most cases to the establishment of new sets of rules, contracts or distributional coalitions. The interaction of actors motivated to produce or design change may, however, lead to unintended outcomes. When change is designed by different parties across time and space, it will lead to divergent outcomes. Designed outcomes may also adjust or evolve over time so as to improve economic efficiency (see Rutherford 1994:83-127 and 179).

In the second group are approaches concerned with historical changes and grounded in methodological holism. Institutional theories grew out of criticisms of the neo-classical theories when the latter were in their infancy at the turn of the century. The evolutionary multi-linear processes emphasised by institutional theories have been adopted by many of the new institutional theories (Foster 1991:208-209). In institutional theories, change evolves out of the dynamic interactions of individuals and institutions in which institutions mould the individual behaviour. This contrasts with new institutional theories that consider institutions as either given constraints or arising out of the self-interested action of individuals (Rutherford 1994:175). In institutional theories, the processes of change can be a designed as well as an unintended process of institutional evolution (1994:93 and 126). Transitional changes involve the evolution of the entire legal, social and/or economic system.

Figure 5.1 Explaining Change

Methodological criteria	Time scale	Causes	The mechanism	Path - Direction: theories
Individualism	At one point or different points in time	Self-interested actions of individuals	Spontaneous processes guided by the invisible hand	Uni-linear - Equilibrium: Neo-classical theories
	Longer term	Self-interested actions of individuals	Evolutionary and/or designed processes	Multi-linear: New institutional theories
Holism	Historical changes	Individuals whose actions are shaped by institutions	Evolutionary and designed processes	Multi-linear: Institutional theories
	Historical changes	In-built economic and structural logic	Evolutionary processes Evolutionary and designed processes	Uni-linear - teleological: Evolutionary theories Multi-linear - teleological: Convergence theories
	Historical changes	*Interaction of:* Ideas Economic activity Technology Political and social relations	Evolutionary and designed processes passing through stages/ forms/orders/ systems	Uni-linear - teleological: Hegel Orthodox Marxism Multi-linear - non-teleological : *a. Capital-labour relations* Neo-Schumpeterian theories Regulation theories *b. Gender relations* Dual System theory Theory of Patriarchal Structures Gender Order Theory The Gender System theory Regimes of Gender Relations

The evolutionist theories of the nineteenth century claimed there was a uni-linear path along which societies would evolve (usually from the primitive to the civilised states). Kerr et al. (1962) rejected the uni-linear path and argued for multi-linear paths to universal structures. According to Kerr et al., modern industrialism has its own 'logic' which will ultimately lead to a convergence between industrial societies. However, elites have some choice as concerns the path to convergence (Sklair 1991:30; Hyman 1994:2). Hegel and Marx developed evolutionary theories of change but they differ as concerns the 'primus motor' of change. Hegel emphasised the role of human ideas in driving change while Marx believed that different forms of economic activity that affect human behaviour may lead to transformation of societies. According to Hegel, human ideas come in conflict with each other at different stages of history. These conflicting ideas or thesis and antithesis are then resolved through a process of synthesis. When a synthesis occurs, society moves into the next historical stage and this process of change will repeat itself. The process of change involves a continuous development of the human intellect and thereby society towards perfection. According to Marx, different forms of economic activity are accompanied by different forms of exploitation and conflict that creates a dialectic which propels societies to higher stages (see Midgley 1995:42; Scott 1991:235). The transitional changes are not products of uniform process but involve certain historically specific patterns of development. Hence, no particular transitional change can be taken as a model for another because each transition has its own history of struggle. Orthodox Marxism abstracts from these historically specific social struggles and presents a fixed model for all societies (see Kiely 1995:29).

Regulation theories (for example, Leborgne and Lipietz 1987) and neo-Schumpeterian theories (for example, Freeman and Perez 1988) also view transitional changes as passing through stages or waves of growth and crises. The stages of development refer in most cases to distinct historical periods in the development of capitalism and are employed to explain historical changes that have or are taking place (see Leborgne and Lipietz 1991). Although national and regional configurations as well as historical specificity are emphasised, these theories identify universal laws behind the processes of change. In neo-Schumpeterian theories the stages of development are termed 'long waves' while the regulation theories describe them as 'models (patterns) of development'. Long waves are characterised by a specific techno-economic paradigm and models of development have similarly a specific regime of capital accumulation (see Jonsson 1989). According to Freeman and Perez (1988:38), a shift in the techno-economic paradigm leads to long waves in economic development[1]. Leborgne and Lipietz (1987:3) claim that when one or several countries have adopted variants of the same model of development, it has become the dominant model or pattern of development[2]. The main difference between the two schools is that the neo-Schumpeterian theories consider the driving force to be technology changes or diffusion of new technology to which social relations and institutions adjust while the regulation theories claim that changes involve interrelated alterations in social, economic and political and cultural structures (Jonsson 1989:24).

The focus of the above discussed approaches has been on the behaviour of individuals (neo-classical theories), interest/elite groups (new institutional and convergence theories), institutions (institutional theories) and on social structures (Marxist and regulation theories). Analyses of gender relations have primarily focused on identifying universal social structures whose interaction may generate changes in the hierarchical relations between men and women. Hartmann (1981) claims in her dual system theory that capitalism and patriarchy are the two systems or social structures enabling men to exercise control over women. However, Hartmann's use of patriarchy has been criticised for being tautological as men's control over women's labour power is explained by men's control (see, for example, Pollert 1996; Tong 1989:181-183). Walby (1990) has responded to the problems of tautology by fragmenting patriarchy or the social structures and practices in which men oppress women into six sub-structures that are: 1) the patriarchal mode of production (in households); 2) patriarchal relations in paid work; 3) the patriarchal state, 4) male violence; 5) patriarchal relations in sexuality; 6) patriarchal relations in cultural institutions. Hirdman, on the other hand, has added the political realm to Hartmann's dual structures in her theory of the gender system (genussystemet). Hence, the three social structures affecting the relations between men and women are capitalism, democracy and the gender system. Capitalism and democracy involve forces that integrate women into men's psychological and physical areas such that women start to question the primacy of men's norms. The gender system on the other hand has two logics - gender segregation of all areas and primacy of men's norms. Although Walby and Hirdman have made improvements to Hartmann's analysis of women's subordination, they have not been able to overcome the problem of explaining the origin of men's power. Connell (1987), on the other hand, rejects the notion that there are some underlying structures as patriarchy with no origin/roots that subordinate women and superordinate men. Instead, the relationship between men and women consists of three structures or the division of labour, the structure of power and the structure of cathexis[3]. Moreover, these structures are the major elements of any gender regime and gender order where the former refers to the institutional levels and the latter to the societal level.

In our analysis of the regimes of gender relations, we focus also on the patterns/forms of gender relations in order to avoid tautological explanations of men's control over women's labour (see Mósesdóttir 1995 and chapter 1). However, there are important differences between our analysis of regimes of gender relations and Connell's gender order theory[4]. First, our analysis is limited to the patterns/forms gender relations take at the societal level. Connell's theory, on the other hand, includes the personal relationship between men and women (cathexis) into his analysis of the patterns/forms gender relations at the national level. Secondly, Connell is not concerned with country-specifities, although he acknowledges variations across space. Our study is based on a comparative study involving three countries but a comparison of patterns of gender relations across countries with different history of social relations and institutional settings reveals the importance of context in shaping gender relations. Thirdly, instead of dividing gender relations into three structures as done by Connell, we are primarily concerned with how the hierarchical division of work between men and women is regulated through norms, institutional arrangements and power relationships in the production sphere, social reproduction sphere/the household and by the state. In other words, how actors, cultural norms and structures interrelate and affect the relative position of men and women. Finally, the role of political agency is not sufficiently accounted for in Connell's account as well as in Hartmann's, Walby's and Hirdman's theories of structures/systems. Our analysis of the state involved both political struggles and political strategies in order to highlight women's role in shaping the regulation of gender relations over time (see chapter 1 and chapter 2). However, our analysis needs more theoretical and empirical work on how gender relations change over time.

The approaches explaining historical changes offer valuable insights into the processes of change over time and across space. Based on our analysis so far, changes in gender relations arise from the dynamic interaction of social, political and economic institutions and actors (social structures) creating both designed and unintended processes that are not uniform (new institutional theories and institutional theories). The outcomes of these evolutionary processes will be multi-linear across space and involve over-lapping trends over time (evolutionary theories). Hence, countries will adopt variants of a historically specific model of gender relations, for example, the dual breadwinner model (neo-Schumpeterian theories and regulation theories). Moreover, the shift from the male breadwinner household model to the dual breadwinner household model is not dichotomous. Instead the movement from one stage/phase in the development of gender relations will involve both continuities and discontinuities.

Hirdman's theory of the gender system focuses also on stages or on gender contracts (genuskontrakt) which refer to certain forms/orders the relations between men and women take[5]. According to Hirdman, gender contracts are different historical compromises made to solve the reoccurring gender conflict created by the interaction of capitalism, democracy and the gender system. The different contracts in each society create a social pattern or a gender system. These gender contracts ensure the reproduction of the gender system (genussystemet). The greater the integration of women, the more serious the gender conflict as it is approaching the real essence of the gender system - the power relations between men and women. Hence, the gender conflict has a revolutionary character that has so far been successfully channelled into a reform in which women and not men are regarded as the problem. Each period involves some fundamental solutions to the gender conflict and new patterns of segregation or division between men and women. The gender conflict can never be completely solved as each new solution contains contradictions that progress with time into new conflicts.

There are two problems with Hirdman's gender contracts. First, it may not be such a smooth process to solve reoccurring gender conflicts as assumed by Hirdman who relies on the development of gender relations in Sweden where conflicts have been solved through consultation instead of confrontation. Alliances across political parties and social groups may block the integration and implementation of solutions to the gender conflict at the state level such that conflicts proceed over a long period of time. As discussed in chapter 2, the German Catholic Church and the CDU (Die Christlich-Demokratische Union Deutschlands) have, for example, successfully blocked women's initiatives to liberalise the abortion law. Moreover, institutional arrangements such as the state form (federal versus unitary state) will influence how comprehensive and coherent the new solutions to the gender conflict will be (see Mósesdóttir 1997). Hence, changes in gender relations will not be universal across space implying that women's success in challenging their subordination will vary across countries. Secondly, the move from one stage to another will not necessarily involve progress or revolutionary elements but may instead lead to backsliding or deterioration of women's rights/position relative to men.

In our analysis of changes in gender relations in Sweden, Germany and the United States, we will apply insights from theories explaining historical changes. The processes of change will be seen as evolutionary, creating multi-linear developments across space and overlapping trends over time. Stages or phases in the development of gender relations are the male breadwinner model and the dual breadwinner model. The shift from the male breadwinner model to the dual breadwinner model will be related to the feminisation of the labour force, decentralisation and international regionalisation. However, the time-span of our empirical analysis is much shorter than that of approaches used to explain historical changes due to lack of comparable historical data. Hence, it is difficult to evaluate Pollert's (1991) claim that we are neither seeing a break nor historical continuities. However, our empirical analysis in chapter 3 covering the period 1960-1995 shows that incremental changes have accumulated into a shift from the male breadwinner model to the dual breadwinner model. This shift has been facilitated by the feminisation of the labour force, decentralisation and international regionalisation. These three developments were generated by the interaction of technology, economic conditions and political and social relations at the national and the international level (cf. theories based on holism). Ideology has also played an important role. As demonstrated in chapter 2, the egalitarian principle has been an important drive in Sweden for achieving a high participation rate among women. Moreover, the Catholic family ideology in Germany has hindered the full integration of women into paid work while the market/liberal ideology has served as an important incentive for women in the United States to participate in work at the same time as welfare services have been almost non-existent as compared to, for example, Sweden. The main focus of our empirical analysis will now be on the role of the industrial system and the industrial relations system in facilitating the feminisation of the labour force and decentralisation which in turn has stimulated a move from the male breadwinner model to the dual breadwinner model. Moreover, the role of the state in mediating between competing interests and the implications of supranational regulation/deregulation of labour markets will also be considered.

Moving from the Male Breadwinner Model

After the Second World War, countries in North America and Western Europe went back to 'normality' by supporting women in their role as wives and/or mothers and men in their role as breadwinners. Wages were in most cases high enough to enable men to support a wife and/or family and women were granted rights as wives and/or mothers. Women's labour force participation was in most cases discontinuous and depended on the financial needs of the family and the overall labour demand in the economy. The economic structure was increasingly based on industrial mass production around which the industrial relations system and welfare state developed. The relations between industries, industrial relations and the welfare state were not necessarily functional or coherent as they were shaped by political actors as discussed in chapter 3. The demand for labour grew as industrial mass production and consumption expanded. Foreign labour and/or the large reserve of married women were used to meet the rising demand. In Sweden, women's labour force participation expanded fast during the 1960s and 1970s and women became concentrated in the public sector. In 1960, women's paid employment in the United States was at lower level than in Sweden and West Germany. However, public sector expansion during the 1960s and continuous private sector expansion stimulated women's labour force participation in the United States. American women are now more likely than German women to engage in paid work. The labour force participation of German women was relatively high during the early part of the post-war period as West Germany was slower to move to 'normality' than most other Western European countries. It was not until the mid-1980s when the service sector started to expand that women's labour force participation in West Germany showed signs of a continuous increase.

We will now analyse in more details how the interaction of the industrial system and the industrial relations system in Sweden, Germany and the United States has shaped the feminisation of the labour force which in turn has contributed to a move from the male breadwinner model to the dual breadwinner model.

Industrial Development

During the early 1960s, there existed a shortage of labour in manufacturing and services in Sweden, West Germany and the United States. This shortage was met by activating immigrant workers and/or married women. The main Swedish trade union, the LO, and the main governing political party, the Social Democratic Party, responded to the labour shortage and demands of women's groups for equal opportunities by encouraging directly and indirectly women's labour force participation. In Sweden, a growing number of women were employed in skilled jobs in manufacturing (see Gonäs and Lehto 1997:58). The highly export-orientated manufacturing sector was an important generator of employment opportunities in the private sector. Manufacturing consisted primarily of resource-based industries exploiting domestic raw materials, mass-production industries (textiles, ships and car) and of engineering industries. During the late 1960s and early 1970s, Swedish mass-production industries started to lose market shares in international markets as a result of growing competition from low-cost producing countries and rising oil prices (Swedish Institute 1997). Instead of lowering pay to enhance the competitiveness of these export industries, the state implemented active labour market measures. Firms and labour received generous subsidies and public assistance to move out of the uncompetitive industries into more dynamic sectors (Ryner 1994). Women went from skilled jobs in manufacturing industries to temporary jobs in the service sector. Most of the service sector jobs were created in the public sector and involved cleaning and care assistance (see Gonäs and Lehto 1997:58). Hence, women moved into the public sector while men continued to be employed in the private sector. During the 1970s and 1980s, the Swedish state expanded paid employment through direct employment creation at the local level in the public sector where mostly women were employed. The private sector has, on the other hand, had limited employment growth which has been attributed to the solidaristic wage policy aimed at 'pricing-out' low productivity firms and to the progressive taxation of small firms that hindered the entrance of, e.g. new family firms (see Mósesdóttir and Eydal 1998).

In West Germany, manufacturing was also an important industry during the early 1960s but it was to a greater extent based on crafts technology than the Swedish manufacturing sector (see Swenson 1991:532). Moreover, a production growth took place in the German manufacturing sector during the early 1960s that created a shortage of labour. This labour shortage was intensified by the introduction of compulsory military or community service in 1956 and its extension in early 1960s (Smith 1994:256). The labour shortage could not be met to the same extent by the female labour reserve in West Germany as in Sweden. The West German state was committed by a clause in the Basic Law to defend and preserve the family and the Constitutional Court had also ruled that functional difference in the family and in the employment could justify different treatment of women and men (Ferree 1995:97). In order to meet the labour shortage, the state promoted short term immigration of labour and the immigrants coming from 1962 to 1985 were unskilled workers from Turkey and Yugoslavia (Smith 1994:256-264). The West German state supported the industrial sector by allowing temporary immigration as well as by providing educational system that reinforces craft skills which form the basis for the grading of jobs (Lane 1993; Rubery et al. 1997). The unions were able to ensure that it was only temporary and that the immigrant workers did not pose a threat to male-breadwinner jobs. The industrial sector experienced difficulties during the late 1960s and the 1970s as a result of falling competitiveness in foreign markets and rising oil prices. Early retirement schemes were implemented in order to enable older workers to leave the labour market and foreign workers were encouraged to leave the country. Moreover, the labour unions accepted gradually wage constraints due to rising unemployment. From 1970s to the mid-1980s, women's paid employment in manufacturing contracted. The extensive transfers and high labour costs hindered growth in both public and private services until the mid-1980s (see Esping-Andersen 1990). From the mid-1980s, social and financial services expanded and a rising number of women were able to find jobs (Meyer 1994).

The continuous flow of immigrants into the labour market in the United States reduced employers' interest in activating the large reserve of married women. Hence, the expansion of employment in the welfare state during the 1960s was the most important stimulus behind the greater economic mobility of women and minorities (Ginsburg 1992:111). Employment growth during the 1960s occurred mainly in education, distribution and government administration while producer services, health and other services expanded during the 1970s (Esping-Andersen 1990:119). The industrial policy has been much more selective in the United States than in Sweden and the West Germany. During the early part of this century, an active farm policy was pursued enabling the development of a highly productive agricultural sector. During the early part of the post-war period, the expanding mass production industries, for example, cars, machinery and consumer electronics fought for less state regulation. Sectors producing high technology military products lobbied on the other hand vigorously and successful for government support and they were therefore not as hard hit by the industrial crisis of the 1970s (Howes 1995). The American industrial sector encountered falling profits arising from cheaper manufacturing products by pressing wages further down than its competitors (see Brenner 1998:94). Employers' attack on wages had an adverse effect on the unions that have always been relatively weak due to the large surplus of labour in the labour market created by the continuous immigration. In the 1980s, the share of the workforce represented by unions contracted more rapidly than in the previous several decades (Mishel and Bernstein 1993:187-190). Moreover, the federal government allowed during the 1980s an historically unprecedented repression of wages which enabled employers to make large-scale transition into low productivity services (Brenner 1998:156). Hence, the industrial restructuring was primarily structured by employers in the United States and not by the state as in Sweden and to a lesser extent in West Germany. The fastest growth in women's paid employment occurred during the 1980s, facilitated by growing employment opportunities in the private sector, falling real wages of married men and a rise in female real wages (see Mishel and Bernstein 1993:79).

The Industrial Relations System

The system of industrial relations in the three countries played also an important role in facilitating and conditioning women's paid employment. In Sweden, centralised bargaining became a regular practice around the mid-1950s and it involved negotiation between representatives of large trade union confederations and representatives from different employer associations on how much all workers in a particular confederation of unions should receive (Wise 1993:78). Centralised pay rates were not set

173

according to productivity or the ability of individual firms to pay but according to what was regarded as 'just pay' at full employment (Standing 1988; Ryner 1994:400). During the early 1960s, separate women's pay classifications were ended and the aim of the centralised pay system was to ensure fair pay distribution by narrowing the pay gap between sectors and jobs (Hirdman 1990:235-236; Standing 1988). Women benefited from the narrowing of difference between women's and men's pay rates, improvement in the position of the low paid and from a reduction in pay dispersion across sectors. Hence, women's real pay rose more than men's during the 1960s and 1970s (Löfström 1995:43). Rising female pay facilitated further women's labour force participation. The solidaristic pay policy and the progressive taxation of small firms hindered, on the other hand, the employment growth in the private sector (see Fölster and Peltzman 1995).

The aim of the industrial relations system in West Germany has been to ensure high productivity by linking pay with productivity (Smith 1994). The German central bargaining system has two levels. At the first level, trade unions and employers' associations negotiate agreements that are legally binding in order to ensure the broad application of negotiated wage contracts through the whole branches of the economy. At the second level, grievance handling and supplementary bargaining on a statutory basis between the works council and the individual employer take place (see Thelen 1993)[6]. The main role of the unions has been to negotiate pay and other conditions of employment at the regional level and the agreements served as a statutory minimum (Smith 1994:292). The unions have paid limited attention to gender inequalities in the labour market. The central bargaining system has ensured a relatively high pay level and women have benefited from special measures aimed at improving the pay level of the lowest wage groups. However, the gap between the highest and the lowest wage groups remains wide. Moreover, the German labour unions have not fought for greater equality across sectors. Hence, jobs in the less unionised private service sector where women are concentrated pay less than jobs in the industrial sector (see Maier et al. 1993; Blossfeld and Rohwer 1997).

The industrial relations system in the United States has been much more market-determined than in Sweden and Germany and both low productivity jobs paying low wages and high productivity jobs paying high wages have been created. Capital has always been very mobile within and outside their large home markets and the continuous flow of immigrant workers provided them with large pools of surplus workers (Swenson 1991:540). The labour unions have, therefore, not managed to organise on a mass scale. The labour law has also encouraged single-employer bargaining and employer associations play virtually no role in the bargaining system (OECD 1994d:172). In the early 1960s, the federal government enforced anti-discrimination legislation but women's rights groups had fought for its passing. The legislation led to a modest reduction in male-female pay gaps, especially during the 1970s that contributed to a growth in women's labour force participation (see Blau 1993:88). During the 1980s, many states implemented comparable worth programmes for their employees that were successful in closing the pay gap between female and male jobs (Hartmann and Aaronson 1994). These measures and union agreements have been less effective in improving the relative position of low paid workers than their counter-parts in Europe (Blau and Kahn 1996:796). Hence, the gender pay gap has been relatively wide in the United States as compared with Sweden and West Germany (United Nations 1995:128).

The Feminisation of the Labour Force and the Implications

In Sweden, women's groups managed during the 1960s to press the main federation of labour, the LO, and the main governing party, the Social Democratic Party to incorporate women into their commitment to equality beyond the market and full employment (see Ginsburg 1992). Women's integration into paid work became a part of the class equality project. Various measures were undertaken by the LO and the Social Democratic Party to enable women to participate in paid work. These measures involved an increase in women's real pay, the individualisation of taxation (1971), parental leave (1974) and subsidised public child care (see Persson 1990; Löfström 1995). As it took time to build up a sufficient level of welfare services, extensive use of part time work was necessary to attract women to the labour market. The unions ensured that this new employment form enjoyed the same benefits and rights as full-time work. Expanding welfare services created employment opportunities for women entering the labour market as well as for those women who were no longer able to find jobs in the industrial sector due to restructuring. Hence, women's paid employment grew and their labour force participation reached in 1990 almost 83 per cent (OECD 1997a). Moreover, men were able to obtain employment in the private sector that has had limited employment growth.

Hence, women have seldom been in direct competition with men for jobs. The solidaristic pay policy made it also difficult for employers to use women as low paid labour to displace men from the labour market. Hence, the shift towards the dual breadwinner model was driven by a permanent shortage of labour and by demands for greater equality. Moreover the unions were able to ensure that women's integration into paid work did not distort class relations in the labour market.

In West Germany, the unions, employers and the state created conditions for the male breadwinner families/households by pursuing an industrial development based on high productivity and by enforcing pay setting system linking pay with productivity. Moreover, the male breadwinner family has been supported through the tax system and the pension system (see Buchholz-Will 1992; Ginsburg 1992). The labour shortage during the early 1960s could not be met by greater participation of married women as the state was committed to defend and preserve the family. Hence, short-term immigration was allowed which postponed women's large scale inroad into paid until the mid-1980s. When the industrial sector underwent restructuring during the 1970s, the state implemented measures to reduce the size of the labour force. Hence, it was not until the service sector started to expand that women's paid employment expanded continuously. Policies such as the joint taxation involving splitting of the income (since 1958) and derived rights to pension benefits for wives were used to enable married women to become homemakers (see Buchholz-Will 1995). During the 1970s and 1980s, autonomous women's groups started to demand a greater say in decisions concerning abortion and whether or not to become housewives (see Kaplan 1992). These demands, rising unemployment and the process of unification between East and West Germany induced the state to support the creation of part-time jobs on the one hand and women's part-time employment by providing subsidised child care facilities with short opening hours on the other hand. Hence, the need for more a flexible workforce in, especially, the service sector was an important driving force behind women's integration into paid work. The state has at the same time implemented measures to ensure that women continue to provide family-care by recognising care of children and the elderly in the pension system. Women's integration into paid employment has not undermined male breadwinner wages in the industrial sector as the unions have been successful in their fight against non-standard employment in the industrial sector (see Blossfeld and Rohwer 1997).

During the early part of the post-war period, paid employment of married women in the United States was constrained in various ways. From 1920 to 1950, many large firms applied a 'marriage bar' to occupations such as clerical work (Goldin 1990:147). Moreover, the state supported indirectly married women in their role as homeworkers through tax policy of splitting of the income (since 1948) and derived rights to pension benefits for wives (see Nelson 1991:16-17)[7]. In addition, the state has always encouraged a continuous flow of immigrants into the labour market to provide the industrial sector with sufficient supply of labour. In spite of these constraints, the paid employment of married women rose due to increased education, falling fertility and growing importance of clerical work (Goldin 1990:159). In 1960, women's labour force participation in the United States was at lower level than in Sweden and West Germany. During the 1960s, women fighting for equality in terms of non-discrimination in the United States were strengthened by the achievements of the civil rights movement that managed to press for employment expansion in the public sector. This public sector expansion opened up employment opportunities for women in education, welfare and governmental administration (Ginsburg 1992:111).

During the 1970s, employers in the United States responded to falling profits in the industrial sector by pressing wages down and the state supported this development throughout the 1980s by repressing the minimum wage. Hence, the private sector employment expanded and women's labour force participation accelerated. The state encouraged the employment of women during the 1980s by granting tax deductions on private child care. At the same time, a support was given to low income families through the Earned Income Tax Credit. During the early 1990s, this family support was expanded by the Clinton administration. The rise in the income of married women was not, however, enough to stop the overall growth of inequality (Mishel and Bernstein 1993:79). The rise in inequality during the 1980s reversed three decades of declining income inequality. The lower and middle income families either lost ground or struggled to stay even by working harder through longer hours and more family members working (Mishel and Bernstein 1993:20). Employers' attack on wages and the repression of the federal minimum wage during the 1980s weakened the labour unions and there has been a rapid growth of low paid jobs with little or no employer-provided health and pension benefits. American women have, therefore, entered a vicious circle where falling real wages are forcing them to participate or increase their work effort at the same time as greater availability of labour in terms of numbers and hours enables employers to cut wages further.

To sum up, gender relations in Sweden, Germany and the United States have been in the process of change. During the post-war period, incremental changes have accumulated into a shift from the male breadwinner model towards the dual breadwinner model. Moreover, the shift has involved overlapping developments with male and dual breadwinner models coexisting at the same time as well as multi-linear development across space as the speed at which the three countries have adopted their variant of the dual breadwinner model differs. This overlapping trend over time and the multi-linear development is the outcome of the interaction between economic, social, political actors and institutions that have country-specific features. Hence, each country has been in the process of developing its own variant of the dual breadwinner model. Decentralisation and international regionalisation have enhanced this development.

Decentralisation

During the 1980s and 1990s, the industrial relations system in Sweden, Germany and the United States underwent changes that had implications for gender relations. In Sweden, pay flexibility and high levels of unemployment began to threaten the dual breadwinner model. Meanwhile in Germany, employment flexibility has involved the creation of part-time jobs which has enabled many women to obtain paid work. Women's paid employment and falling incomes of low and middle income households are undermining further the male breadwinner model in Germany. In the United States, greater decentralisation of the already decentralised industrial relations system has led to growing inequalities that have stimulated the paid employment of married women and thereby strengthened the trend towards the dual breadwinner model. International regionalisation has enhanced the trend towards the dual breadwinner model in the three countries, although it involves greater supranational regulation in Sweden and Germany on the one hand and intensified market-influences in the United States on the other hand.

The structural changes occurring during the 1960s and 1970s involved a decline or a slow down in the employment growth in mass production industries and a tremendous employment expansion in the service sector.

According to Piore and Sabel (1984), employers have responded to the declining industrial mass production and greater market pressures by implementing new production technology enabling more flexible production[8]. Atkinson (1986) claims that employers have also responded to market stagnation and increased uncertainty by deploying a more flexible manpower policy. The new manpower policy involves more flexibility in the number of workers and hours of work to meet fluctuations in demand on the one hand and a more functional flexible workforce on the other hand. Pay flexibility has also been utilised to encourage more functional flexibility and to individualise pay. These production and employment strategies have intensified the demand for skilled workers and blurred the division between blue and white collar functions.

Pay Flexibility in Sweden

During the early 1980s, Swedish employers in the export engineering industry wanted greater flexibility in pay to attract more skilled workers as well as to increase productivity and product quality through incentive pay (Pontusson and Swenson 1996:236). The centralised bargaining system in Sweden broke down when these employers managed to get one of the most powerful unions in the LO, the Metalworkers Union, to agree to bargain separately in order to achieve higher than average pay increases in the profitable industries (Ryner 1994:404). According to Thelen (1993), the two institutional links between central and local bargaining were the main reasons for the breakdown or decentralisation of the bargaining system in Sweden. First, bargaining had never been unified across blue-collar and white-collar workers within, for example, manufacturing as the LO bargained for blue-collar workers and the white-collar bargaining unit called the PTK (Privattjänstemannakartellen) for white collar workers[9]. In addition new production technology and employers' employment strategies involving functional flexibility blurred in some cases the distinction between white-collar and blue-collar work. The tensions created by the organisational divisions and blurring of the blue-collar and white-collar distinction contributed to willingness of the metalworkers' union to withdraw in 1983 from the national confederation bargaining level. Secondly, employers wanted a greater pay decentralisation as the centralised negotiations had centred around effective wages, i.e. including the wage drift during the previous year at each of the three levels (the national confederation level, the national union/association level and the firm level). This created a spiral of pay increases resulting in a very compressed pay structure across, for example, skill groups. In order to prevent pay from increasing at each of the three levels, employers wanted to reduce the number of bargaining levels or the confederation level. The LO gradually accepted this development of decentralised bargaining and proposed a modified solidarity policy of 'different pay for different work' (Delsen and Van Veen 1992:87-88). In 1991, the employers' federation SAF dismantled its own central bargaining unit and started to concentrate on broad political and ideological concerns (Pontusson and Swenson 1996:230).

In Sweden, the centralised bargaining system until 1983 was used to achieve a solidaristic pay structure such that the income distribution was relatively compressed both at the bottom (50/10) and at the top (90/50) (see table 5.1).

Table 5.1 Earnings Inequality *

	Sweden	Germany	United States
Early 1980s**			
50/10	1.30	1.65	1.78
90/50	1.57	1.63	1.96
Late 1980s***			
50/10	1.35	1.50	2.07
90/50	1.57	1.64	2.10
Mid 1990s****			
50/10	1.34	1.44	2.00
90/50	1.59	1.61	2.21

*Includes only earnings of full-time workers. Inequality is measured as the ratio of the earnings of the 90th percentile worker to those of the 50th percentile worker (90/50) and of the 50th percentile worker to those of the 10th percentile earner (90/10).

**Sweden: 1980, W. Germany: 1983, United States: 1979.

***Sweden: 1989, W. Germany: 1989, United States: 1989.

****Sweden: 1993, Germany 1994, United States: 1995.

Source: Mishel et al. 1997:400.

The effect of the compressed income distribution was to narrow the gender pay gap such that it has been smaller in Sweden than in Germany and the United States (United Nations 1995). Greater decentralisation of the centralised pay setting system has, on the other hand, reduced the inter-sectoral levelling of pay such that the notion of 'just pay' at full employment has been weakened. Hence, the income dispersion at the bottom and the top increased slightly during the 1980s. One effect of the reduced inter-sectoral levelling has been that the gender pay gap ceased to narrow during the mid-1980s and grew for the first time since women entered the labour market in the 1960s. This unfavourable trend in the gender pay gap may be attributed to a slower rise of pay in the public sector where the majority of women work (see Mahon 1991:305). Moreover, full employment has lost its centrality in pay settings and the employment growth lagged behind the population growth for the first time during the early 1990s (see Mishel et al. 1997:411). During the early 1990s, economic recession and public budget constraints have made it increasingly difficult for the state to implement measures to sustain full employment. Unemployment for both men and women has reached record high levels and those hardest hit are young people who have had difficulties finding a job, especially a permanent job. Hence, the break-down of the solidaristic pay policy and a weaker commitment to full employment has enhanced gender and generational divisions in Sweden. During the early 1990s, the high level of unemployment has deprived many men and women of the opportunity to fulfil their dual breadwinner role. The Social Democratic government which entered power in 1994 reduced some of the pressures on the dual breadwinner model by enrolling a large share of the unemployed in active labour market measures, education and in early retirement programmes[10]. These measures have also destroyed some of the tensions between young people and those already in the labour market.

Employment Flexibility in Germany

Contrary to Sweden, employment flexibility was the main concern in West Germany as strong co-determination rights of the works council made it hard for employers to lay off workers[11]. Thelen (1993) claims that the West German industrial relations system was better able to deal with demands for flexibility than the more centralised industrial system in Sweden. In

Sweden, the demands for pay flexibility came mainly from large export firms while small and medium-sized firms were in most cases against concessions on working time as demanded by unions. In addition, West German employers were less dissatisfied with the dual industrial relations system. Higher unemployment in West Germany had forced the unions to be more moderate in their pay demands. In addition, the pay policy has never had a strong solidaristic component such that pay differentials between skilled and unskilled workers have been more pronounced in Germany than in Sweden[12]. Bargaining within individual sectors was also more unified than in Sweden as industry contracts cover both blue-collar and white-collar workers. The traditional bargaining system in Germany was therefore not attacked to the same degree as in Sweden and the pressures for decentralisation were resolved by renegotiating relations between the sectoral level and the firm level. Flexibility was incorporated into central contracts and new functions delegated to the works councils. Hence, the firm level bargaining has become increasingly important even though the formal structure of collective bargaining has been unchanged since the late 1970s (see also Pontusson and Swenson 1996:245; Maier et al. 1996:66-67). The German unification, on the other hand, poses a new threat to the dual industrial relations system that was extended almost unchanged to East Germany. First, pressures toward pay harmonisation across West and East Germany and pay restraints in the West broke down the link between pay and productivity growth (see Flockton and Esser 1992:282). Hence, pay of those at the lower end of the labour market has fallen in relation to the return to capital and in relation to the costs of living (see Smith 1992:203). Secondly, East German workers are less likely to be covered by collective agreements than their counterparts in the West (Maier et al. 1996:42). Pay in East Germany has also been lower and working hours longer than in the West since unification (Moody 1997:65). Thirdly, agreements at the firm level in East Germany have been made to allow firms to ignore the binding regulations of the sectoral contract and to undercut its provisions in order to save jobs (Fichter 1997:402)[13]. Hence, unification has intensified the trend towards firm-based bargaining. The labour movement has, so far, resisted employers' demands for more pay flexibility that should make the economy more 'competitive'.

In Germany, pay policy has never had a strong solidaristic component and the income dispersion has been wider than in Sweden, although it has become more compressed at the bottom during the 1980s and early 1990s (see table 5.1). Contributing to the narrowing of the income distribution at the bottom are union agreements on pay increases above sectoral levels for low paid workers in order to raise the minimum floor (see Blau and Kahn 1996:802). The effect of narrowing income dispersion at the bottom during the 1980s and early 1990s has benefited women with low income. According to Maier et al. (1996:60-71), the gender pay gap in West Germany was stable during the early 1990s but it rose sharply in East Germany after unification. The gender pay gap in manufacturing remained unchanged from 1991 to 1994 while it widened in the service sector and narrowed in the public sector[14]. The gender pay gap in East Germany has widened due to a more favourable revaluation of men's jobs compared to women's jobs and a falling share of women in higher and better paid positions. Employment flexibility in Germany has not prevented unemployment from growing. In addition, real disposable incomes of low and middle income households have been on the decline resulting in a growing need for more than one income earner (see Maier et al. 1996:29). Greater employment flexibility in Germany involving reduced working hours and increased availability of part time work has enabled many married women to increase their labour force participation, such that the number of housewives has been falling. Hence, the sustainablity of the male breadwinner model has come under a strain and more and more women are finding it necessary and desirable to intensify their participation in the labour market.

Market-determined Flexibility in the United States

In the United States, the industrial relations system in the United States has not been used to the same extent as in Sweden and Germany to reduce the number of low productivity jobs[15]. During the 1980s and early 1990s, the decentralised industrial relations system in the United States underwent further decentralisation and employment became more precarious. The share of the workforce represented by unions has contracted and pay-settings have become more individualised at the same time as real pay has deteriorated and income inequality widened. Fewer workers are now covered by health and pension plans and jobs are less secure[16]. Mishel et al. (1997:7-8) attribute the downward shift in the pay structure to a growing number of low paid and precarious jobs (temporary and part time) in the service sector, a decline of high paying manufacturing jobs, a falling

183

real value of the minimum wage and to an inflow of immigrant workers. The individualisation of the pay system in the United States has meant that regular jobs do not necessarily pay high enough wages to enable a person to provide for himself/herself and/or dependants. Hence, a growing number of persons have been forced into multiple job holding and involuntary part time work (Moody 1997:66; Mishel et al. 1997:262).

Among the three countries, the United States has had the widest income distribution both at the bottom and at the top (see table 5.1). During the post-war period, there was a trend towards less income inequality that turned around during the 1980s when a dramatic rise in the income gap between high and low income families took place (Mishel et al. 1997:43). The dispersion at the bottom widened during the 1980s but narrowed slightly again in the early 1990s due to the rise in minimum wage (1997: 4 and 146). There has, on the other hand, been a continuous widening at the top during the period. The greater inequalities in the United States have been attributed to higher returns to skills, greater number of people with low skill levels in employment and a decentralised pay system that does not ensure as compressed pay structure at the bottom as centralised pay system (Rowthorn 1992; Blau and Kahn 1996). During the period 1979-1995, there was a general downward shift in the entire pay structure in the United States. The gender pay gap narrowed during the 1980s as a result of both improvements in real hourly pay for women and real pay reduction for men. Moreover, the gap widened between women earning high pay and women earning low pay during the 1980s but this trend slowed down during the early 1990s (Mishel et al. 1997:chapter 3). The falling pay of men during the 1980s and early 1990s stimulated the work effort of married women and dual breadwinner families have become more common. The growing inequalities have especially undermined male breadwinner and single parent families whose income continued to fall during the 1980s and early 1990s (1997:chapter 1). However, the hardest hit by growing income inequalities are younger families whose earnings are lower and have grown more slowly than the previous generations (1997:5).

To sum up, the move towards the dual breadwinner model in the United States has increasingly been driven by a survival strategy of families hard hit by employers' and the government's attack on pay. Moreover, the implementation of the Temporary Assistance for Needy Families (TANF) in 1996 or workfare instead of welfare for single parents will further enhance the trend towards greater participation of mothers in paid work. In Sweden, on the other hand, the shift towards the dual breadwinner model was a class equality project and a response to permanent labour shortage. When full employment was no longer a sustainable goal in Sweden, active labour market measures were implemented in order to keep the unemployed in paid activity. Hence, the unemployed have, so far, not undermined class and gender relations that were established during the post-war period and involved greater equality than in, for example, Germany and the United States. Although the Swedish employment system involving paid work, paid training or early retirement has put a strain on the public finances during the early 1990s, there are no signs that the system will be abandoned. In Germany, employers' demands for more flexibility are undermining the male breadwinner model as many women are now able to find paid work. At the same time, various policies were implemented in order to enable women to continue to provide care in the family. Employers' demands to cut wages further will continue to meet opposition from the male-dominated unions that are strongest represented in the industrial sector. The German 'consensus model' involving consultation and negotiations between the major interest parties has, so far, not allowed confrontation between employers and labour on the same scale as in the United States. Instead, the solution to the competing interests of employers and the labour union will probably involve further divisions of the private sector into a highly productive industrial sector paying male breadwinner wages on the one hand and into a service sector with low productivity and low paid jobs employing many women on a part-time basis on the other hand. This development towards a two-tier private service sector is likely to be faster and more extensive in the East than in the West of Germany.

International Regional Integration

National states have increasingly facilitated international regionalisation in order to enhance economic growth and to ensure that their national model is reproduced at the international regional level. Examples of regionalisation are the EU and the NAFTA. Inter-regional trade has increased between the three NAFTA member countries, i.e. Canada, Mexico and the United States on the one hand and between the EU member countries on the other hand (Weiss 1997). The United States has been less affected domestically by international regionalism than Germany and Sweden as the scope of the NAFTA is limited to the promotion of free trade rather than to design common standards in order to ensure 'fair competition' in a common market as is the case of the EU. International regionalism has thus exacerbated differences between the United States on the one hand and Sweden and Germany on the other hand. The NAFTA has implications for labour and gender relations as it has legalised some of the flow of illegal immigrants from Mexico to the United States. Growing immigration puts a downward pressure on wages that in turn will intensify women's paid employment.

While the NAFTA is an extension of the free trade market model with a very limited role of the state, the EU is a more integrated model with active supra, national and local alliances and networks as well as regulation. The EU membership has obliged Sweden, the late-comer and Germany, one of the founding states, to implement universal and common values that in turn have made them more pluralistic (see Hantrais 1995:35). The EU's directives in the economic area enforce universal principles that give very limited scope for national variations, while directives in the social area only impose common principles and allow some variation in implementation in order to acknowledge different national systems (1995:23; Duncan 1996:410). Hence, national differences across the EU member states have been more pronounced in the social area than in the economic area. Moreover, the EU equality law has exclusively focused on promoting women's rights as workers rather than as citizens. By concentrating on workers' rights in paid employment, the EU has imposed the employment-insurance principle on the member states which is one of the cornerstones of the German welfare state (Clasen and Freeman 1994). The EU has on the other hand pressed the German authorities to consider women as workers in need of equality legislation and not only as housewives by extending the employment-insurance principle to women (see Hoskyns 1996:197).

The founders of the EU included in the Treaty of Rome (1957) article 119 that committed the member states to apply the principle of equal pay for work of equal work. Directives that are secondary to the treaties have since then been established to expand on article 119 (Hantrais 1995:106-108; Duncan 1996:399). During the period 1974-1986, Directives on equal treatment for men and women at work and in social security were negotiated and adopted (Hoskyns 1996:97)[17]. The EU equality legislation has slowly started to recognise that women may need special treatment as working mothers (Hantrais 1995:112). In the Social Agreement of the Maastrict Treaty from 1992, member states were allowed to undertake special measures in order to promote women's progression in the labour market. In 1992, a Directive was passed that established minimum maternity leave rights or 14 weeks of maternity leave with pay for employed and registered unemployed women (Duncan 1996:399; Hantrais 1995:106-108). The emphasis of the EU equality legislation appears to be expanding once again as the EU has started to stress the importance of reconciling work and family life for both men and women. A Directive on parental leave was first proposed in 1983 and then included in the social protocol of the Maastricht agreement (Rubery et al. 1996:239). The directive that comes into effect in 1998 grants each parent an individual right to three months of leave on the birth or adoption of a child until it reaches the age of eight. The Directive does not, however, include provisions on payments during the leave. Finally, a Directive on part-time work was also adopted under the Social Protocol that has the purpose of preventing any form of discrimination against part-time workers and to facilitate the creation of quality part-time work.

At the same time as Germany has been moving towards more universal welfare policies, the emphasis of the Swedish welfare policies has been shifting towards more employment-related principles. Examples of universal welfare policies in Germany are the 'social supplement' funded federally and made available to East German minimum pension holders without test of need to bring their benefits up to subsistence level. Moreover, care of the elderly and children is now recognised in the insurance system as a means of improving the situation of those involved in unpaid care. The establishment of non-contributory insurance credits/payments for care work has introduced a more universal access to otherwise very exclusive social security system in Germany. A trend towards what Kangas (1994) calls 'Europeanization' of the Swedish social security system started before Sweden joined the EU in 1995 and became especially apparent in 1996 when the compulsory supplementary or earnings-related pension scheme ATP was reformed. The reform involved two major changes to the ATP pension scheme. First, the funding of the ATP scheme moved from an employer tax to contributions from both employers and employees. Secondly, there was a shift from defined benefits that related the amount of the benefits to previous earnings towards benefits depending more on contributions (Stephens 1996:46; Mósesdóttir and Jonsson 1996). This reform brought the Swedish ATP pension scheme in line with the dominant employment-insurance social security system both in terms of funding and benefits.

The move towards the non-egalitarian insurance based social security system does not imply a major change in gender relations in Sweden. Public services are still relatively extensive and universally provided, although state activities have been cut and replacement rates of most benefits have been lowered considerably[18]. Women's labour force participation is very similar to that of men in Sweden which will reduce the polarisation effect of the employment-insurance model. However, polarisation may increase among the elderly due to high levels of unemployment and lower life time earnings of women. The greatest challenge to the prevailing form of gender relations is unemployment and fiscal pressures which may force the state to cut further public services and thereby female employment. Moreover, gender inequalities in pay are likely to grow if the pay-setting in Sweden becomes more individualised or market-determined. In Germany, the recognition of caring in the social insurance system does not compensate women fully for their loss of earnings as care work is evaluated at a very basic level in the calculation of pension benefits and the period covered for child care is three years while the average mother interrupts her paid employment for six years (see Maier et al. 1996:264). The inclusion of women as providers of care in the family does not challenge but rather reinforces the underlying assumptions shaping gender relations during the post-war period in Germany. Women's primary role is still to be wives and/or mothers who not only support their husbands but also care for children, the elderly and the disabled. A challenge to prevailing gender relations is women's desire to reconcile work and family life as well as the persistent high level of unemployment which is depriving many German men of the opportunity to fulfill their male breadwinner duty.

To sum up, changes interact with a national-specific institutional framework, such that national trajectories or a multi-linear path of development is created. Decentralisation has, for example, taken place in the three countries but its effect on gender inequalities has been different across the three countries due to different institutional pay settings. Moreover, decentralisation has shifted the locus of decision making from national/regional level to the firm/individual level. In addition, the national level is increasingly cross-cut by the international level through regional integration. Hence, the locus of regulation appears to be shifting away from the national level to the local level on the one hand and from the national level to the international level on the other hand. Regionalisation has led to more pluralistic institutional framework in Sweden and Germany but enhanced the national trajectory in the United States.

Conclusion

The aim of this chapter was to analyse changes affecting gender relations over time and across Sweden, Germany and the United States. We have argued that it is possible to identify two stages/phases during post-war period in the development of gender relations. The first stage was the male breadwinner model which was the outcome of a dynamic interaction between economic development and polices of the state and the labour unions. The state supported women directly and indirectly in the role as mothers and wives and employers increasingly accepted male breadwinner wages demanded by the labour unions. Women had very limited influence on the process of change due to their weak position within the political system in the three countries (see discussion in chapter 2). Labour shortage and women's demands for greater inclusion into the economic and political spheres facilitated soon another trend that accumulated into a shift towards a dual breadwinner model. The shift to the dual breadwinner model has, however, not been uni-linear across space. The dual breadwinner model is well established in Sweden while Germany is only slowly moving away from the male breadwinner model. Moreover, the trend towards the dual breadwinner model has been strengthened by employers' drive for greater decentralisation involving either pay flexibility or employment flexibility as well as by international regionalisation. The changes in gender relations has also involved reproduction of gender inequalities as unpaid work is still the main responsibility of women and women's paid work is undervalued in the labour market. However, gender inequalities have become intertwined with other social relations in the labour market. Pay flexibility has, for example, led to enhanced generational and gender inequalities in Sweden and greater individualisation of pay in the United States has intensified class divisions among women.

In Sweden, the shift towards the dual breadwinner model was driven by a permanent shortage of labour and demands for greater equality across class and gender. The labour unions ensured that women's integration into paid work did not distort class relations and the state implemented measures to enable women to reconcile work and family life. High unemployment threatens now the dual breadwinner model as many men and women are not able to find paid employment. In West Germany, it was not until employers managed to press through greater employment flexibility and women's groups demanded greater autonomy in their own affairs that the state started to promote the creation of part-time jobs and women's part-time employment. These measures have stimulated women's integration into paid work but the state has ensured that women only participated during periods of lighter domestic activities by acknowledging unpaid work in the pension system. The main concern of the German labour unions has been to protect the male breadwinner jobs in the industrial sector. In the United States, employers' attack on wages and the repression of the federal minimum wage during the 1980s weakened the labour unions and there has been a rapid growth of low paid jobs with little or no employer-provided health and pension benefits. The private sector expansion and lower earnings of men led to an acceleration in married women's labour force participation and dual breadwinner families have become more common.

The shift towards the dual breadwinner model has had pronounced implications for gender relations as well as for industrial relations in Sweden, Germany and the Untied States. Greater labour force participation of women has given women some economic independence from men and greater opportunities for equality. However, economic independence has been achieved through an intensified work effort from women. Women's labour force participation has also involved advantages for men who have been able to withdraw (voluntarily) from the labour force and/or reduce their hours of work. However, high and persistent male unemployment has robbed many men of their privileges provided by the labour market. The dual breadwinner model has been beneficial to employers who are no longer being forced to provide male breadwinner pay and the feminisation of the labour force has enlarged their labour pull. Finally, the greater work effort of women has put a pressure on the state to expand its provision of care services on the one hand and enabled it to tighten its welfare services by restricting access and cutting replacement rates without endangering the livelihood of many families on the other hand. The number of dual breadwinner families has increased in Sweden, Germany and the United

States. Hence, men and women are no longer segregated in the two worlds of work, i.e. in the household and the labour market. Instead gender segregation has been established within the labour market that is becoming more complicated as it is no longer only affected by hierarchical relations between men and women but also cross-cut by other social relations such as class, race and generational divisions. The more fused labour market divisions pose a problem for the organisational structure of labour unions that is based on blue-collar and white-collar divisions.

Employers' preferences for greater flexibility, women's aspirations to work and a growing need for a two-earner household due to the destruction of many breadwinner jobs and falling real wages have put pressure on the 'coherence' between the labour market, household and the welfare state in the three countries. The incoherence has led to growing gender tensions. During the early 1990s, many men and women have been deprived of the opportunity to fulfil their dual breadwinner role due the high level of unemployment. The Social Democratic government has reacted to high unemployment and fiscal pressures in Sweden by expanding active labour market measures and by cutting jobs in the public services. The cut in public sector jobs has led to a rise in women's unemployment and to greater work pressures on those providing welfare services. At the same time, active labour market measures involving paid training have been used to keep the 'unemployed' active which in turn has reduced some of the pressures on the dual breadwinner model. These training measures have increasingly come under attack as they have not led to greater employment growth. Hence, the labour market is no longer able to generate enough employment opportunities for a welfare state based on the dual breadwinner model. There are, however, no signs that the dual breadwinner model will be abandoned. The strong position of the left parties that are supported by the majority of women will ensure that the active labour market measures will continue to be used to activate the unemployed.

The gender relations institutionalised by the German state are that of a male breadwinner whose wife is either homeworking or is engaged in part-time work during periods of lighter domestic activities. However, high unemployment and women's growing desire to enter paid employment are putting a pressure on the male breadwinner wages which the labour unions have fought hard to maintain. The outcome of the competing interests between employers and the labour union will probably involve further divisions of the private sector into a highly productive industrial sector paying male breadwinner wages on the one hand and into a service sector with low productivity and low pay jobs employing many women on a part-time basis on the other hand. This development towards a two-tier private service sector is likely to be faster and more extensive in the East than in the West of Germany. In the United States, women's employment has been expanding at the same time as fewer jobs are providing workers with employment and welfare rights. In addition, the American state has enhanced single mothers' reliance on work (workfare), although the number of workers with earnings below the poverty level has increased (see Mishel and Bernstein 1993:307). Hence, American women have entered a vicious circle where falling real wages are forcing them to participate or increase their work effort at the same time as greater availability of labour in terms of numbers and hours enables employers to cut wages further. This vicious circle will continue to exist while labour relations are governed by employers. Intensified divisions may, on the other hand, unify the working poor and lead to greater confrontations between the various interest groups. The federal government will intervene when the confrontations start to threaten the internal coherence of the nation.

In this chapter, we have focused on overlapping trends over time and multi-linear development across countries which are the outcome of inter-action between economic, social, political actors and institutions that have country-specific features. Moreover, we have argued that each of the three countries is in the process of developing its own variant of the dual bread-winner model. In the following chapter, we will incorporate the results of our analysis into the regimes of gender relations that were developed in chapter 1.

Notes

[1] A new techno-economic paradigm is established when a diffusion of certain type of technology is accompanied by a major structural adjustment involving deep social and institutional changes necessary to bring about a better match between the new technology and the system of social management or regime of regulation. The successive techno-economic paradigm starts to develop within the preceding stage or paradigm and only takes over when it has demonstrated its comparative advantages (Freeman and Perez 1988:58).

[2] A model or pattern of development consists of three main elements: a technical model or paradigm of industrialisation, a regime of accumulation and a mode of regulation. A technical model of industrialisation refers to what is thought to be the

best practice technology. Moreover, a regime of accumulation is a systematic mode of distribution and allocation of the social product, that over a long period generates a balance between the changes in the relations of productions and the changes of the eventual conditions of consumption. A regime of accumulation is first established when there is a systematic coupling with the mode of regulation that refers to the ensemble of the state forms, social norms political parties and institutional networks (see Tickell and Peck 1995:357-358; Kiely 1995:91).

[3]Cathexis refers to the construction of emotionally charged social relations with other people (Connell 1987:112).

[4]Our regimes of gender relations were developed without any prior knowledge of Connell's gender order theory.

[5]The gender contract has three different levels, i.e. metaphysical, institutional and individual levels and its content and completeness vary across space and time. The class system, family situation and age operate also at the second and the third levels (Hirdman 1990).

[6]The unions made some gains in regaining and consolidating the real living standards during the 1950s and 1960s and in improving non-pay benefits during the 1970s (see Smith 1994:254-287).

[7]The marriage benefit obtained by splitting the income curbed considerably in 1952 and 1969 since its introduction (see Nelson 1991:16).

[8]In mass production, product-specific machines and semi-skilled workers were used to produce standardised goods for standarised consumer markets. The new flexible production is based on information technology and involves offering product diversity and/or high quality as well as adopting quickly to changing market demands (Piore and Sabel 1984).

[9]This bargaining unit was formed by the TCO and SACO. The TCO (Tjänstemännens Centralorganisation) refers to the Confederation of Professional Employees and SACO (Sveriges Akademikers Centralorgansation) is the Confederation of Academics in Sweden.

[10] In 1996, 6.3 were unemployment, 2.8 per cent were in labour market programs and those outside the labour force were 19.3 (see the Swedish Institute 1997).

[11]In the famous agreement between LO and the Employers' Confederation SAF at Saltsjöbaden, the former recognised the 'management right to manage' (Standing 1988:2).

[12]The main public sector union (ÖTV) also followed the metalworkers' in terms of percentage increases but the contracts have not promoted wage leveling between the two. Tenured civil servants do not have the right to strike or even bargain collectively (Thelen 1993:37).

[13]In 1993, IG metal and the employers' association changed the pay agreement in 1991 for East Germany in order to delay the wage equalisation measure for two years or until the summer of 1996, In addition, provisions were included that

allowed companies with economic problems to pay wages below the agreed wage (Maier et al. 1996:43).

[14]The positive effects of more women entering high paying jobs have not outweighed the negative effects of greater number of women working for low pay in the service sector. A growing share of women in the public sector on the other hand has gone in hand with a decreasing gender pay gap (Maier et al. 1997:60-71).

[15] During the period 1960-1994, the growth rates in worker productivity (GDP per employed) to the US standard of living was 2.1 per cent in Sweden, 2.7 per cent in Germany and 1.1 per cent in the United States (Mishel et al. 1997:384).

[16]The percentage of the workforce represented by unions was close to 25 per cent in the early 1970s and by 1994 it had dropped to around 15 per cent (Mishel et al. 1997:199).

[17]These Directives are on equal opportunities in respect of equal pay (1975) that later developed into equal pay for work of equal value, equal treatment at work (1976) and equal treatment in employment-related social insurance rights (1979, implemented in 1984) that was extended to include private occupational pension schemes and self-employment in 1986 (Duncan 1996:399; Hantrais 1995:106-108).

[18]In 1995, social expenditures (pension payments not included) as a percentage of GDP was still higher in Sweden than in the other Nordic countries (NOSOSKO 1997:136).

6 Regimes of Gender Relations

The various themes and arguments developed so far in this work will now be brought together. We will return to the regimes of gender relations presented in chapter 1 and incorporate the main results in the proceeding chapters. Our aim in this chapter is to introduce time into our analysis of regimes of gender relations that was developed to highlight the forms/patterns of gender relations prevailing during the early 1990s in Sweden, Germany and the United States. We will start our discussion by integrating our main analytical contributions into the framework of the regimes of gender relations. We will then summarise the results of our empirical analysis within two periods. The first period involves mounting tension over the male breadwinner model in the three countries. The second period is characterised by compromises or by the establishment of the dual breadwinner model in Sweden, a move towards the dual breadwinner model in the United States and modifications to the male breadwinner in Germany. The chapter will conclude with a discussion of the new contradictions and tensions created by the these country-specific compromises.

Conceptualising Patterns/Forms of Gender Relations

When analysing gender relations, we have primarily been concerned with how the hierarchical division of work between men and women is regulated through norms, institutional arrangements and power relationships in the production sphere, social reproduction sphere/the household and by the state. In other words, how actors, cultural norms and structures interrelate and affect the relative position of men and women creating certain patterns/forms of gender relations that vary across countries and change through time. Central to our analytical framework of the regimes of gender relations is the mode of regulation which is a concept applied within the regulation theories (see, for example Leborgne and Lipietz 1991). As stated in chapter 1, the regimes of gender relations rest on the general principle of work organised along gender lines in the sphere of social reproduction and the sphere of production. Gendered organisation of work involves hierarchical relationships between men and women in which women are subordinated to men. The main mechanism to adjust the behaviour of individuals to a gendered organisation of work is the mode of regulation. The concept of mode of regulation refers to explicit and implicit norms of institutions that constantly adjust the expectations and behaviour of individuals to a certain form of hierarchical relations between men and women as, for example, the male breadwinner model. As the relations between the family, market and the state are relatively autonomous, not all people will behave in accordance to the dominant pattern of gender relations. The consolidation of a mode of regulation will depend on political and social struggles, agreements and institutional compromises. Social forces will not devote themselves to endless struggle but build a stable system of relations or social blocks around a certain mode of regulation. A country-specific mode of regulation can be identified by studying norms and institutional arrangements underlying activities of the state, labour unions and employers.

The concept of mode of regulation is more suitable than most feminist approaches (Hartmann 1981; Walby 1990; Hirdman 1990) as it escapes tautological explanations of men's control over women by focusing on how a particular mode of regulation arises through social and political struggles on the one hand and on the country-specific elements of the mode of regulation on the other hand. As the concept of mode of regulation has not been developed to analyse how a particular form of hierarchical relationships between men and women are established and reproduced, further theoretical work is needed on the concept of the state as gendered social relations and on the processes of change which lead to new patterns of gender relations or to a new form of hierarchical relations between men and women as, for example the dual breadwinner model. By studying the state as a site of gendered strategies, regulator of gender relations and the product of past gender relations, we are able to map out how a particular mode of regulation arises and is reproduced. The role of the state in regulating gender relations has increased during the post-war period due to women's greater participation in paid work. Moreover, economic internationalisation and regional co-operation have reduced variations accounted for by developments in the economic spheres. Hence, the state has become the most important regulator of gender relations and the main source of divergencies in the forms/patterns of gender relations across space.

In the following, we will incorporate our discussion of the state as gendered social relations and of the processes of change into the framework of regimes of gender relations. We will conclude with remarks about the difficulties involved in classifying countries according to the mode of regulation involving norms, institutional arrangements and political relations underlying the mode of regulation.

The State as Gendered Social Relations

In chapter 1, we developed a new 'feminist-relational' approach to the study of the state that sees the state as gendered social relations or a site of gender strategies and a regulator of gender relations as well as a product of past gender struggles. This contrasts with other economic and feminist approaches that are mainly concerned with how capitalists, capitalist development, state-managers and patriarchs mould the policies and activities of the state. We developed our approach further by studying women's struggles in relation to other social and political relations in chapter 2 and by examining in chapter 3 the role of the state in regulating employment changes in the labour market that have affected gender relations or the patterns/forms of gender relations. In addition, the implications of these employment changes for gender relations were analysed in chapter 4.

In order to understand the drives behind the state's activities and policies, our analysis in chapter 2 starts at the level of the individual and proceeds to the collective level. Individuals have a variety of interests or perceive themselves as belonging to a variety of groups organised around, for example, class, religion and race that may represent conflicting interests. An individual may join a group(s) in order to make new claims and/or support old claims or simply to reap the benefits involved, i.e. to be a free-rider and/or to fight subordination. The mechanisms of group identity and interest shape and are shaped by social institutions which on the other side systematically strengthen certain groups and weaken others. Societal changes (economic, social and/or political) leading to growing contradictions between individuals/groups/countries will induce new collective actions that are in most cases a collective attempt outside established institutions to promote a common interest. Although the activities of the new collective action or social movements may be outside the establishment, they may promote their interest through formal channels. Groups fighting women's subordination have adopted a variety of strategies towards the state that involve certain interests and forms of mobilisation. As the state is a product of country-specific political and social struggles, a strategy adopted in one country may not be successful in another country. The success of women's struggles is also affected by social blocks that only recognise new groups and social contexts or agency when the system of social relations can no longer by reproduced or regulated due to societal changes.

Women as well as men constitute major political forces that have struggled to shape the way the state regulates gender relations. The women's movement is not independent of other political ideas and activities but rather a response to the particular political configuration. As political actors, women have fought for recognition by the prevailing social blocks and for a place in the forming of social blocks but political and social actors will after a period of struggles form alliances and agreements as well as institutional compromises around a certain mode of regulation. The particular form of integration or exclusion from political influences will determine to what extent women are able to influence/challenge norms about their role in society but these norms become embedded in institutional settings. The state is active in regulating men's and women's behaviour through social norms underlying their family policies and employment policies. As the state is the most important force in regulating gender relations, political influences will always be an important goal in women's struggle for improvements in their position. However, the success of women's struggle is affected by the institutional arrangements of the state that are the product of past struggles. Institutional arrangements influencing women's struggle are the form of the state (unitary versus federal state), policy formation (institutionalised form of interest mediation versus bargaining between the most influential interest groups) and policy implementation (unified or flexible at the various levels). Moreover, the institutional arrangements of the state influence how homogenous the conditions of women are within the national borders.

In chapter 3, we argued that the measures available to the state to regulate employment in the labour market are to alter the volume of labour/jobs and/or create incentives/disincentives to engage in paid work. The extent to which the state engages in the creation of welfare services may affect the volume of jobs and immigration will increase the size of the labour force. The state adjusts the behaviour of men and women to certain patterns/forms of gender relations by creating incentives/disincentives that are based on certain norms about men's and women's roles that are then supported by the appropriate institutional arrangements in the area of production and reproduction. However, it is not possible to read off supply responses from the state policies aimed at regulating the labour supply. The decisions of women and men to be inactive or active part-time or full-time in the labour market are in continuous non-accommodating interaction with social norms, family structures, structures of paid employment and employers' policy as well as structures and policies of the state. Moreover, the state has made greater efforts to influence women's paid employment than men's paid employment. Family-obligations have prevented employers' demand pressures stimulating women's paid work to the same extent as men's paid work.

Employment changes are the outcome of dynamic interactions between demand pressures and supply responses that are conditioned by collective actors and institutional arrangements. The state has become an important source of variations in labour market outcomes across space as economic internationalisation and regional co-operation in the economic spheres has reduced variations accounted for by the structure and the functioning of the industrial system. The interrelationship between the welfare state, the household and the labour market is relatively autonomous as there is not necessarily a smooth accommodation between policies adopted by the state and participation patterns in the labour market. Moreover, the degree of relative autonomy will differ as responses are shaped by the dominant social blocks at the state level. Hence, the responses of the state to structural changes and/or demands made by actors may be more extensive in one country than in another country where the dominant social block has been successful in fighting for less state intervention.

Employment changes have implications for gender relations as they may affect the hierarchical relationships between men and women in which women are subordinated to men. In chapter 4, we claimed that gender segregation is the outcome of a dynamic interaction between individual tastes and country-specific social structures. Gender segregation indicates to what extent men's and women's occupational choices are restricted but constraints on the behaviour of individuals violate the assumption that labour markets are competitive. The segmentation processes resulting in gender segregated labour markets are affected by employers, labour unions and the state who may affect the size of the labour force as well as the allocation of jobs and rewards. The degree to which gender segregation is influenced by country-specific social structures is the outcome of technological progress, country-specific capital-labour struggles and the role the state in the interest mediation. The size of the labour force will influence how much power employers have over the segmentation processes. Immigration also affects the composition of the labour force and thereby the scope for segregation. When the working population consists of more than one race, differences between men and women become infused with race. Hence, labour markets with relatively high shares of immigrants or minority workers may be less gender segregated as these disadvantaged workers may be given jobs at lower levels in the job hierarchy where many women are also situated. Moreover, continuous immigration may also contribute to a fall in the gender segregation over time. Employers' scope for discrimination will, however, be constrained by laws on equal pay and equal access to jobs as well as unions' pay settlements. Country-specific social structures will create variations in gender segregation across space. Moreover, changes through time may involve desegregation or less hierarchical division of work between men and women as well as resegregation or more hierarchical division of work.

In chapter 5, we claimed that changes in gender relations arise from the dynamic interaction of country-specific social, political and economic institutions and actors (social structures) creating both designed and unintended processes that are evolutionary. The outcomes of these evolutionary processes will be multi-linear across space and involve over-lapping trends over time. The movement from one stage/phase in the development of gender relations includes both continuities and discontinuities. During the post-war period, incremental changes have, for example, accumulated into a shift from the male breadwinner model towards the dual breadwinner model. The shift has involved overlapping developments with male and dual breadwinner models coexisting at the same time. Moreover, the development has been multi-linear across space as the speed at which countries adopt variants of the dual breadwinner model differs. In addition, the locus of the regulation of gender relations appears to be shifting away from the national level to the local level on the one hand and from the national level to the international level on the other hand.

Our analysis of regimes of gender relations developed in chapter 1 included some thoughts about processes of change over time. Our main assertion was that regimes are not constants as the societal environment undergoes frequent changes that give rise to new demands by social forces. These new changes and demands put a pressure on the state to adjust or even change its activities and policies concerning the sphere of production and sphere of social reproduction. Conflicts and growing tensions may induce regime transition or transformation. In the case of regime transition the mode of regulation will change. Transition may either entail a change leading to the creation of a new regime of gender relations or a move from one existing regime to another. Institutional and policy changes/adjustments will not necessarily resolve tensions as they may generate conflicting social forces and different societal situations. Hence, regimes are under constant pressure to change and/or adjust its norms and institutional arrangements.

If we integrate our analysis of changes in gender relations into our regimes of gender relations that were developed to capture the main features of patterns/forms of gender relations prevailing during the early 1990s, we can see that the shift from the male breadwinner model towards the dual breadwinner generated a transition that led to the establishment of the egalitarian regime of gender relations in Sweden. The modified male breadwinner model in Germany is captured by the ecclesiastical regime of gender relations. The liberal regime of gender relations in the United States is positioned between the other two regimes with male and dual breadwinner models coexisting, although the latter is becoming more dominant than the former. Divorces have become more common in the three countries that may be the start of a shift towards a one-headed household model involving either female-headed or male-headed households with or without children.

The forms/patterns of gender relations prevailing after World War Two involving women as wives and/or mothers and men as breadwinners came under pressure to change as a result of the interaction between the various social structures that create tensions and conflicts. The economic pressures to integrate women into the labour force and women's demands for greater participation in public life created gender tensions as men were not willing to share with women the burden of unpaid work and to accept women's full integration into paid work. A period of heightening gender conflicts occurred during the 1960s and 1970s as employers pressed for a greater supply of labour and women's desire to break out of their exclusion from public life mounted. Labour shortage facilitated the integration of women into paid work which in turn put a pressure on the patterns/forms of gender relations established immediately after World War Two which involved the separation of men and women into two different spheres. The notion of gender equality became the focus of women's political struggles and greater educational attainment provided the drive behind women's greater desire to engage in paid work. The flow of women into the labour market resulted in the break-down of the sharp division between the sphere of production and the sphere of reproduction but involved gender divisions in the area of paid work (cf. chapter 4). The state reacted to the tensions arising from the integration pressures by altering the volume of labour/jobs and/or by creating incentives/disincentives for women to engage in paid work. The behaviour of men and women was adjusted to certain patterns/forms of gender relations through norms and institutional arrangements that either involved adjustments within the mode of regulation (Germany) or a transition to a new mode of regulation or to the dual breadwinner model

(Sweden). In the United States, the adjustments to the mode of regulations underlying the breadwinner model have been much more extensive than in Germany.

Classification of Countries

Two problems become evident when classifying countries into regimes of gender relations. First, gender relations are under constant pressure to change. As pointed out by Hirdman (1990:80), gender relations are socially constructed and they are therefore open to questioning and destruction. If the mode of regulation can not adjust the behaviour of men and women to new pressures, the regime of gender relations starts to dissolve. Then, the classification becomes less applicable to the actual conditions prevailing in the particular country. Although welfare policies in Germany support extensively the homeworking wife, the majority of women are now engaged in paid work. As the mode of regulation is increasingly being adjusted to women's paid work, our classification of Germany as the ecclesiastical regime of gender relations will become less relevant. Secondly, the mode of regulation of gender relations is incomplete and contradictory. The mode of regulation is incomplete as it does not extend to all areas and include all groups. Activities in the sphere of social reproduction are often less regulated than those taking place in the sphere of production. Moreover, state policies are often incomplete as institutional arrangements necessary for the pursuit of certain policies will take time to development. It is also possible that the state's policies and activities are contradictory as the state attempts to mediate between competing interests. The Swedish state pursued, for example, egalitarian polices in the area of work but encouraged concentration of capital ownership. Incomplete and contradictory mode of regulation is an important source of divergences across countries that more or less cluster around similar patterns of hierarchical gender relations. Although political and social struggles have country-specific characteristics and institutional outcomes, there are not infinite numbers of regimes of gender relations. Countries will cluster around certain patterns. The close and extensive Nordic co-operation has contributed to similar patterns of gender relations across the countries. In the Nordic countries, female labour force participation is, for example, high and women are treated as individuals in most welfare policies. In the early 1990s, the Nordic countries decided collectively to abolish the widow pension which was the only remaining differentiation between men and women in their welfare policies (NOSOSKO 1995; Mósesdóttir and Eydal forthcoming). There are, however, important divergences as concerns gender relations across the Nordic countries that are due to incomplete and contradictory modes of regulation[1].

Patterns/Forms of Gender Relations during the Post-War Period

During the post-war period, the patterns of gender relations have gone through periods of heightening conflicts and periods of compromises that have stabilised the conflicts for a while. Women's political struggles surged during periods of heightening conflicts and subsided during periods of consolidation when some of women's demands were absorbed into the mode of regulation. We will now summarise our empirical study of the development of gender relations in Sweden, Germany and the United States by dividing the post-war period into a period of mounting tension over the male breadwinner model and a period of compromises involving the establishment of the dual breadwinner model in Sweden, modifications to the male breadwinner in Germany and a move towards the dual breadwinner model in the United States. Finally, contradictions and tensions created by the these country-specific compromises will be discussed.

When the Swedish and American women entered the electoral systems from 1919 to 1921, new social groups were not recognised such that the suffragette movements were forced to disintegrate. The consequence of women's exclusion from politics in Sweden, West Germany and the United States was twofold (see chapter 2). First, women did not become a part of the dominant social blocks built around class, regional and religious divisions. Secondly, women were not able to challenge state measures reinforcing their status as mothers (Sweden and the United States) and wives (West Germany). Nevertheless, not all women were willing and/or able to leave the labour market. These reinforcing measures involved family-orientated social polices in Sweden, protective legislation and the mothers' pension in the United States and a clause in the West German Basic

Law committing the state to defend and preserve the family (see Jenson and Mahon 1993; Kaplan 1992; Skocpol 1995). The exclusion of women from political influences and a period of economic prosperity set the ground for the male breadwinner model. Norms assigning the role of a mother or a wife to women and a breadwinner to men became engraved in the norms and the institutional structure of the state during the early part of the welfare state's development.

Heightening Conflicts over the Male Breadwinner Model

During the early 1960s, there existed a shortage of labour in manufacturing and services in Sweden, West Germany and the United States (see chapter 5). Moreover, the exclusion of women from political power as well as their integration into paid work and education sparked off a new rise in women's political activities during the 1960s and 1970s. The state responded to the labour shortage by enabling women to participate in paid work (Sweden) and/or to encourage immigration of workers (West Germany and the United States). In the early 1960s, women's groups and other social groups in Sweden demanded greater equality of outcome in terms of both class and gender. The Social Democratic government that had close ties with the largest confederation of labour, the LO, responded to these demands by integrating women into their class equality program. Equality across class and gender was to be achieved through full employment and solidaristic pay policy (see Persson 1990). Hence, active labour market measures and welfare services were expanded to ensure maximum employment integration. During booms and recessions, mobility grants, training and early retirement schemes were used to keep the unemployed in paid activity (see chapter 3). The expansion of welfare services created new employment opportunities for women while men continued to be employed in the private sector. Hence, women became increasingly concentrated in the public sector and men in the private sector. The solidaristic pay policy made it, however, difficult for employers to use women as low paid labour in order to displace men from the labour market (see chapter 4).

During the post-war period, the unions, employers and the state in West Germany created conditions for the male breadwinner families/households by pursuing an industrial development based on high productivity and by enforcing pay determination system linking pay with productivity (see chapter 5). Moreover, the male breadwinner family was supported through the tax and the pension systems (Buchholz-Will 1992; Ginsburg 1992). The labour shortage prevailing during the early 1960s could not be met by greater participation of married women as the state was committed to defend and preserve the family (see Ferree 1995). Hence, the state allowed temporary immigration and the unions made sure that the immigrant workers did not threaten the male-breadwinner jobs. Immigrant workers were, therefore, segregated into low paid jobs that were in most cases below their level of skills (see Smith 1994; Maier et al. 1996). During the 1970s and 1980s, autonomous women's groups started to demand a greater say in decisions concerning abortion and whether or not to become housewives (Kaplan 1992). It was, however, not until the service sector started to expand in the mid-1980s that women's labour force participation in West Germany showed signs of a continuous increase (see our discussion in chapter 3).

In the United States, employers have been able to secure a continuous flow of immigrant labour into the labour market. The continuous immigration, 'marriage bar', derived pension rights of wives and a tax policy involving splitting of the income contributed to a relative slow integration of women into paid work until the 1980s (see chapter 3 and 5). During the 1960s, women fighting for equality in terms of non-discrimination in the United States were strengthened by the achievements of the civil rights movement that managed to press through employment expansion in the public sector. This public sector expansion during the 1960s opened up employment opportunities for women in education, welfare and governmental administration (Ginsburg 1992). During the 1970s, employers in the United States responded to falling profits in the industrial sector by pressing wages down and the state supported this development throughout the 1980s by repressing the minimum wage (Brenner 1998). The fastest growth in women's paid employment occurred during the 1980s, facilitated by growing employment opportunities in the private sector, falling real wages of married men and a rise in female real wages (see Mishel and Bernstein 1993).

The Role of the State in Solving the Gender Conflict

The inroad which women made into education and paid work led to growing dissatisfaction among women with welfare polices treating women as wives and/or mothers on the one hand and differential wages based on the assumption that women were additional earners on the other hand. This discrepancy between social norms and institutional arrangements or the mode of regulation and the greater inclusion of women into the public sphere led to an upsurge in women's struggles during the 1960s and 1970s (cf. chapter 2). The state and the labour movement incorporated some of women's demands into their welfare and pay policies in order to resolve the growing gender tensions over the male breadwinner model. In Sweden, measures were implemented that could be incorporated into the class equality project. These measures led to the development of the dual breadwinner model. In Germany, the state and the unions were not willing to retreat from the male breadwinner model, such that the male breadwinner model had to be modified in order to make it more acceptable to women. The move towards the dual breadwinner model in the United States has increasingly been driven by a survival strategy of families hard hit by employers' and the state's attack on pay. Moreover, the implementation of the Temporary Assistance for Needy Families (TANF) in 1996 or workfare instead of welfare for single parents will further enhance the trend towards greater participation of mothers in paid work (see chapter 5).

In Sweden, the state played an important role in smoothing the transition from the male breadwinner model to the dual breadwinner model. The state's solution to the gender tensions created by the integration pressures of capitalism was to expand the welfare rights and welfare services. The individual taxation, generous statutory leave of absence for parenthood, rights to reduced hours work for parents and the extensive availability of subsidised public child care services has enabled Swedish women to attain similar participation rates to those of men (see chapter 3). Moreover, the centralised bargaining system has been used to achieve a relatively compressed income distribution which has benefited women. The school-based training system has also contributed to the compressed wage structure as the cost of training is to a large extent paid by the state (see chapter 4). Today, most

Swedish women work full-time up to and after the birth of their first child and thus remain classified as full-time. After completing the parental leave, most mothers shift to part-time work until the youngest child enters school at the age of 7 years (see Gonäs and Lehto 1997). Hence, the solutions to the gender tensions around the male breadwinner model have primarily involved measures enabling working mothers to travel between paid and unpaid work without any major changes in status and income. The 'Daddy-month' that was introduced in 1994 as a part of the parental leave arrangements signals a gesture on behalf of the state to ensure that working fathers engage in the care of children at home.

In West Germany, short term immigration as well as the favourable treatment of the homeworking wife in tax and pension policies postponed women's inroads into paid work until the mid-1980s. The unions managed during the 1980s and early 1990s to get employers to agree on special measures to improve the pay level of the lowest wage groups, thereby benefiting women (Blau and Kahn 1996). The dual vocational system which is partly financed by the state has in general served to exclude women from large number of male-dominated occupations. However, the system gives status protection to those women who complete training within the system as it forms the basis for ranking of jobs (Maier et al. 1996). The German state supported during the 1980s and the early 1990s the creation of part-time jobs and women's part-time employment in order to reduce women's dissatisfaction with the male breadwinner model as well as the tensions arising from high unemployment, the unification process between East and West Germany and employers' demands for more flexible labour. Hence, the need for a more flexible workforce in, especially, the service sector was an important driving force behind women's integration into paid work since the mid-1980s. The state has at the same time implemented measures to ensure that women continue to provide family-care by recognising care of children and the elderly in the pension system (see Daly 1998; Ostner 1998). Hence, the traditional work pattern of German women is paid employment, marriage, withdrawal when children are born and then re-entry six or more years later. When women re-enter paid employment normally they enter into part-time work (Maier et al. 1996).

In the United States, the flow of women into paid employment was slowed down by the continuous immigration and the favourable

208

treatment of the homeworking wife in the tax and pension systems. The American state has, however, reduced its support for the homeworking wife by eroding the advantages of joint taxation implemented in 1948 (Nelson 1991). The unions have been weak or had limited control over the pay determination system due to the continuous flow of immigrant workers into the labour market. The civil rights movement and women's groups have, therefore, had to rely on the state to ensure improvements in pay of minority and women workers. The federal government has enforced anti-discrimination legislation since the 1960s that has led to some improvements in women's pay and access to occupations (Blau 1993). During the 1980s, many states implemented comparable worth programme for their employees that were successful in closing the pay gap between female and male jobs (Hartmann and Aaronson 1994). However, these measures and the union pay agreements have been less effective in improving the relative position of the low paid workers, such that the gender pay gap has been wider in the United States than in Sweden and West Germany (United Nations 1995). The falling pay of men during the 1980s and early 1990s stimulated women's employment. Hence, the state has facilitated the development of the dual breadwinner model by restricting the scope for gender discrimination in pay and by allowing real wages of men to fall. Moreover, the state passed legislation on family leave in 1993 that requires employers to grant their employees twelve weeks of unpaid leave in connection with a birth of a child (see Albelda et al. 1997).

While the state in the United States has increased its direct and indirect support for women's labour force participation, families with children have been given greater assistance through the tax system. The growing number of poor families and families headed by women has led to renewed support for families with children through Earned Income Tax Credit (EITC) during the 1980s and the early 1990s. The effect of the EITC is that families with low income face the highest marginal tax on their additional income[2]. Moreover, women are still able to gain access to the public pension system or social security through their husbands' contributions. Hence, the state gives some support to the male breadwinner model through its family policies at the same time as the employment policies implemented by the state have contributed to a tremendous reduction in the number of jobs paying male breadwinner wages. Although many American women still interrupt work at marriage and/or as a result of child birth and child rearing, their interruption from paid work is short and the majority returns to full time work (see Drobnic and Wittig 1997).

Growing Tensions over the Compromises

Women's inclusion into public life involved both greater integration into paid work and politics. The shift from the male breadwinner model has contributed to a weakening of the social blocks formed during the early part of this century (cf. chapter 2). The disintegration of the social blocks prevailing since the early part of this century has made the process of interest mediation more complicated at the same time as supranational regulation has increasingly cross-cut national regulation. Slow-down in economic growth, stronger position of capital and regional integration are now the main constraints on the options available to the state to solve some of the gender conflicts arising from the growing importance of the dual breadwinner model. The fragmentation of social and political groups also means that it has become difficult to separate gender conflicts from class, race/ethnicity, regional and generational conflicts as these divisions cut across women as a political group.

During the 1980s and early 1990s, the parliamentary party system in Sweden and Germany started to fragment, first on the left and then on the right (see chapter 2). Women's groups have contributed to the fragmentation of the political system by engaging in the establishment of new parties and making alliances that have cut across the established party system. Moreover, women in Sweden, Germany and the United States have started to use their right to vote to a greater extent then before which has forced the state in the three countries to pay closer attention to women's demands. In Sweden, women are more likely than men to use their right to vote. Women have as voters attempted to pressure the Social Democrats to refrain from cutting welfare rights and services. The Social Democrats have, on the other hand, tried to obtain a larger share of women's voting by increasing the number of women on their party lists and in government. In Germany, the CDU/CSU has been successful in appealing to women by increasing its number of female candidates and by implementing policies enabling women to reconcile family work with part-time work.

Hence, more women have since 1983 voted for the CDU/CSU than men (Molitor 1991). Since 1980, women in the United States have been much more likely than men to vote for the Democratic party. The pro-family stance and the anti-feminist appointments of the Reagan administration have contributed to women's dissatisfaction with the Republican Party. In 1992, women voted for Clinton to a greater extent than men but young, single women are most likely to vote Democratic (see chapter 2).

In Sweden, greater decentralisation of the centralised pay setting system has, on the other hand, reduced the inter-sectoral levelling of pay such that the notion of 'just pay' at full employment has been weakened. One effect of the reduced inter-sectoral levelling has been that the gender pay gap ceased to narrow during the mid-1980s and grew for the first time since women entered the labour market in the 1960s. Moreover, the economic recession during the early 1990s and public budget constraints has made it increasingly difficult for the state to implement measures to sustain full employment. Unemployment for both men and women has reached record high levels and those hardest hit are young people who have had difficulties finding a job, especially a permanent job. Hence, the break-down of the solidaristic pay policy and a weaker commitment to full employment has enhanced gender and generational divisions in Sweden. During the early 1990s, persistent high unemployment and pay flexibility began to threaten the dual breadwinner model. The Social Democratic government which entered power in 1994 reduced some of the pressures on the dual breadwinner model by enrolling a large share of the unemployed in active labour market measures, education and in early retirement programs. These measures have also destroyed some of the tensions between young people and those already in the labour market. Although the Swedish employment system involving paid work, paid training or early retirement had put a strain on the public finances during the early 1990s, there are no signs that the system will be abandoned (see chapter 5).

Persistent high levels of unemployment have, on the other hand, robbed many German men of the opportunity to become male breadwinners. Moreover, many East German women have lost their dual breadwinner status at the same time as their husbands have not been able to find male breadwinner jobs and unemployment has been much higher in the East than the West. In addition, the support of employers for the system of breadwinner wages involving extensive employment rights has been eroding. The inability of the German economy to create a sufficient number of jobs, especially male breadwinner jobs, will put further pressure on the German 'consensus' model which has so far been very successful in withstanding demands for fundamental changes. The solution to the competing interests will probably involve further divisions of the private sector into a highly productive industrial sector paying male breadwinner wages on the one hand and into a service sector with low productivity and low paid jobs employing many women on a part-time basis on the other hand. This development towards a two-tier private service sector is likely to be faster and more extensive in the East than in the West of Germany as East German unions have demonstrated greater willingness to give in to employers' demands (see chapter 5).

Growing polarisation of American Society during the 1980s contributed to the success of the Democrats in entering the Presidency in 1993. Clinton's presidency has, however, not led to any radical reduction in the growing polarisation of American Society. Clinton's health reforms and the welfare reforms became watered-down compromises as they had to be negotiated with the Republicans who have since 1994 been the majority party in Congress (see chapter 2). Although the passing of the unpaid parental leave measure was an important achievement for the women's movement, it has only assisted a very small group of women who want to reconcile work and family life. The Clinton administration has enhanced the gender tensions already existing from the greater labour force participation of women by intensifying pressures on women on welfare to participate in paid work. Many unskilled men have not been able to find jobs while women's labour force participation has been rising. The depressed labour market for unskilled men during the 1980s and early 1990s has forced many unskilled men to turn to crime as a mean to support themselves. From the mid-1970s to the mid-1990s, the number of men convicted of crime and sent to prison or jail tripled. In 1993, the share of American men in prison or jail was comparable with the share of long-term unemployed men in many Western European countries (Freeman 1996).

Women's greater engagement in paid work has put a strain on the gender division of work in the private sphere as many men have at the same time lost their breadwinner status. Moreover, the integration of women into paid work has not changed fundamentally the division of work between men and women as women still do bulk of the unpaid work. In the labour market, occupations with a high level of female employment correspond to stereo-typed characteristics of female workers that have been used to justify lower pay to women. Hence, women have moved from the private sphere to the public sphere without challenging men's subordination of women's work (see chapter 4). Hence, women have increasingly become dissatisfied with the prevailing patterns of gender relations. Men, on the other hand, have started to feel threatened by women's inroads into the public sphere. High unemployment among men (Germany and Sweden) and male imprisonment (the United States) have intensified pressures on women to return to the home. Moreover, the economic recession during the early 1990s induced the state to cut welfare benefits (the United States), public sector employment (Sweden) or to maintain its limited support for women's labour force participation (Germany).

International and regional integration is putting pressure on the national modes of regulation that has prevailed during most of the post-war period. Economies have become more interrelated due to growing importance of international trade and regional co-operation. The EU and the NAFTA are examples of regional co-operation while the General Agreement on Trade and Tariffs, the GATT, has been successful in removing some of the barriers to international trade. The EU has used treaties, directives and recommendations to push member-countries into similar directions or to cluster around a certain mode of regulation in the economic sphere. During the early 1990s, tax cuts and a more earnings-related pension system were implemented in order to move Sweden closer to the EU member countries. Hence, the EU membership has been used to justify a less egalitarian society. This development has put a strain on the class compromise prevailing during the post-war period as it was based on redistribution across class and gender. In Germany, pressures from the EU to acknowledge women's rights as workers have been integrated as far as possible into the 'modified' male breadwinner model. The emphasis of the EU on women as workers and the high level of unemployment, especially in East Germany, are putting a strain on the viability of the German male breadwinner model. The United States, on the other hand, holds a hegemonic position in the world, such that its liberal ideology has not been challenged by outside pressures and the NAFTA is an extension of US liberal mode of regulation. The greater dependence on market forces in the United States has led to growing polarisation across class and gender. American women have entered a vicious circle where falling real wages are forcing them to participate or increase their work effort at the same time as greater availability of labour in terms of numbers and hours enables employers to cut wages further.

Conclusion

Hirdman (1990) claims that a new gender contract needs to be established when women have moved into the men's world. The prevailing patterns of hierarchical gender relations do not only come under strain when women are making progress into traditional male areas but also when polarisation across class and gender increases. During the 1960s and 1970s, women's inroads into paid work constituted the main challenge to the male breadwinner model prevailing immediately after World War II. The convergence in women's and men's labour force participation rates has contributed to polarisation across class, especially, where the majority of women have been used to undermine class relations. Moreover, polarisation among women has intensified as they have become integrated into paid work. The extent to which women are able to influence the development of the dual breadwinner model in the near future will depend on their ability to overcome divisions among themselves and on their capacity to build alliances with other disadvantaged groups. The greatest threat to the dual breadwinner model is employers' growing ability to drive wages down. Conflicts over the dual breadwinner model will surge when the income of the dual breadwinner family no longer provides its members with the basic 'necessities' of life.

Women's dissatisfaction is once again mounting as their inclusion into paid work has not brought about gender equality in terms of pay and access to occupations. The solutions to the present gender conflicts will depend on how the divisions among women develop as well as on the ability of the state to initiate settlements. The desire to fight women's subordination is still a unifying force among women but pay and occupational divisions in the labour market have created divisions among women. Many working class women see the male-breadwinner mode as a means to escape physically demanding and low paid work. Female-dominated occupations are in most cases low paid jobs but may offer good career opportunities. Women in male-dominated sectors are, on the other hand, segregated in jobs at the lower end of the male job-hierarchy. Hence, the road to greater equality for women in female-dominated occupations is through equal pay for comparable work while the main concern of women in male-dominated occupations is that of equal access to high paying jobs. What happens in the future will depend on the size of the three groups of women but the interaction of social structures will determine how labour markets develop. The greater the number of 'bad' jobs, the greater the number of women pulling into the direction of the male breadwinner model. The pressure towards the dual breadwinner model will intensify the greater the number of women regarding paid work as a road to gender equality.

In Sweden, the labour market has become divided into the female-dominated public sector and the male-dominated private sector. However, gender equality has been attained by high labour force participation of women and compressed wage structure across sectors. This pattern of gender relations or the egalitarian regime of gender relations is based on the state's commitment to full employment and the union's commitment to solidaristic pay policy. The gender and class equality project has, however, come under strain. High unemployment and greater pay differentials have led to growing gender and generational tensions. In addition, the state has become more sensitive to the needs of capital as employers have been able to strengthen their position. The economic recession of the early 1990s and Sweden's membership of the European Union have contributed to this shift in the capital-labour relations. Hence, the state has intensified the trend towards gender and class inequality by curtailing redistribution through the tax system and by placing greater emphasis on labour market status in welfare policies. The growth in inequality is, however, not likely to lead to fundamental changes in the egalitarian regime of gender relations. The Social Democrats need the support of women and the unions to remain in power and thus they will try to limit the growth in inequality.

While the development in the United States has been towards greater integration of women into paid work, the trend in Germany has been towards interrupted labour force participation. The German state has sought to ensure that women continue to take on their caring responsibilities within the family as advocated by the Catholic Church. The state has, thereby, counteracted some of the integration tendencies of capitalism and the growing aspirations of women to work. Hence, the ecclesiastical regime of gender relations is still based on the male breadwinner model but with important adjustments. Women are no longer constrained to the private sphere but engage in paid work before and after periods of domestic responsibilities. The sustainablity of the modified male breadwinner model will depend on the state's ability to find resources to subsidise care work within the family. If the state is not able to expand its support for care within the family, the pressures for greater integration of women into paid work can no longer be withheld and the modified male breadwinner model will move towards the dual breadwinner model.

After unification, the East German mode of regulation of gender relations underwent a transition from the dual breadwinner model back to the West Germany male breadwinner model. This transition was made possible through massive financial transfers from the West to the East Germany. However, the transition is not as stable as it appears. The German state is now being pressed through its membership in the European Monetary Union EMU to cut its budget deficit. Moreover, the high level of unemployment in East Germany has hindered many East German men from becoming male breadwinners. In addition, wages in East Germany are still lower than in West Germany. Hence, the male breadwinner model is more of an ideology in the East than in the West of Germany. In addition, many East German women have been forced to withdraw involuntarily from paid work but their work commitment is still greater than that of West German women. Hence, the support for the male breadwinner model in East Germany is likely to erode when the German state reduces its financial support for the East German economy. Hence, we are likely to see growing regional differences in the patterns of gender relations in Germany.

In the United States, the trend has been towards greater labour force participation of women that the state has enhanced through its employment policies. Hence, the influences of the market forces have been increased in the liberal regime of gender relations. The state has, however, not eroded its support for families in the tax and pension systems. Moreover, the move from the male breadwinner model has not led to greater equality for all women since it has involved polarisation across class and gender. Hence, a group of women has lost out as they have not kept up with women moving up the job-ladder. Moreover, many unskilled men have been pushed out of the labour market, while women have increased their participation in paid work. The need of capital for cheap and flexible labour has not been counteracted as the state has been more open to the interests of capital than labour and other interest groups. The polarisation across class and gender has resulted in a growing number of people living in poverty in the United States. Hence, the state has had to increase its spending on policing and imprisoning the poor to prevent social unrest to take place. It will, however, become increasingly difficult to repress the growing number of deprived people who will soon be joined by poor mothers. Growing social unrest may force the federal government to implement new programs aimed at improving the deficiencies of the workfare programs.

In the future, gender tensions will increasingly involve conflicts between the parliamentary system and the market (the stock market). Women have started and will continue to use their vote and political influences to achieve higher levels of service provisions and protection against discrimination in the labour market. As these measures involve in most cases increases in the state's expenditures and an active role of the state in the labour market, the stock market will protest each time political parties promoting women's demands come into power. An effective way to protest is to move money out of the economy which will lead to lower share values and may drive the interest-rate up. Moreover, employers in North-America and Western Europe appear to be pressing for the expansion of low paid jobs as a means to deal with greater international competition. This low pay policy can not be carried out without the active support of the state involving cuts in taxes and welfare benefits as well as measures to prevent social unrest, i.e. greater expenditure on policing. As a reaction to this development, men will with the support of the labour unions demand that the state and capitalists spend more on promoting growth in the male-dominated industrial sector, i.e. high technology industries. Women, on the other hand, will protest against this industrial policy as it requires the state to remove resources from services where the majority of women work to the industrial sector. In addition, ideology will increasingly come to shape gender relations in the future. Religious groups feeling threatened by the break-up of the family as well as political parties rejecting the selfishness fostered by the market are becoming popular among those dissatisfied with the capitalist development. The size of these groups will grow as the polarisation of societies increases. Moreover, the regulation of gender relations appears to be shifting away from the national level to the local level on the one hand and from the national level to the international level on the other hand. The consequence of weaker national states is likely to be greater regional differences as they have played an important role in equalising resources across communities. Growing regional inequalities will add another dimension to the polarisation of societies. Future research on gender relations focusing on actors and structures at the collective level needs to be ware of the growing conflicts between the parliamentary system and the market on the one hand and between groups adhering to religious family values and parties fighting for a more just society on the other hand. Finally, the implications of greater supranational and local regulation for the development of gender relations need to be explored.

Notes

[1]In Iceland, the transformation to more egalitarian gender relations has been much more incomplete and contradictory than in Sweden as the Icelandic state has been much more reluctant to intervene in the private sphere or to provide services previously performed in the family. During the independence struggle which ended with independence from Denmark in 1944, images were used that emphasised motherhood as the most noble role of Icelandic women (see Björnsdóttir 1989). Today, the main governing political party, the Independent Party, and the Women's List still refer to women as mothers in their political agenda (Kristmundsdóttir 1996). Permanent labour shortage and employers' unwillingness/inability to pay male breadwinner wages and women's greater educational attainments have been the main factors contributing to a high labour force participation Icelandic women. In 1996, 77 per cent of women were engaged in paid work. At the same time, a fertility rate of 2.1 was the highest in Iceland among the Nordic countries (Mósesdóttir 1998). The gender pay gap has been relatively wide as women have first and foremost mothers earning additional income and the unions' regulation of

wages has been weak (Mósesdóttir 1989; Mósesdóttir 1993). Hence, Iceland has high female labour force participation, highly gender segregated labour market and a relatively large gender pay gap.

[2]The EITC means that a family with two children earning in 1996 between $11.610 and $28.490 faces higher marginal tax rate than the richest Americans (McIntyre 1996). The median family income of female-headed households in was $19.691 (Mishel et al. 1997:51).

Bibliography

Albelda, R.P., Lalbelda, R. and Tilly, C. (1997), *Glass Ceilings and Bottomless Pits: Women's Work, Women's Poverty*, South End Press, New York.

Anker, R. (1998), *Gender and Jobs. Sex Segregation of Occupations in the World*, International Labour Organisation, Geneva.

Arrow, K. J. (1951), *Social Choice and Individual Values*, Cowles Foundation, John Wiley and Sons, New York.

Atkinson, J. (1986), 'Employment Flexibility in Internal and External Labour Markets', in R. Dahrendorf, E. Köhler and F. Piotet (eds.), *New Forms of Work and Activity*, European Foundation for the Improvement of Living and Working Conditions, New York.

Badgett, M.V.L. and Hartmann, H. (1995), 'The Effectiveness of Equal Employment Opportunity Policies', in M. C. Simms (ed.), *Economic Perspectives on Affirmative Action*, Joint Center for Political and Economic Studies, Washington DC.

Bailey, K. D. (1994), *Typologies and Taxonomies. An Introduction to Classification Techniques*, Sage University Paper series on Quantitative Applications in the Social Sciences, Sage, London.

von Baratta, M. (1995), *Der Fischer Weltalmanach 1996*, Fischer Taschenbuch Verlag, Berlin.

Becker, G. S. (1957), *The Economics of Discrimination*, University of Chicago Press, Chicago.

Becker, G. S. (1964), *Human Capital*, Columbia University Press, New York.

Becker, G. S. (1965), 'A Theory of the Allocation of Time', *Economic Journal*, vol. 75, pp. 493-517.

Becker, G. S. (1981), *A Treatise on the Family*, Harvard University Press, Cambridge.

Begg, D., Fischer, S. and Dornbusch, R. (1994), *Economics*, 4th ed., McGraw-Hill Book Company, London.

Bergqvist, C. (1994), *Mäns makt och kvinnors intressen*, Acta Universitais Upsaliensis, Uppsala.

Bernstein, J. (1997), *The Challenge of Moving from Welfare to Work. Depressed Labor Market Awaits Those Leaving the Rolls*, EPI Issue Brief, no. 116, Economic Policy Institute, Washington DC.

Bertramsen, R. B. (1991), 'From the Capitalist State to the Political Economy', in R. B. Bertramsen, J. P. Frölund Thomsen and J. Torfing (eds.), *State Economy and Society*, Unwin Hyman, London.

Bettio, F., Prechal, S., Bimonte, S. and Giorgi S. (1998), *Care in Europe*, joint report of the Gender and Employment Network of Experts and the Gender and Law Network of Experts for the Equal Opportunities Unit, DGV, of the European Commission.

Betz, H. and Welsh, H. A. (1995), 'The PDS in the New German Party System', *German Politics*, vol. 4, pp. 92-111.

Björnsdóttir, I. D. (1989), 'Public View and Private Voices', in P. Durrenberger and G. Pálsson (eds.), *The Anthropology of Iceland*, Iowa University Press, Iowa.

Blackbrun, R., Jarman, J. and Siltanen, J. (1991), *International Comparison in Occupational Gender Segregation: Assessing Two Popular Measures*, working Paper no. 9, Sociological Research Group, Social and Political Sciences, University of Cambridge, Cambridge.

Blau, F. D. (1993), 'Gender and Economic Outcomes: the Role of Wage Structure', *Labour*, vol. 7, pp. 73-92.

Blau, F. D. and Hendricks, W. (1979), 'Occupational Segregation by Sex: Trends and Prospects', *The Journal of Human Resources*, vol. 14, pp. 197-210.

Blau, F. D. and Kahn, L. M. (1996), 'International Differences in Male Wage Inequality: Institutions versus Market Forces', *Journal of Political Economy*, vol. 104, pp. 791-837.

Blossfeld, H. and Rohwer, G. (1997), 'Part-Time Work in West Germany', in H. Blossfeld and C. Hakim (eds.), *Between Equalisation and Marginalization. Women Working Part-Time in Europe and the United States of America*, Oxford University Press, Oxford.

Boje, T. P. (1993), *Women between Work and Family*. Paper presented at the Conference on Comparative Research on Welfare States in Transition, Oxford 9-12 September.

Bonefeld, W. (1993), 'Crisis of Theory', *Capital & Class*, vol. 50, pp. 25-48.

Borchorst, A. (1989), *The Scandinavian Welfare States - Patriarchal, Gender Neutral or Women-friendly?*, Institute of Political Science, University of Aarhus, Aarhus.

Borchorst, A. (1994), 'Welfare State Regimes, Women's Interests, and the EC', in D. Sainsbury (ed.), *Gendering Welfare States*, Sage, London.

Borchorst, A. and Siim, B. (1987), 'Women and the Advanced Welfare State - A New Kind of Patriarchal Power?', in A. S. Sassoon (ed.), *Women and the State. The Shifting Boundaries of Public and Private*, Unwin Hyman, London.

Braudel, F. (1979), *The Wheels of Commerce*, Harper and Row, New York.

Brenner, R. (1998), 'The Economics of Global Turbulance', *New Left Review*, vol. 229, pp. 1-264.

Brosnan, P., Rea, D., and Wilson, M. (1995), 'Labour Market Segmentation and the State: the New Zealand Experience', *Cambridge Journal of Economics*, vol. 19, pp. 667-696.

Buchholz-Will, W. (1995), 'Wann wird aus diesem Traum Wirklichkeit? Die gewerkschaftliche Frauenarbeit in der Bundesrepublik', in F. Hervé (ed.) *Geschichte der Deutschen Frauenbewegung*, Papyrossa, Köln.

Büchtemann, C. F. and Quack, S. (1990), 'How Precarious is "Non-Standard" Employment? Evidence for West Germany', *Cambridge Journal of Economics*, vol. 14. pp. 315-329.

Campbell, C. and Rockman B. A. (1996), *The Clinton Presidency. First Appraisals*, Catham House Publishers, New Jersey.

Chamberlayne, P. (1994), 'Women and Social Policy', in J. Clasen and R. Freeman (eds.), *Social Policy in Germany*, Harvester Wheatsheaf, Hemel Hempstead Hertfordshire.

Chapman, J. (1993), *Politics, Feminism and the Reformation of Gender*, Routledge, London.

Charles, M. (1992), 'Cross-National Variation in Occupational Sex Segregation', *American Sociological Review*, vol. 57, pp. 483-502.

Charles, M. and Grusky, D. B. (1995), 'Models for Describing the Underlying Structure of Sex Segregation', *American Journal of Sociology*, vol. 4, pp. 931-971.

Clasen, J. (1994), 'Social Security - the Core of the German Employment-Centred Social state', in J. Clasen, and R. Freeman (eds.), *Social Policy in Germany*, Harvester Wheatsheaf, Hemel Hempstead, Hertfordshire.

Cochrane, A. and Clarke, J. (1993), *Comparing Welfare States. Britain in International Context*, Sage, London.

Cockburn, C. (1985), *Machinery of Dominance. Women, Men and Technical Know-How*, Pluto Press, London.

Compston, H. (1995), 'Union Participation in Economic Policy Making in Scandinavia, 1970-1993', *West European Politics*, vol. 18, pp. 98-115.

Connell, R. W. (1987), *Gender and Power*, Polity Press, Cambridge.

Connell, R. W. (1990), 'The State, Gender, and Sexual Politics. Theory and Appraisal', *Theory and Society*, vol. 19, pp. 507-544.

Conradt, D. P. (1993), 'Part Three: Germany', in M. D. Hancock et al., *Politics in Western Europe*, Macmillian Press, London.

Craig, C., Rubery, J., Tarling, R. and Wilkinson, F. (1985), 'Economic, Social and Political Factors in the Operation of the Labour Market', in B. Roberts, R. Finnegan and D. Gallie (eds.), *New Approaches to Economic Life. Economic Restructuring: Unemployment and the Social Division of Labour*, University Press, Manchester.

Crompton, R. (1997), *Women & Work in Modern Britain*, Oxford University Press, Oxford.

Crompton, R. and Harris, F. (1998), 'Explaining Women's Employment Patterns: "Orientations to Work" Revisited', *British Journal of Sociology*, vol. 49, pp. 118-149.

Dahlerup, D. (1986), *The New Women's Movement. Feminism and Political Power in Europe and the USA*, Sage, London.

Dahlerup, D. (1987), 'Confusing Concepts - Confusing Reality: a Theoretical Discussion of the Patriarchal State', in A. S. Sassoon (ed.), *Women and the State. The Shifting Boundaries of Public and Private*, Unwin Hyman, London.

Daly, M. (1996), *The Gender Division of Welfare: The British and German Welfare States Compared*, doctoral thesis submitted at the European University Institute, Florence.

Daly, M. (1997), 'Welfare States under Pressure: Cash Benefits in European Welfare States over the Last Ten Years', *Journal of European Social Policy*, vol. 7, pp. 129-149.

Deakin, S. and Muckenberger, U. (1992), 'Deregulation and European Labour Markets', in A. Castro, P. Méhaut and J. Rubery (eds.), *International Integration and Labour Market Organisation*, Academic Press, London.

Deakin, S. and Wilkinson, F. (1991/2), 'Social Policy and Economic Efficiency: The Deregulation of the Labour Market in Britain', *Critical Social Policy*, vol. 33, pp. 40-61.

Delsen, L. (1998), 'When do Men Work Part-Time?', in J. O'Reilly and C. Fagan (eds.), *Part-Time Prospects. An International Comparison of Part-Time Work in Europe, North America and the Pacific Rim*, Routledge, London.

Delsen, L. and Van Veen, T. (1992), 'The Swedish Model: Relevant for Other European Countries?', *British Journal of Industrial Relations*, vol. 30, pp. 83-105.

Dex, S. and Shaw, L. (1986), *British and American Women at Work. Do Equal Opportunities Policies Matter?*, Macmillan, London.

Drobnic. S. and Wittig, I. (1997), 'Part-Time Work in the United States of America', in H. Blossfeld & C. Hakim (eds.), *Between Equalisation and Marginalization. Women Working Part-Time in Europe and the United States of Amercia*, Oxford University Press, Oxford.

Duncan, S. (1996), 'Obstacles to a Successful Equal Opportunities Policy in the European Union', *The European Journal of Women's Studies*, vol. 3, pp. 399-422.

Duncan, O. D. and Duncan, B. (1955), 'A Methodological Analysis of Segregation Indices', *American Sociological Review*, vol. 20, pp. 210-217.

Edelman, P. (1997), 'The Worst Thing Bill Clinton has done', *The Atlantic Monthly*, vol. 279, pp. 43-58.

Eduards, M. L. (1991), 'The Swedish Gender Model: Productivity, Pragmatism and Paternalism', *West European Politics*, vol. 14, pp. 96-121.

Eduards, M. L. (1992), 'Against the Rules of the Game. On the Importance of Women's Collective Actions', in M. L. Eduards (ed.), *Rethinking Change. Current Swedish Feminist Research*, Humanistisk-Samhällsvetenskapliga Forskningsrådet, Stockholm.

Eisenstein, Z. R. (1981), *The Radical Future of Liberal Feminism*, Longman, New York.

Eisenstein, Z. R. (1984), *Feminism and Sexual Equality: Crisis in Liberal America*, Monthly Review Press, New York.

Ellingsæter, A. L. (1995), *Gender, Work and Social Change. Beyond Dualistic Thinking*, Institute for Social Research, Oslo.

Elman R. A. (1995), 'The State's Equality for Women: Sweden's Equality Ombudsman', in D. M. Stetson and A. G. Mazur (eds.), *Comparative State Feminism*, Sage, London.

Esping-Andersen, G. (1985), *Politics Against Markets*, Princeton University Press, Princeton.

Esping-Andersen, G. (1990), *The Three Worlds of Welfare Capitalism*, Polity Press, Cambridge.

Esping-Andersen, G. (1992), 'The Three Political Economies of the Welfare State', in J. E. Kolberg (ed.), *The Study of Welfare State Regimes,* M. E. Sharpe, New York.

Ferree, M. M. (1995), 'Making Equality: The Women's Affairs Offices in the Federal Republic of Germany', in D. M. Stetson and A. G. Mazur (eds.), *Comparative State Feminism*, Sage, London.

Fichter, M. (1997), 'Institutional Transfer and the Transformation of Labour Relations in East(ern) Germany: Lessons for Central and Eastern Europe?', *Transfer,* vol. 3, pp. 390-407.

Firestone, S. (1970), *The Dialectic of Sex*, Bantam Books, New York.

Flockton, C. and Esser, J. (1992), 'Labour Market Problems and Labour Market Policy', in G. Smith, W. E. Paterson, and P. H. Merkl (eds.), *Developments in German Politics*, Macmillan, London.

Folbre, N. (1994), *Who Pays for the Kids?*, Routledge, New York.

Foster, J. (1991), 'The Institutionalist (Evolutionary) School', in D. Mair and A. G. Miller (eds.), *A Modern Guide to Economic Thought. An Introduction to Comparative Schools of Thought in Economics*, University Press, Cambridge.

Fölster, S. and Peltzman, S. (1995), 'Samhällsekonomiska kostnader av regleringar och bristande konkurrens i Sverige', in R. B. Freeman, B. Swedenborg and R. Topel (eds.), *Välfärdsstat i omvandling. Amerikanskt perspektive på den svenska modellen*, NBER rapporten, SNS Forlag, Stockholm.

Franzway, S., Court, D. and Connell, R. W. (1989), *Staking a Claim. Feminism, Bureaucracy and the State*, Allen & Unwin, Sydney.

Fraser, N. (1989), *Unruly Practices. Power, Discourse and Gender in Contemporary Social Theory*, Polity Press, Oxford.

Freeman, C. and Perez, C. (1988), 'Structural Crises of Adjustment: Business Cycles and Investment Behaviour', in G. Dosi, C. Freeman, R. Nelson, G. Silverberg and L. Soete (eds.), *Technical Change and Economic Theory*, Pinter, London.

Freeman, R. and Clasen J. (1994), 'The German Social State: An Introduction', in J. Clasen, and R. Freeman (eds.), *Social Policy in Germany*, Harvester Wheatsheaf, Hemel Hempstead, Hertfordshire.

Freeman R. B. (1996), 'Why Do so Many Young American Men Commit Crimes and What Might We Do about It', *Journal of Economic Perspectives*, vol. 10, pp. 25-42.

Furåker, B., Johansson, L. and Lind, J. (1990), 'Unemployment and Labour Market Policies in the Scandinavian Countries', *Acta Sociologica*, vol. 33, pp.141-164.

Ganssman, H. (1993), 'After Unification: Problems Facing the German Welfare State', *Journal of European Social Policy*, vol. 3, pp. 79-90.

Gibowski, W. G. (1995), 'Election Trends in Germany. An Analysis of the Second General Election in Reunited Germany', *German Politics*, vol. 4, pp. 26-53.

Giddens. A. (1993), *Sociology*, 2nd ed., Polity Press, Oxford.

Ginn, J., Arber, S., Brannen, J., Dale, A., Dex, S., Elias, P., Moss, P., Pahl, J. Roberts, C., and Rubery, J. (1996), 'Feminist Fallacies: A Reply to Hakim on Women's Employment', *British Journal of Sociology*, vol. 47, pp. 167-174.

Ginsburg, N. (1992), *Divisions of Welfare. A Critical Introduction to Comparative Social Policy*, Sage, London.

Ginsburg, H. L., Zaccone, J., Goldberg, G. S., Collins, S. D. and Rosen, S. M. (1997), 'Editorial Introduction', *Economic and Industrial Democracy*, vol. 18, pp. 5-34.

Gitter, R. J. and Scheuer, M. (1997), 'U.S. and German Youths: Unemployment and the Transition from School to Work', *Monthly Labor Review*, March, pp. 16-20.

Goldin, C. (1990), *Understanding the Gender Gap. An Economic History of American Women*, Oxford University Press, Oxford.

Gonäs, L. and Lehto, A. in collaboration with Sjørup K. and Mósesdóttir, L. (1997), 'Overview of Literature - Scandinavian Languages Area', in J. Plantenga and J. Rubery (eds.), *State of the Art Review on Women and the Labour Market*, Report for the Equal Opportunities Unit, DG V of the European Commission, University of Utrecht, Utrecht.

Gonäs, L. and Spånt, A. (1996), *Trends and Prospects for Women's Employment in the 1990s. The Swedish Report.* Report for the European Commission, EC Network on the Situation of Women in the Labour Market, UMIST, Manchester.

Goodman, W. (1995), 'Boom in Day Care Industry the Result of many Social Changes', *Monthly Labor Review*, August, pp. 23-28.

Gordon, L. (1990), *Women, the State, and Welfare*, The University of Wisconsin Press, Madison.

Gough, I. (1979), *The Political Economy of the Welfare State*, Macmillan, London.

le Grand, C. (1994), 'Löneskillnaderna i Sverige: förändring och nuvarande struktur', in Fritzell, J. and Lundberg (eds.), *Vardagens villkor.*

Levnadsförhållanden i Sverige under tre decennier, Brombergs Bokförlag, Stockholm.

Grimshaw, D. and Rubery, J. (1996), *The Concentration of Women's Employment and Relative Occupational Pay: A Statistical Framework for Comparative Analysis*, OECD discussion paper, Directorate for Education, Employment, Labour and Social Affairs, Paris.

Gustafsson, S. (1991), 'Ekonomisk teori för tvåförsörjarfamiljen', *Ekonomisk Debatt*, vol. 91, pp. 503-514.

Hagen, E. and Jenson, J. (1988), 'Paradoxes and Promises', in J. Jensson, E. Hagen and C. Reddy (eds.), *Feminization of the Labour Force. Paradoxes and Promises*, Polity Press, Cambridge.

Hakim, C. (1995), 'Five Feminist Myths about Women's Employment', *British Journal of Sociology*, vol. 46, pp. 429-455.

Hancock, M. D. (1993), 'Part Five: Sweden', in M. D. Hancock, D. P. Conradt, B. Guy Peters and W. Safran (eds.), *Politics in Western Europe*, Macmillian Press, London.

Hanmer, J. and Saunders, S. (1984), *Well-Founded Fear: A Community Study of Violence to Women*, Croom Helm, London.

Hantrais, L. (1995), *Social Policy in the European Union*, London, Macmillian Press.

Hartmann, H. (1979), 'Capitalism, Patriarchy and Job Segregation by Sex', in Z. R. Eisenstein (ed.), *Capitalist Patriarchy*, Monthly Review Press, New York.

Hartmann, H. (1981), 'The Unhappy Marriage of Marxism and Feminism: Towards a More Progressive Union', in L. Sargent (ed.), *Women and Revolution. A Discussion of the Unhappy Marriage of Marxism and Feminism*, Pluto Press, London.

Hartmann, H. and Aaronson, S. (1994), 'Pay Equity and Women's Wage Increases: Success in the States. A Model for the Nation', *Duke Journal of Gender Law & Policy*, vol. 69, pp. 69-87.

Hernes, H. M. (1987a), *Welfare State and Woman Power. Essays in State Feminism*, Norwegian University Press, Oslo.

Hernes, H. M. (1987b), 'Women and the Welfare State: The Transition from Private to Public Dependence', in A. S. Sassoon (ed.), *Women and the State. The Shifting Boundaries of Public and Private*, Unwin Hyman, London.

Hirdman, Y. (1990), 'Genussystemet' in Statens Offentliga Utredningar *Demokrati och makt i Sverige*, no. 44, Statens Offentliga Utredningar (SOU), Stockholm.

Hirdman, Y. (1994), *Women - from Possibility to Problem? Gender Conflict in the Welfare State - The Swedish Model*, research report no. 3, The Swedish Center for Working Life, Stockholm.

Holton, R. J. (1993), *Economy and Society*, Routledge, London.

Hoskyns, C. (1992), 'The European Community's Policy on Women in the Context of 1992', *Women's Studies International Forum*, vol. 15, pp. 21-28.

Hoskyns, C. (1996), *Integrating Gender. Women Law and Politics in the European Union*, Verso, London.

Howes, C. (1995), 'Long Term Economic Strategy and Employment Growth in the US: An Analysis of Clintons' Economic Policies', *Contributions to Political Economy*, vol. 14, pp.1-31.

Humphries, J. (1995), 'Economics, Gender and Equal Opportunities', in J. Humphries and J. Rubery (eds.), *Economics of Equal Opportunities*, Manchester: Equal Opportunities Commission.

Humphries, J. and Rubery, J. (1984), 'The Reconstitution of the Supply Side of the Labour Market: The Relative Autonomy of Social Reproduction', *Cambridge Journal of Economics*, vol. 8, pp. 331-346.

Humphries, J. and Rubery, J. (1988), 'Recession and Exploitation. British Women in a Changing Workplace', in J. Jenson, E. Hagen and C. Reddy (eds.), *Feminization of the Labour Force*, Polity Press, Cambridge.

Humphries J. and Rubery, J. (1995), 'Introduction', in J. Humphries and J. Rubery (eds.), *Economics of Equal Opportunities*, Equal Opportunities Commission, Manchester.

Hutchens, R. (1994), 'The United States: Employer Policies for Discouraging Work by Older People', in F. Naschold and B. de Vroom (eds.), *Regulating Employment and Welfare. Company and National Policies of Labour Force Participation at the End of Worklife in Industrial Countries*, Walter de Gruyter, Berlin.

Hyman, R. (1994), 'Introduction: Economic Restructuring, Market Liberalism and the Future of National Industrial Relations Systems', in R. Hyman and A. Ferner (eds.), *New Frontiers in European Industrial Relations*, Blackwell, Oxford.

International Labour Office (1990), *Yearbook of Labour Statistics*, ILO, Geneva.

International Labour Office (1996), *Yearbook of Labour*, ILO, Geneva.

International Labour Office (1997), *Yearbook of Labour*, ILO, Geneva.

Jacobs, K. and Rein, M. (1994), 'Early Retirement: Stability, Reversal, or Redefinition', in F. Naschold and B. de Vroom (eds.), *Regulating Employment and Welfare. Company and National Policies of Labour Force Participation at the End of Worklife in Industrial Countries*, Walter de Gruyter, Berlin.

Jacobsen, J. P. (1994), *The Economics of Gender*, Blackwell, Oxford.

Jenson, J. (1989), 'Paradigms and Political Discourse: Protective Legislation in France and the United States Before 1914', *Canadian Journal of Political Science*, vol. XXII, pp. 235-258.

Jenson, J. (1990), 'Was it for "Want of Courage"? The Ebbing of Canada's Maternal Feminism after Entering the Electoral Institutions', in M. F. Katzenstein and H. Skjeie (eds.), *Going Public. National Histories of Women's Enfranchisement and Women's Participation within State Institutions*, Institute for Social Research, Oslo.

Jenson, J. and Mahon, R. (1993), 'Representing Solidarity: Class, Gender and the Crisis in Social-Democratic Sweden', *The New Left Review*, vol. 201, pp. 79-100.

Jessop, B. (1982), *The Capitalist State*, Martin Robertson, Oxford.

Jessop, B. (1990), *State Theory*, Polity Press, Cambridge.

Jessop, B. (1991), 'The Welfare State in the Transition from Fordism to Post-Fordism', in B. Jessop, H. Kastendiek, K. Nielsen and O. K. Pedersen (eds.) *The Politics of Flexibility. Restructuring State and Industry in Britain, Germany and Scandinavia*, Edward Elgar, Aldershot.

Jessop, B. (1995), 'The Regulation Approach, Governance and Post-Fordism', *Economy and Society*, vol. 24, pp. 307-333.

Jones, C. (1993), *New Perspectives on the Welfare State in Europe*, Routledge, London.

Jonsson, I. (1989), 'Hegemonic Politics and Capitalist Restructuring' *Þjóðmál: Yearbook of Political Economy and Social Sciences*, Félags- og hagvísindastofnun Íslands, vol. 1, pp. 216-349.

Jonsson, I. (1991), *Hegemonic Politics and Accumulation Strategies in Iceland 1944-1990. Long Waves in the World Economy, Regimes of Accumulation and Uneven Development. Small States, Microstates and Problems of World Adjustment*, Doctoral Dissertation, University of Sussex, Brighton.

Jonsson, I. (1993), 'Regimes of Accumulation, Microeconomies and Hegemonic Politics', *Capital and Class*, vol. 50, pp. 49-97.

Jonung, C. (1984), 'Patterns of Occupational Segregation by Sex in the Labour Market', in G. Schmid and R. Weitzel, *Sex Discrimination and Equal Opportunity. The Labour Market and Employment Policy*, St. Martin's Press, New York.

Jonung, C. and Persson, I. (1993), 'Women and Market Work: The Misleading Tale of Participation Rates in International Comparison', *Work, Employment & Society*, vol. 7, pp. 259-274.

Kalberg, S. (1994), *Marx, Weber's Comparative - Historical Sociology*, University of Chicago Press, Chicago.

Kangas, O. (1994), 'The Merging of Welfare State Models? Past and Present Trends in Finnish and Swedish Social Policy', *Journal of European Social Policy*, vol. 4, pp. 79-94.

Kaplan, G. (1992), *Contemporary Western European Feminism*, Allen & Unwin, Sydney.

Katzenstein, M. F. (1987), 'Comparing the Feminist Movements of the United States and Western Europe: An Overview', in M. F. Katzenstein and C. McClurg Mueller (eds.), *The Women's Movements of the United States and Western Europe*, Temple University Press, Philadelphia.

Katzenstein, M. F. (1990), 'Feminism within American Institutions: Unobtrusive Mobilization in the 1980s', *Signs*, vol. 16, pp. 27-54.

Katzenstein, M. F. (1992), 'Die Instituionalisierung des amerikanischen Feminismus: Kampf innerhalb des Systems', *Berl. J. Soziol*, vol. 1, pp. 29-37.

Kerr, C., Dunlop, J. T., Harbison, F. H. and Myers, C. A. (1960), *Industrialism and Industrial Man*, Harvard University Press, Cambridge.

Kiely, R. (1995), *Sociology & Development. The Impasse and Beyond*, UCL Press, London.

Koistinen, P. and Ostner, I. (1994), 'Comparing and Learning about Differences', in P. Koistinen, and I. Ostner (eds.), *Women and Markets*, University of Tampere, Tampere.

Kolinsky, E. (1992), 'Women in the New Germany; The East-West Divide', in G. Smith et al., (eds.), *Developments in German Politics*, Macmillan, London.

Kristmundsdóttir, S. D. (1996), 'Fjölskylda, frelsi og réttlæti', *Ný Félagsrit*, Reykjavík.

Lane, C. (1991), 'Industrial Reorganization in Europe: Patterns of Convergence and Divergence in Germany, France and Britain', *Work, Employment and Society*, vol. 5, pp. 515-539.

Lane, C. (1993), 'Gender and the Labour Market in Europe: Britain, Germany and France Compared', *The Sociological Review*, vol. 41, pp. 274-301.

Lane, C. (1994), 'Is Germany Following the British Path? A Comparative Analysis of Stability and Change', *Industrial Relations Journal*, vol. 25, pp. 187-198.

Lash, S. and Urry, J. (1987), *The End of Organised Capitalism*, Polity Press, Cambridge.

Layard, R. (1997), 'Sweden's Road Back to Full Employment', *Economic and Industrial Democracy*, vol. 18, pp. 99-118.

Leborgne, D. and Lipietz, A. (1987), *New Technologies, New Modes of Regulation; Some Spatial Implications*, CEPREMAP, Paris.

Leborgne, D. and Lipietz, A. (1991), 'Two Social Strategies in the Production of New Industrial Spaces', in G. Benko and M. Dunford (eds.), *Industrial Change & Regional Development*, Belhaven Press, London.

Leira, A. (1993), 'The "Women-Friendly" Welfare State?: The case of Norway and Sweden', in J. Lewis (ed.), *Women and Social Policies in Europe. Work, Family and the State*, Edward Elgar, Aldershot.

Lewis, J. (1992), 'Gender and the Development of Welfare Regimes', *Journal of European Social Policy*, vol. 2, pp. 159-173.

Lewis, J. and Åström, G. (1992), 'Equality, Difference, and State Welfare: Labour Market and Family Policies in Sweden', *Feminist Studies*, vol. 18, pp. 56-87.

Lindblad, I., Stalvant, C., Wahlback D. and Wiklund, D. (1984), *Politik i Norden. En Jämförande Översikt*, Liber, Stockholm.

Lovenduski, J. and Randall, V. (1993), *Contemporary Feminist Politics. Women and Power in Britain*, Oxford University Press, Oxford.

Löfström, Å. (1995), *Women and the European Employment Rate: The Causes and Consequenses of Variations in Female Activity and Employment Patterns,* report for the European Commission, the EC Network on the Situation of Women in the Labour Market, UMIST, Manchester.

Mahon, R. (1991), 'From Solidaristic Wages to Solidaristic Work: A Post-Fordist Historic Compromise for Sweden?', *Economic and Industrial Democracy*, vol. 12, pp. 295-325.

Maier, F. (1995), 'Skill Formation and Equal Opportunity - A Comparative Perspective', in J. Humphries and J. Rubery (eds.), *Economics of Equal Opportunities*, Equal Opportunities Commission, Manchester.

Maier, F., Quack, S., Carl. A., and Strunk, S. (1993), *Wage Determination and Sex Segregation in Employment in West Germany*, report for the European Commission. Working Paper, the EC Network on the Situation of Women in the Labour Market, UMIST, Manchester.

Maier, F., Quack, S., Martschink, A., and Rapp, Z. (1996), *Trends and Prospects for Women's Employment in the 1990s*, report for the European Commission, the EC Network on the Situation of Women in the Labour Market, UMIST, Manchester.

Maleck-Lewy, E. (1995), 'Between Self-Determination and State Supervision: Women and the Abortion Law in Post-Unification Germany', *Social Politics*, vol. 2, pp. 62-75.

Marklund, S. (1992), 'The Decomposition of Social Policy in Sweden', *Scandinavian Journal of Social Welfare*, vol. 1, pp. 2-11.

McDonagh, E. L. (1990), 'The Gendered American State and Women's Right to Vote: The Nexus of Power Politics and Republican Motherhood in the Progressive Era', in M. F. Katzenstein and H. Skjeie (eds.), *Going Public. National Histories of Women's Enfranchisement and Women's Participation within State Institutions*, Institute for Social Research, Oslo.

McIntosh, M. (1978), 'The State and the Oppression of Women', in A. Kuhn and A. M. Wolpe (eds.), *Feminism and Materialism*, Routledge and Kegan Paul, London.

McKay, D. (1993), *American Politics & Society*, 3rd edition, Blackwell, Oxford.

Melling, J. (1991), 'Industrial Capitalism and the Welfare of the State: the Role of Employers in the Comparative Development of Welfare States. A Review of Recent Research', *Sociology*, vol. 25, pp. 219-239.

Meyer, M. H. (1996), 'Making Claims as Workers or Wives: The Distribution of Social Security Benefits', *American Sociological Review*, vol. 61, pp. 449-465.

Meyer, T. (1994), 'Emancipatory or Patriarchal? The Impact of the German and British Welfare States as Employers on Female Economic Independence', in D. Sainsbury (ed.), *Gendering Welfare States*, Sage, London.

Michon, F. (1992), 'The Institutional Forms of Work and Employment: Towards the Construction of an International Historical and Comparative Approach?', in A. Castro, P. Méhaut and J. Rubery (eds.), *International Integration and Labour Market Organisation*, Academic Press, London.

Midgley, J. (1995), *Social Development. The Development Perspective in Social Welfare*, Sage, London.

Millar J. and Warman, A. (1996), *Family Obligations in Europe*, Family Policy Studies Centre, London.

Mincer, J. (1962), 'Labor Force Participation of Married Women: A Study of Labor Supply', in H. G. Lewis (ed.), *Aspects of Labor Economics*, Universities-National Bureau Committee for Economic Research, Princeton University Press, Princeton, NJ.

Mincer, J. (1985), 'Intercountry Comparisons of Labor Force Trends and of Related Developments: An Overview,' *Journal of Labor Economics*, vol. 5, pp. S1-S32.

Mishel, L. and Bernstein, J. (1993), *The State of Working America. 1992-93*, Sharpe, New York.

Mishel, L. and Schmitt, J. (1997), *Cutting Wages by Cutting Welfare. The Impact of Reform on the Low-Wage Labor Market*, Economic Policy Institute Brief Paper, Economic Policy Institute, Washington D.C.

Mishel, L., Bernstein, J. and Schmitt, J. (1997), *The State of Working America 1996-7*, M. E. Sharpe, Armonk.

Molitor, U. (1991), *Wählen Frauen anders? Zur Soziologie eines frauenspezifischen politischen Verhältens in der Bundesrepublik Deutschland*, Nomos Verlagsgesellschaft, Baden-Baden.

Moody, K. (1997), 'Trade Unions Across Borders', *New Left Review*, vol. 225, pp. 52-72.

Mósesdóttir, L. (1989), *Women in the Icelandic Labour Market*, Working Paper no. 1, Háskólinn á Akureyri, Akureyri.

Mósesdóttir, L. (1991), 'Hagfræðikenningar um stöðu kvenna á vinnumarkaði' *Þjóðmál: Yearbook of Political Economy and Social Sciences*, Félags- og hagvísindastofnun Íslands, vol. 1, pp. 3-25.

Mósesdóttir, L. (1993), *Íslenskur vinnumarkaður í ljósi efnahags-og stofnanaþróunar*, Working Paper, Félags- og hagvísindastofnun Íslands.

Mósesdóttir, L. (1993), 'Vad vet vi och vad vet vi inte om mäns och kvinnors lön på Island' *Kvinnelønnas mysterier - myter og fakta om lønnsdannelsen*, Nord 1993:16, Nordic Council of Ministers, Copenhagen.

Mósesdóttir, L. (1994), *Regimes of Gender Relations and the State. A Comparative Framework*, Working Paper no. 9407, Manchester School of Management, University of Manchester Institute of Science and Technology, Manchester.

Mósesdóttir, L. (1995), 'The State and the Egalitarian, Ecclesiastical and Liberal Regimes of Gender Relations', *British Journal of Sociology*, vol. 46, pp. 623-642.

Mósesdóttir, L. (1997), *Breaking the Boundaries. Women's Encounter with the State in Sweden, Germany and the United States*, Working Paper no. 4, Feminist Research Centre, Aalborg University, Aalborg.

231

Mósesdóttir, L. in collaboration with Björgvinsson, D. T. (1998), *Reconciling Work and Family Life in Iceland*, a study done for the joint report of the 'Gender and Employment Network of Experts' and the 'Gender and Law Network of Experts' for the Equal Opportunities Unit, DGV, of the European Commission.

Mósesdóttir, L. and Eydal, G. B. (forthcoming), 'The Swedish Economy, Welfare State, Tax System and the Educational System', in B. A. Cook (ed.), *Europe since 1945: An Encyclopaedia*, Garland Publishing, New York.

Mósesdóttir, L. and Jonsson, I. (1996), *Pensionssystemerne i Danmark, Island og Sverige*, report written for the Home Rule Minister of Work and Social Affairs in Greenland.

Munoz, G. and Carey, E. (1997), *Differential Impact of the Electoral Systems on Female Political Representation*, Women's Rights Series, W-10, Directorate-General for Research, European Parliament.

Naschold, F., de Vroom, B. and Casey, B. (1994a), 'Regulating Employment and Retirement: An International Comparison between Firms and Countries', in F. Naschold and B. de Vroom (eds.), *Regulating Employment and Welfare. Company and National Policies of Labour Force Participation at the End of Worklife in Industrial Countries*, Walter de Gruyter, Berlin.

Naschold, F., Oppen, M., Peinemann, H. and Rosenow, J. (1994b), 'Germany: The Concerted Transition from Work to Welfare', in F. Naschold and B. de Vroom (eds.), op.cit.

Nätti, J. (1993), 'Temporary Employment in the Nordic Countries: A "Trap" or a "Bridge"?', *Work, Employment and Society*, vol. 7, pp. 451-472.

Nelson, J. A. (1991), 'Tax Reform and Feminist Theory in the United States: Incorporating Human Connection', *Journal of Economic Studies*, vol. 18, pp. 11-29.

Nordic Council of Ministers, *Yearbook of Nordic Statistics*, various years, Nordic Council of Ministers, Copenhagen.

NOSOSKO (1997), *Social tryghed i de nordiske lande 1995. Omfang, udgifter og finansiering*, NOSOSKO, Copenhagen.

O'Connor, J. S. (1993a), 'Gender, Class and Citizenship in the Comparative Analysis of Welfare State Regimes: Theoretical and Methodological Issues', *The British Journal of Sociology*, vol. 44, pp. 501-518.

O'Connor, J. S. (1993b), *Labour Market Participation in Liberal Welfare State Regimes - Issues of Quantity and Quality*, paper presented at Conference on Comparative Research on Welfare States in Transition, Oxford 9-12 September.

OECD (1973), *Labour Force Statistics 1960-1971*, OECD, Paris.

OECD (1984), *Labour Force Statistics 1962-1982*, OECD, Paris.

OECD (1985), *Labour Force Statistics 1964-1983*, OECD, Paris.

OECD (1988), *Employment Outlook*, OECD, Paris.

OECD (1993), *Employment Outlook*, OECD, Paris.

OECD (1994a), *Labour Force Statistics 1972-1992*, OECD, Paris.

OECD (1994b), *OECD Jobs Study*, OECD, Paris.

OECD (1994c), *Women and Structural Change. New Perspectives*, OECD, Paris.

OECD (1994d), *Employment Outlook*, OECD, Paris.

OECD (1995), *Education at a Glance. OECD Indicators*, OECD, Paris.

OECD (1996a), *Employment Outlook*, OECD, Paris.

OECD (1996b), *Labour Force Statistics 1974-1994*, OECD, Paris.

OECD (1997a), *Labour Force Statistics 1976-1996*, OECD, Paris.

OECD (1997b), *Employment Outlook*, OECD, Paris.

Olafsson, G. and Petersson, J. (1994), 'Sweden: Policy Dilemmas of the Changing Age Structure in a "Work Society"', in F. Naschold and B. de Vroom (eds), *Regulating Employment and Welfare. Company and National Policies of Labour Force Participation at the End of Worklife in Industrial Countries*, Walter de Gruyter, Berlin.

Oláh, L. S. (1998), '"Sweden, the Middle Way". A Feminist Approach', *The European Journal of Women's Studies*, vol. 5, pp. 47-67.

Olofsson, P. (1998), 'Unga kvinnor samhällets förlorare', *Dagenshydeter* 24/8:A4.

O'Reilly, J. (1995), 'Le travail a temps partiel en Allemagne de l'Est et en Allemagne de l'Ouest: Vers un "modele societal sexue"', *Cahiers des MAGE (Marche du Travail et Genre)*, vol. 1, pp. 77-88.

O'Reilly, J. and Fagan, C. (1998), 'Conceptualising Part-Time Work: The Value of an Integrated Comparative Perspective', in J. O'Reilly and C. Fagan (eds.), *Part-Time Prospects. An International Comparison of Part-Time Work in Europe, North America and the Pacific Rim*, Routledge, London.

Orloff, A. S. (1993), 'Gender and the Social Rights of Citizenship: The Comparative Analysis of Gender Relations and Welfare States', *American Sociological Review*, vol. 58, pp. 303-328.

Oskarson, M. and Wängnerud, L. (1995), *Kvinnor som väljare och valda*, Studentlitteratur, Lund.

Ostner, I. (1998), 'The Politics of Care in Germany', in J. Lewis (ed.) *Gender, Social Care and Welfare State Restructuring in Europe*, Avebury, Aldershot.

øyen, E. (1990), 'The Imperfection of Comparison', in E. øyen (ed.), *Comparative Methodology. Theory and Practice in International Social Research*, Sage, London.

Padgett, S. and Paterson, W. (1994), 'Germany: Stagnation of the Left', in P. Anderson and P. Camiller (eds.), *Mapping the West European Lefts*, Verso, London.

Persson, I. (1990), 'The Third Dimension - Equal Status Between Swedish Women and Men', in I. Persson (ed.), *Generating Equality in the Welfare State. The Swedish Experience*, Norwegian University Press, Oslo.

Pfau-Effinger, B. (1994), 'Women's Work and New Form of Employment in Germany', in P. Koistinen and I. Ostner (eds.), *Women and Markets*, University of Tampere, Tampere.

Pierson, C. (1991), *Beyond the Welfare State? The New Political Economy of Welfare*, Polity Press, Cambridge.

Piore, M. J. and Sabel, C. F. (1984), *The Second Industrial Divide*, Basic Books, New York.

Piven, F. F. (1991), 'Structural Constraints and Political Development: The Case of the American Democratic Party', in F. F. Piven (ed.), *Labour Parties in Postindustrial Societies*, Polity, Oxford.

Piven, F. F. (1995), 'Is it Global Economics or Neo-Laissez-Faire', *The New Left Review*, vol. 213, pp. 107-114.

Polachek, S. W. (1980), 'Occupational Self-Selection: A Human Capital Approach to Sex Differences in Occupational Structure', *The Review of Economics and Statistics*, pp. 60-69.

Polanyi, K. (1944), *The Great Transformation*, Beacon Press, Boston.

Pollert, A. (1996), 'Gender and Class Revisited; or, the Poverty of "Patriarchy"', *Sociology*, vol. 30, pp. 639-659.

Pontusson, J. (1994), 'After the Golden Age', in P. Anderson and P. Camiller (eds.), *Mapping the West European Lefts*, Verso, London.

Pontusson, J. and Swenson, P. (1996), 'Labor Markets, Production Strategies, and Wage Bargaining Institutions. The Swedish Employer Offensive in Comparative Perspective', *Comparative Political Studies*, vol. 19, pp. 223-250.

Power, M. (1988), 'Women, the State and the Family in the US: Reaganomics and the Experience of Women', in J. Rubery (ed.), *Women and Recession*, Routledge, London.

Regini, M. (1995), *Uncertain Boundaries. The Social and Political Construction of European Economics*, Cambridge University Press, Cambridge.

Reskin, B. F. and Roos, P. A. (1990), *Job Queues, Gender Queues. Explaining Women's Inroads into Male Occupations*, Temple University Press, Philadelphia.

Rosen, S. (1995), *Public Employment and the Welfare State in Sweden*, Occasional Paper, no.61, SNS Forlag, Stockholm.

Rosenberg, S. (1989), 'From Segmentation to Flexibility', *Labour and Society*, vol. 14, pp. 363-407.

Rosenberg, F. (1991), 'Shock Therapy: GDR Women in Transition from a Socialist Welfare State to a Social Market Economy', *Signs*, vol. 17, pp. 129-151.

Rosenfeld, R. A. and Birkelund, G. E. (1995), 'Women's Part-Time Work: A Cross-National Comparison', *European Sociological Review*, vol. 11, pp. 111-134.

Rowthorn, R. E. (1992), 'Centralisation, Employment and Wage Dispersion', *The Economic Journal*, vol. 102, pp. 506-523.

Rubery, J. (1988a), 'Preface', in J. Rubery (ed.), *Women and Recession*, Routledge, London.

Rubery, J. (1988b), 'Introduction', in J. Rubery (ed.), op.cit.

Rubery, J. (1988d), 'Women and Recession: a Comparative Perspective', in J. Rubery (ed.), op.cit.

Rubery, J. (1989), 'Precarious Forms of Work in the United Kingdom', in G. Rodgers and J. Rodgers (eds.), *Precarious Jobs in Labour Market Regulation. The Growth of Atypical Employment in Western Europe*, ILO, Geneva.

Rubery, J. (1992), 'Productive Systems, International Integration and the Single European Market', in A. Castro, P. Méhaut and J. Rubery (eds.), *International Integration and Labour Market Organisation*, Academic Press, London.

Rubery, J. (1994), 'The British Production Regime: A Societal-Specific System?', *Economy and Society*, vol. 23, pp. 335-354.

Rubery, J. and Fagan, C. (1993), *Occupational Segregation of Women and Men in the European Community*, report written for the European Commission, the EC Network on the Situation of Women in the Labour Market, UMIST, Manchester.

Rubery, J. and Fagan, C. (1994), 'Does Feminization Mean a Flexible Labour Force?', in R. Hyman and A. Ferner (eds.), *New Frontiers in European Industrial Relations*, Blackwell, Oxford.

Rubery, J. and Fagan, C. (1995), 'Gender Segregation in Societal Context', *Work Employment & Society*, vol. 9, pp. 213-240.

Rubery, J., Bettio, F., Fagan, C., Maier, F., Quack, S., and Villa P. (1997), 'Payment Strutures and Gender Pay Differentials: Some Societal Effects', *International Journal of Human Resource Management*, vol. 8, pp. 131-149.

Rubery, J., Smith, M., Fagan, C. and Grimshaw, D. (1996), *Women and the European Employment Rate: the Causes and Consequences of Variations in Female Activity and Employment Patterns in the European Union*, report written for the European Commission, the EC Network on the Situation of Women in the Labour Market, UMIST, Manchester.

Rudolph, C. (1993), *Die andere Seite der Frauenbewegung. Frauengleichstellungsstellen in Deutschland*, Aktuelle Frauenforschung, Bd.17, Centaurus-Verlagsgesellschaft: Pfaffen-weiler, Rosch-Buch, Hallstadt-Bamberg.

Rutherford, M. (1994), *Institutions in Economics. The Old and the New Institutionalism*, Cambridge University Press, Cambridge.

Ryner, M. (1994), 'Assessing SAP's Economic Policy in the 1980s: The "Third Way", the Swedish Model and the Transition from Fordism to Post-Fordism', *Economic and Industrial Democracy*, vol. 15, pp. 385-428.

Sapiro, V. (1986), 'The Women's Movement, Politics and Policy in the Reagan Era', in D. Dahlerup (ed.) *The New Women's Movement. Feminism and Political Power in Europe and the USA*, Sage, London.

Sayer, A. (1984), *Method in Social Science. A Realist Approach*, Hutchinson, London.

Scheiwe, K. (1994), 'Labour Market, Welfare State and Family Institutions: The Links to Mothers' Poverty Risks', *Journal of European Social Policy*, vol. 4, pp. 201-224.

Schmid, G. (1991), *Women and Employment Restructuring. Women in the Public Sector*, OCDE/GD(91)213, OECD, Paris.

Schmid, G. (1992), *Is the State a Model Employer for Women?*, paper presented at the Annual Conference of the European Association of Labour Economists, 3-6 September.

Schmid, G. and Ziegler, C. (1992), *Die Frauen und der Staat. Beschäftigungspolitische Gleichstellung im öffenlichen Secktor aus internationaler Perspektive*, Discussion Paper, Wissenschaftscentrum Berlin für Sozialforschung, Berlin.

Schmidt, M. G. (1995), 'The Parties-Do-Matter Hypothesis and the Case of the Federal Republic of Germany', *German Politics*, vol. 4, pp. 1-21.

Scott, A. G. (1991), 'Marxian and Radical Economics', in D. Mair and A. G. Miller (eds.), *A Modern Guide to Economic Thought. An Introduction to Comparative Schools of Thought in Economics*, University Press, Cambridge.

Seiz, J. A. (1995), 'Epistemology and the Tasks of Feminist Economics', *Feminist Economics*, vol. 1, pp. 110-118.

Sklair, L. (1991), *Sociology of the Global System*, Harvester Wheatsheaf, London.

Skocpol, T. (1995), *Social Policy in the United States. Future Possibilities in Historical Perspective*, Princeton University Press, Princeton.

Smith, E. O. (1994), *The German Economy*, Routledge, London.

Smith, G. (1992), 'The Nature of the Unified State', in G. Smith, W. E. Paterson, and P. H. Merkl (eds.), *Developments in German Politics*, Macmillan, London.

Smith, J. P. and Ward, M. P. (1984), *Women's Wages and Work in the Twentieth Century*, Rand Corporation, Santa Monica, CA.

Standing, G. (1988), *Unemployment and Labour Market Flexibility: Sweden*, ILO, Geneva.

Statistics Sweden (1995), *Women and Men in Sweden. Facts and Figures 1995*, Statistics Sweden, Örebro.

Statistics Sweden (1997), *Kvinnor och män på arbetsmarknaden*, Statistics Sweden, Örebro.

Statistisches Bundesamt, *Statistisches Jahrbuch*, various years.

Stephens, J. D. (1996), 'The Scandinavian Welfare States: Achievements, Crisis, and Prospects', in G. Esping-Andersen (ed.), *Welfare States in Transition. National Adaptations in Global Economies*, Sage, London.

Stetson, D. M. (1995), 'The Oldest Women's Policy Agency: The Women's Bureau in the United States', in D. M. Stetson and A. G. Mazur (eds.), *Comparative State Feminism*, Sage, London.

Stivers, C. (1993), *Gender Images in Public Administration. Legitimacy and the Administrative State*, Sage, London.

Stoesz, D. and Karger, H. J. (1984), *Reconstructing the American Welfare State*, Rowman & Littlefield Publishers, Lanham, MD.

Sturm, R. (1992), 'The Changing Territorial Balance', in G. Smith, W. E. Paterson, and P. H. Merkl (eds.), *Developments in German Politics*, Macmillan, London.

Sundström, M. (1993), 'The Growth in Full-Time Work Among Swedish Women in the 1980s', *Acta Sociologica*, vol. 36, pp. 139-150.

Sundström, M. (1997), 'Managing Work and Children: Part-Time Work and the Family Cycle of Swedish Women', in H. Blossfeld and C. Hakim (eds.), *Between Equalisation and Marginalization. Women Working Part-Time in Europe and the United States of America*, Oxford University Press, Oxford.

Swedish Institute (1997), *The Swedish Economy and Swedish Industry*, http://www.si.se/eng/esverige/economy.html, May.

Swenson, P. (1991), 'Bringing Capital Back in or Social Democracy Reconsidered. Employer Power, Cross-Class Alliances, and Centralization of Industrial Relations in Denmark and Sweden', *World Politics*, vol. 43, pp. 513-544.

Tanda, P. (1994), 'Marital Instability, Reproductive Behaviour and Women's Labour Force Participation Decisions', *Labour*, vol. 8, pp. 279-301.

Tarullo, D. K. (1992), 'Federalism Issues in United States Labour Market Policies and Employment Law', in A. Castro, P. Méhaut and J. Rubery (eds.), *International Integration and Labour Market Organisation*, Academic Press, London.

Thelen, K. (1993), 'West European Labor in Transition', *World Politics*, vol. 46, pp. 23-49.

Therborn, G. (1987), 'Welfare State and Capitalist Markets', *Acta Sociologica*, vol. 30, pp. 237-254.

Therborn, G. (1991), 'Swedish Social Democracy and the Transition from Industrial to Postindustrial Politics', in F. F. Piven (ed.), *Labor Parties in Post-industrial Societies*, Polity Press, Oxford.

Thomson, L. and Norries, D. F. (1995), 'Introduction: The Politics of Welfare Reform', in D. F. Norries and L. Thompson (eds.), *The Politics of Welfare Reform*, Sage, London.

Tickell, A. and Peck J. A. (1995), 'Social Regulation after Fordism: Regulation and Re-Regulating the Local State', *Economy and Society*, vol. 24, pp. 357-386.

Tong, R. (1989), *Feminist Thought. A Comprehensive Introduction*, Unwin Hyman, London.

United Nations (1995), *The Worlds of Women 1995. Trends and Statistics*, United Nations, New York.

U.S. Department of Commerce (1995), *Statistical Abstract of the United States 1995*, U.S. Government Printing Office, Washington DC.

U.S. Department of Commerce (1997), *Statistical Abstract of the United States 1997*, U.S. Government Printing Office, Washington DC.

Walby, S. (1990), *Theorizing Patriarchy*, Blackwell, Oxford.

Walby, S. (1997), *Gender Transformations*, Routledge, London.

Weiss, L. (1997), 'The Myth of the Powerless State', *New Left Review*, vol. 225, pp. 3-27.

Wilkinson, F. (1983), 'Productive Systems', *Cambridge Journal of Economics*, vol. 7, pp. 413-429.

Wilks, S. (1996), 'Swedish Social Democracy', *Capital and Class*, vol. 58, pp. 89-111.

Williams, F. (1994), 'Social Relations, Welfare and the Post-Fordism Debate', in R. Burrows and B. Loader (eds.), *Towards a Post-Fordist Welfare State?*, Routledge, London.

Wise, L. R. (1993), 'Whither Solidarity? Transitions in Swedish Public-Sector Pay Policy', *British Journal of Industrial Relations*, vol. 31, pp. 75-95.

Woolley, F. R. (1993), 'The Feminist Challenge to Neoclassical Economics', *Cambridge Journal of Economics*, vol. 17, pp. 485-500.

World Bank (1994), *Adverting the Old Age Crisis. Policies to Protect the Old and Promote Growth*, Oxford University Press, Oxford.

Index

240

Van Veen, T. 32, 180

Walby, S. 13-14, 18, 127, 166, 167, 196
Wängnerud, L. 41, 49-51, 68, 76n-77n
Weiss, L. 185
Welsh, H. 55
Wilkinson, F. 32, 124-125, 128
Wilks, S. 50

Williams, F. 38
Wise, L. R. 32, 173
Wittig, I. 114, 117-118, 210
Woolley, F. R. 83-84
World Bank 108, 121n

Ziegler, C. 123